BARRON'S Let's Prepare for the
PARCC

GRADE 7 ELA/LITERACY TEST

Joseph S. Pizzo, M.Ed.

About the Author

Joseph S. Pizzo is a veteran 7th grade language arts teacher of 42 years at the Black River Middle School in Chester, NJ. He also has 24 years of experience as an adjunct professor in the Education, Communications, Business, and English Departments at Centenary College, the English/Modern Language/Fine Arts Department at Union County College, and the Graduate Education Department at the College of Saint Elizabeth.

An experienced writer of language arts and public speaking curricula, Pizzo is an active member of the Scholastic National Teacher Advisory Board. The NJ Association for Middle Level Education's Educator of the Year for 2016, Pizzo is a former Educator of the Year for NJCTE and winner of the NJ Governor's Awards for Arts Education and for Excellence in Education. Pizzo sits on the executive board of NJAMLE and NJCTE while also serving on the Core Team for NJ Schools to Watch. He has received the U.S. President's Award for Community Service and has hosted cable TV's *Education Matters* and radio's *School Bell* series.

With Gratitude

Special thanks are in order for:

- My mother Anna and late father Francis Pizzo, who have provided unwavering support throughout my career in education.
- My mentor Dr. Joseph F. Byrnes, who saw greatness in me during my early years.
- My colleagues Mr. Robert Mullen, Dr. Kenneth Piascik, Mrs. Ilene Heisler, Mrs. Doreen Aiello, Dr. Patricia Schall, media experts Mr. Ron Jaghab and Mr. Patrick Corbitt, and all my fellow teachers, administrators, and board of education members for their continued encouragement and support.
- All of my students at the middle and collegiate levels, the parents/guardians, and community members who continue to support and enhance my efforts.

All inquiries should be addressed to:
Barron's Educational Series, Inc.
250 Wireless Boulevard
Hauppauge, NY 11788
www.barronseduc.com

ISBN: 978-1-4380-0819-6
Library of Congress Control No.: 2016931359

Date of Manufacture: August 2016
Manufactured by: B11R11

Printed in the United States of America
9 8 7 6 5 4 3 2 1

10%
POST-CONSUMER
WASTE
Paper contains a minimum of 10% post-consumer waste (PCW). Paper used in this book was derived from certified, sustainable forestlands.

Contents

Introduction: Overview of PARCC Grade 7

As you prepare to take the PARCC Grade 7 ELA/Literacy Test, you probably have questions. Before we begin preparing for the test, let's try to answer some common questions that you may have.

What Is the PARCC Test?

The PARCC (Partnership for Assessment of Readiness for College and Careers) is a test given by several states to public school students to help indicate the progress being made in mastering the knowledge and skills specified in the Common Core State Standards (CCSS). In grade 7, the two areas being tested are English language arts and math. Here, we will discuss the exam for ELA/Literacy specifically.

When and How Is the PARCC Given?

The PARCC ELA/Literacy test is given each spring. The exam is mainly comprised of reading passages, both literary and informational; multiple-choice questions; and writing responses by way of essays. The PARCC can be given on the computer, so you should be familiar with technology and how to input information. As you answer the Technology-Enhanced Constructed-Response (TECR) questions, you will be asked to select multiple answers to demonstrate that you know which choices are the most important or in what order the choices have occurred. For some of the practice exercises, the directions will include prompts for both paper and computer. For some of the Prose-Constructed-Response (PCR) questions and Evidence-Based Selection (EBS) questions, you may be asked to read two to three passages of text and then view a video before responding to all questions. For more information about the types of questions and what they may look like on screen, please see the following pages. Each type of question has a detailed explanation of what you might be asked to do, either select an answer, select multiple answers, drag and drop, or even highlight.

The passages and the questions seen on the PARCC may be more challenging (covering more difficult material) than you have seen on other tests. There are certain strategies that you can use to help you do your best work.

Before we begin, please understand that on many of the newer tests that are similar to the PARCC, scores are often going to be lower than they were on previously designed tests. The scoring has changed, and the level of difficulty has increased. Do not become frustrated, however. Your teachers understand this challenge, and they are trying to help you earn the best score possible. If you follow the suggestions in this book, you should have a good chance of having your best efforts reflected in your score.

What Do PARCC Online Questions Look Like?

For more on what the online examples or types of questions look like, see below and the following pages.

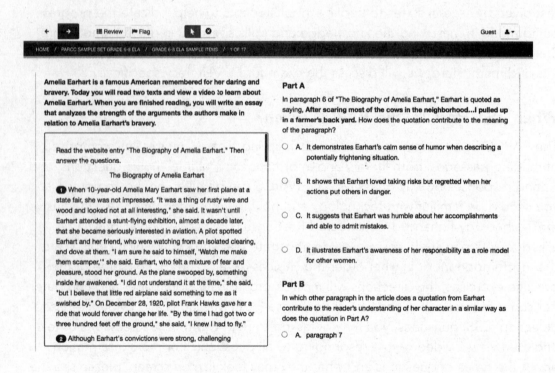

Only part of the passage that you see in these examples is visible. You will need to scroll down on the computer to read the whole passage.

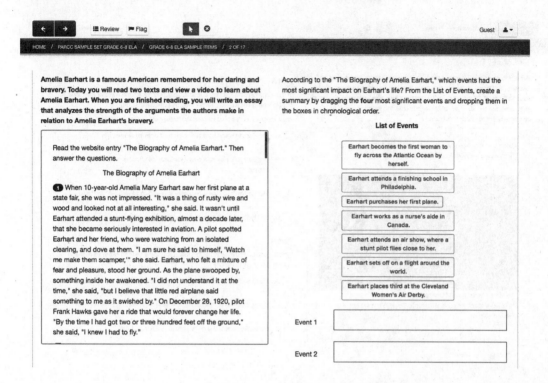

Some questions give you more than four answer choices and require you to click on each correct answer choice or drag them into answer boxes.

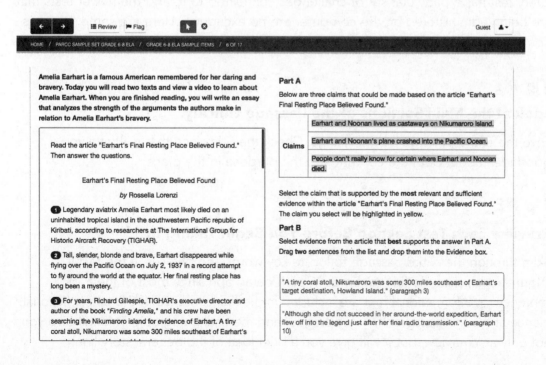

Some essays require you to draw specific information from multiple resources to make specific references.

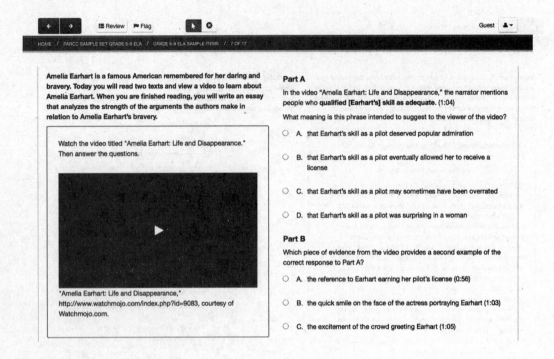

Top 10 Success Tips for PARCC ELA

Every test has a particular set of challenges connected to it, and the newer tests that are being administered on the computer are no exception. Here are some "success tips" to help you on the PARCC.

Tip #1

Look at the Main Sections of the Passage Quickly.

Give the entire passage a brief glance. Check the title since that will give you a good idea about both the content and the purpose in the piece.

Tip #2

Preview Each Test Section Before You Begin Taking It.

Skim through the entire passage to locate key words and phrases. If the text is informational, skim the first sentence in each paragraph since most of the topic sentences in informational text are included in the first sentence. If the text is fictional, glance at the first paragraph, any dialogue, and the final paragraph. This will give you not only an overview, but it will give you a brief idea of the general story line.

Tip #3

Check It Out!

Check out the questions to see what exactly the test is going to ask you to know or think about. With this information, certain questions may become easier to answer since you have already previewed the information.

Tip #4

Read the Passage Carefully.

As you do, take notes on the notepad that is provided on the electronic version of the test. If you are taking the paper version, use a scratch sheet of paper for your notes.

Tip #5

Skip It.

If you are stuck on a question and you don't know the answer, skip that question and return to it later. The electronic version of the test has a way that you can mark a question that you haven't answered and then go back to it when you have finished the other sections of the test. On the paper version, simply make a note on your scratch sheet and remember to skip that answer temporarily on your answer sheet.

Tip #6

Do Not Rush to Finish the Test.

Use as much of the time that you are given to complete the test to the best of your ability. If you rush through the test, you will likely find that you have made many silly mistakes that could have been avoided. The classic expression "Haste makes waste" certainly applies to this situation.

Tip #7

All About Time.

Whenever possible, leave yourself enough time to review your answers. Sometimes, a second look gives you a perspective that you might not have had originally. Also, you may find that a question asked later in the test makes reference to a response that was included earlier.

Tip #8

Answer Questions.

Make sure that you have accurately answered the questions being asked. For example, test makers will sometimes not ask you for the words that best define the theme of a written passage. Rather, they will ask you for the words that are the opposite of the theme of a written passage.

Tip #9

Check Grammar and Spelling.
For any written response, make sure that you check your grammar and spelling. Be sure to address the question being asked, and use direct quotes to cite your evidence. Moreover, make sure that your written responses are lengthy rather than brief. Also, use words that are more difficult and when appropriate, subject-specific. For example, with the phrase "It's better to be a baker," refer to an author's use of alliteration (repeating initial sounds) rather than repetition.

Tip #10

Attitude and Mindset.
Maintain the right attitude both before and throughout the test. Tell yourself that you are going to give your best effort, and then go ahead and do so. If you are too nervous or if you feel that you are not going to do well on the test, then you may actually be programming your human computer (your "brain") not to do well at all.

When I Finish All of the Exercises in This Book, Will I Be Guaranteed to Pass the Grade 7 ELA/Literacy PARCC Test?

Unfortunately, no book can make that guarantee. If you are serious and you complete all of the sections in this book carefully, your chances of doing well on the test should increase. Please remember to review any sections that you find to be difficult ones. The only way to learn is to study the right information properly.

IMPORTANT NOTE

Barron's has made every effort to ensure the content of this book is accurate as of press time, but the PARCC Assessments are constantly changing. Be sure to consult *https://www.parcconline.org/* for all the latest testing information. Regardless of the changes being announced after press time, this book will still provide a strong framework for seventh-grade students preparing for the assessment.

Reading and the Literary Analysis Task

The PARCC Grade 7 ELA/Literacy test contains three units dealing with fiction and non-fiction.

- Unit 1: The Literary Analysis Task
- Unit 2: The Research Simulation Task
- Unit 3: The Narrative Writing Task

Let's look at Unit 1 and the type of reading selections you may see on the exam.

- an excerpt from a novel or short story
- an excerpt from an autobiography
- a poem
- an article
- a letter or editorial
- a speech
- a description of a process
- a review of an event

Let's now examine the section known as "Literary Analysis." You will be given either excerpts from long works or brief works in their entirety. After you have read these works, you will be directed to write analytical essays.

LITERARY ANALYSIS

There is a good chance that you will be given the task of focusing on a certain theme that is covered in the writings. Most likely, the theme will be covered differently in each passage. Therefore, you likely will be asked to compare the way each author developed the theme. You will be required to find similarities, as well as differences. One of the ways this may be done is by having you compare the way a theme is used in a classical piece of literature and in a more modern piece of literature. Moreover, the structure of the piece is important and needs to be addressed. A poem, for example, is written in stanzas while a piece of informational text is written in language that does not necessarily rely on literary devices such as metaphor, simile, alliteration, and onomatopoeia. In addition, the author's purpose for the piece is important. While an informational piece may be written to instruct or to share knowledge, a literary piece may be written to teach a lesson or to resolve a conflict.

Multiple-Choice Questions

The multiple-choice questions that you will be seeing on the PARCC differ greatly from the ones that you have seen in the past. The questions will be paired together, and the answer on the first must be related to the second. For example, you may be asked to select the correct definition of *hubris* (excessive pride) from a list of five or six options. Your next task will be to examine five or more possible supports for your choice. The supports will be based on evidence (examples) from the text. More than one choice may be correct, and you will need to choose all of the correct answers. If you answer the first question correctly but have one or more incorrect answers on the second part, you will receive one-half credit since you answered the first part correctly. However, if you miss the first part of the question and guess correctly on the second part, you will receive no credit for any of your answers to that question.

Multiple-Meaning Words

If a word has more than one meaning when it is used in the passage, then you will be required to choose the correct meanings (two or more) from the list of multiple options of five or more meanings. Let's look at a very simple example. Let's imagine that the weather in a passage may be described as "cool" while a character in the same passage may be referred to by his friends as being "cool." Five or more possible meanings for the word cool may be included as optional answers. The correct answers would refer to a temperature between hot and cold, as well as a desirable quality of one's personality. However, a definition of "cool" as the process to bring down the temperature in food would be incorrect. There likely would be an antonym (opposite) such as raising the temperature of food, as well as a definition such as the sound that a dove makes—which is actually "coo." These two definitions are also incorrect.

> **Remember:** This test can be given on a computer, so you will be asked to click and drag the correct answers to a certain place like a central Venn diagram or a set of boxes into which you will place your answers. You may even be asked to take events from the story and put them in a correct order. There will likely be more events than boxes since some of the events may either not have occurred during the story or they may be from a different part of the story than the one that the question is addressing. The key is to be sure not to rush through your answers. Take a reasonable amount of time while you ensure that you have examined all the possible responses and have chosen the correct ones.

Research, Research, Research

For this exam, you are most likely going to be reading informational (non-fiction) passages. You will be asked questions about what you think the author is trying to communicate to his/her audience and also about the structure of the piece (the way it is arranged). This will include considerations such as chronological order, comparison and contrast, and order of importance. For example, a piece featuring a certain vacation experience may focus on the order in which the events of the vacation occurred. This would be an example of chronological order. A piece using comparison and contrast would possibly showcase the differences of the writer's expectations for the vacation and compare and contrast those with the actual events. Furthermore, a piece written using order of importance would feature the events of the vacation from the most important or memorable to the least important or memorable—without considering the order in which these events occurred.

The PARCC pairs a piece of fiction with a piece of non-fiction. There may even be an additional video to watch. Furthermore, some questions will ask you to compare the information from each passage (and video), as well as the manner in which it is presented. You will be required to find both similarities and differences between not only what is covered in the pieces, but also what you think each author may have intended in his/her piece. You'll complete two major tasks in this section of the test. First, you'll answer questions based on the passage. They'll deal with literary concepts like plot, character, and setting. Second, you'll write both brief and lengthy responses to questions also based on the passages. For these, you'll directly address the questions being raised. Your writing must demonstrate a high ability level.

Using the right strategies can help you to be very successful. We'll begin with the literary questions and move directly to the writing.

USE THE PREVIEW TECHNIQUE (PT) TO BE SUCCESSFUL

Because these tests are timed, you might think that the best strategy is to read the passage(s) and then answer the questions. Actually, that way is NOT the best way to take this test. Instead, use the **Preview Technique (or PT)** before you read each passage. In this way, you will be taking an important step toward determining the author's point of view. By previewing a passage before reading it, you are equipping yourself with the necessary tools to analyze successfully a given piece of text. You may wish to think of this practice as similar to watching a preview of a movie while you are sitting in a movie theater, in your home, or in front of the screen of your computer or device. The preview gives you an idea of what you may expect when you watch the actual movie. The same is true when you preview a writing passage on a standardized test. By the way, this is also an effective technique to use when you are beginning a new chapter in a textbook.

The Key Steps

Step 1—Preview the Questions
Read the questions given for the passage before you read the passage.

Step 2—Preview the Material
Skim through the passage and chunk it into sections. Take notes either with a notepad tool provided on the test or on paper. Keep your notes brief. These may actually help you when you begin to answer the questions. Spending a minute or two to organize yourself may save you many minutes of searching through the text to find the correct answer.

Step 3—Read the Entire Passage
Get all the information you'll need to answer the questions.

Step 4—Address the Prompt Directly
Be sure that you restate the question and make specific text references.

ANSWERING QUESTIONS BASED ON LITERATURE

For Unit 1 of this exam, you will answer questions based mostly on excerpts from long fiction works, short stories, and poetry. Some questions will be based on the text, and others will be inferred (hinted at).

First, let's do a warm-up exercise to become familiar with some important skills you will need not only for this test, but also to help you as you become an effective reader.

Essential Reading Skills: Questioning, Clarifying, and Predicting
Questioning is the effective use of questions to gather information. **Clarifying** is the way to find out further information about a topic. **Predicting** is making educated guesses based on both the information that you have already found out and information that you already know.

Strategy
As you are doing your reading, use these strategies.

- For effective **questioning**, make sure that your questions are designed to bring you the information that you seek. Be specific.
- Use specific questions when you need help **clarifying** information.
- When you are **predicting**, make sure that your predictions are based on logic and common sense.

Practice

The passage that we'll read is a 7th grade student's journal entry entitled *My First Day of School*. The following questions deal with **questioning**, **clarifying**, and **predicting**.

Read the passage, then answer the questions by using the **PT** below.

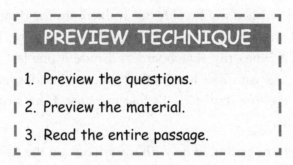

PREVIEW TECHNIQUE

1. Preview the questions.
2. Preview the material.
3. Read the entire passage.

My First Day of School
by Pat Cole

1   When I set my alarm last night, I realized that tomorrow I would be following a different routine for the next few months. Since school had let out last June, I suddenly had a lot more freedom. I could sleep a little later, eat lunch whenever I wanted to, watch my favorite daytime television programs, and just hang out with my friends. Tomorrow morning, it was time to go back to school.

2   The next morning, my mom woke me up even before my alarm rang. She told me that I had to make sure that I was awake. I couldn't go back to sleep. If I did, I would be late for the first day of school. She said, "That's not the way you want to start out your school year, is it?" I just grumbled "No" and slid out of my bed. I found my way to the bathroom and jumped in the shower. During the summer, I never had to take my shower before breakfast. I always made some cereal, poured a glass of juice, and settled in with my favorite television program on one of the music channels. Today, however, I had to finish my shower, dry my hair, and have a little breakfast. Oh, I couldn't do these things in slow motion. My mom kept reminding me to "Hurry up!" so I wouldn't be late. She also reminded me to wear the new outfit we had bought last week. "You should always make a good first impression, especially on the first day of school," she said. It would feel funny dressing up for breakfast after an entire summer of eating while wearing my pajamas.

3 My mom made me hot cereal, toast, and juice for breakfast. She also cut up some melon for me. I was still a little tired and didn't feel like eating much. My mom told me that I would be hungry before lunch if I didn't eat a good breakfast, but I just wasn't hungry. Besides, lunch was only a few hours away, wasn't it?

4 After I had finished my breakfast, I walked out the door. I noticed that my skateboard was hanging from the hook near the door. I wonder what would happen if I took my skateboard and rode it one last time down my driveway. The bus isn't due for another minute. Besides, aren't the buses always late on the first day? Oh, it's just my luck. Here's comes the bus— right on schedule.

5 Well, I least I'm getting to be with my friends on the ride to school. We talk about all the things we always talk about, but it's different today. Before we know it, the bus pulls up to the school. We all get off and head to our homerooms.

6 Classes aren't too bad. Miss Washington is still greeting every one of her students at her front door. Vice-Principal Palmer is disciplining a rowdy student for getting in trouble near the lockers. I only have to carry my math and public speaking textbooks this year because most of our classes let us keep an extra book at home.

7 Things actually didn't go too badly all throughout my day, but I did have one little problem. Around ten o'clock in the morning, I was hungry. Lunch wasn't on my schedule until noon. I had to sit in three different classes and listen to my stomach reminding me that I should have eaten my breakfast. What's worse is we had a discussion in English class of the ways fast food restaurants try to influence us so they can sell us their burgers, fries, tacos, and chicken. I could almost hear the food calling me by my name.

8 After I had lunch, the rest of the day seemed to fly by. I enjoyed my social studies class because Mr. Barns is a great guy. He doesn't hassle his students, and he never makes fun of anyone in his class. Gym was great because I got to blow off a little steam. Miss Springer let us choose an activity today, so my friends and I played dodgeball.

9 When the day was over, I got on the bus and headed home. I didn't think it was fair that we were assigned a one-page journal entry in English class, but I guess I can finish by just writing about my day.

10 Boy, I hope the weekend gets here quickly. I'm going to sleep late on Saturday.

Answer the questions based on this passage using our PT. Fill in or check each correct answer.

1. Select Pat's attitude after setting the alarm for the morning of the first day of school.

   ○ A. happy because the summer was boring
   ○ B. angry because Pat loathed going to school
   ○ C. afraid because the school was in a different town
   ○ D. upset because there would be less freedom in school

2. Which of the following **best** predicts what was likely going to happen when Pat used the excuse "lunch was only a few hours away, wasn't it?" (paragraph 3) to disregard mom's advice to eat a good breakfast?

   ○ A. Pat's mom would be right.
   ○ B. Pat would be right.
   ○ C. Pat's brother would be right.
   ○ D. Pat wanted to watch TV.

3. In paragraph 4, if Pat had taken his skateboard and ridden it "one last time down (his) driveway" before the bus came, which of the following answers would indicate reasons why Pat's mom might be upset?

   ☐ A. Pat had never ridden a skateboard before.
   ☐ B. Pat's new clothes might be ruined.
   ☐ C. Pat might get hurt and miss the first day of school.
   ☐ D. Pat might have to stay away from the class bully on the bus.
   ☐ E. Pat might miss the bus.
   ☐ F. None of the above.
   ☐ G. All of the above.

4. During the morning of the second day of school, what is Pat likely to do?

   ☐ A. sleep late
   ☐ B. eat the breakfast Pat's mother has made
   ☐ C. send a message on social media to his girlfriend
   ☐ D. remember to put the completed diary assignment in the school bag
   ☐ E. walk the dog
   ☐ F. go to the local store and get the morning newspaper

5. In the phrase "the ways fast food restaurants try to influence us" (paragraph 7), what does the word **influence** mean?

○ A. tell a story
○ B. broadcast an idea
○ C. prepare food
○ D. have an effect

Be sure to check your answers with those on pages 217–218.

Essential Reading Skills: Fact vs. Opinion

A **fact** is information that can be measured and proven. An **opinion** shows the way someone feels about a fact.

Strategy

As you are doing your reading, use these strategies.

A **fact** is something that is easy to measure and prove.

- Look for measurements for proof (for example, **gallons**, **days**, and **inches**).
- Look for quotes and citations from books and newspapers.

An **opinion** is an interpretation.

- Look for key words or phrases, such as **Sometimes** or **As I see it**.

A Letter to the Mayor

14 Pleasant Avenue
Springtown, NJ 09151

March 25, 2007

Dear Mayor Patel,

1 I believe that we should have a place in town where all the kids can get together. The park near the river used to have a building where we could play games or just sit with our friends and talk. There was even some blacktop where we used to roller skate or ride our skateboards. Now, the building is closed because there's no one to take care of it. Mr. Ross used to volunteer his time on the weekends to make sure the building was kept up for us kids, but he retired and moved to Florida.

2 A meeting place for us kids is a great idea for our town. Right now, we have no place to go where we can be with our friends. When we go to the movies, the security guards are mean to us. They're always chasing us away.

Sometimes, they even holler at us for laughing too loudly. How can we help it if something's funny? Don't you laugh out loud sometimes, too?

3 Every time we ask for a meeting place for us teens, we're told that large groups of teens cause trouble. Why do people say this to us? We don't look for trouble. Now, I know that some kids can cause problems, but that's why there are adults to watch us. If you put a large group of adults together, don't you think that some of them would get in trouble too? If you don't believe me, just look at the police records for the past month. Are teens the only ones causing trouble?

4 Last month when we came to a town council meeting to ask for a teen center, you became upset with us. You told us that there were too many kids hanging out in the Maple Grove Shopping Center parking lot behind the movie theater. You told us that you were concerned that nine teenagers had been arrested for fighting during the last month. That may be so, but those kids don't represent all of us in town who really want a place to go at night. If you gave us a teen center, there wouldn't be any more trouble in town because we'd be off the streets. We'd all want to be with our friends.

5 Please reconsider my request for a teen center in town. It's a place we really need.

6 Without it, we'll probably just keep having trouble in town.

Sincerely,

Victoria Martinez

1. Which of the following statements from the letter are facts?

☐ A. Mr. Ross continues to volunteer his time so the building where the kids would skate and skateboard is "kept up for us kids."

☐ B. Victoria Martinez wrote the letter to Mayor Patel and requested a new teen center.

☐ C. Victoria Martinez tells Mayor Patel that she has also written a letter to her friends to ask for their support.

☐ D. Mayor Patel is hearing for the first time this request from Victoria Martinez and her friends for a new teen center.

☐ E. Mayor Patel believes that there is already a problem with "too many kids hanging out in the Maple Grove Shopping Center parking lot behind the movie theater."

☐ F. Mayor Patel once agreed to build a new teen center, but the request was not able to be realized because of a budget deficit.

2. Which of these statements are opinion statements?

   ☐ A. "I believe that we should have a place in town where all the kids can get together." (paragraph 1)

   ☐ B. "The park near the river used to have a building where we could play games or just sit with our friends and talk." (paragraph 1)

   ☐ C. "There was even some blacktop where we used to roller skate or ride our skateboards." (paragraph 1)

   ☐ D. "A meeting place for us kids is a great idea for our town. (paragraph 2)

   ☐ E. "When we go to the movies, the security guards are mean to us." (paragraph 2)

   ☐ F. "We don't look for trouble." (paragraph 3)

Be sure to check your answers with those on page 218.

Essential Reading Skills: Following Directions

To do something well, we should make sure that we follow directions carefully. These are our guides for success.

Strategy

As you are doing your reading, use these strategies.
Directions are given in order. We must follow the order to get the desired result.

- Look for key words and phrases—for example, **"first,"** **"next,"** and **"after,"** completing *Step 1.*
- Look for warning phrases—for example, **"before continuing"** and **"be sure to."**
- Only use the directions that are given to write your essay. Do not wander from the topic. Follow the directions that you have been given.

The passage that we'll read contains the guidelines to a Guided Reading Book Report for 7th grade. The focus is on following directions.

Read the passage thoroughly, then answer the questions. **Be sure to**:

```
┌──────────────────────────────────────┐
│  ███ PREVIEW TECHNIQUE ███            │
│                                        │
│  1. Preview the questions.             │
│  2. Preview the material.              │
│  3. Read the entire passage.           │
└──────────────────────────────────────┘
```

Guided Reading Book Report Guidelines

1 Reading a good novel can be exciting. Finding out about the different characters and learning how the author blends each action and scene together are only some of the thrills you can have while reading. This experience can be a good one. If you read your book with a friend, then you can discuss the book together. That means that it's OK to pick out a book to read with a friend, read the book together, and then discuss it too.

2 Once you select your book, you will need to follow these steps.

1. Find a friend who also wants to read the same book.
2. Have your parent/guardian sign your book permission slip.
3. Return your slip to Mr. Rhoades by February 26.
4. Write down the following information in your personal guided reading log:

   a. Your name.
   b. Your reading partner's name.
   c. The title and author of the book that you and your partner are reading.

5. Divide your book into three sections. Enter the page numbers into your reading log.
6. Write down the dates that you plan to discuss each section of your book. Be sure to schedule a meeting at least once a week so you and your partner can complete the assignment no later than March 18.

3 You will be expected to finish reading the book and complete all the discussions with your partner. If you wish to read more quickly than the rest of the class, you may do so without worrying about discussing sections that you were not yet assigned to read. Sometimes when you are really interested in a book, you want to read ahead. This unit has been designed to encourage you to do that.

4 Once a week, you and your partner will form a guided reading small discussion group. You will meet for no more than 20 minutes with another pair of students who are reading a different book. One of you will serve as a group facilitator who will keep the discussion "on track." You will also select a recorder who will take notes that will be signed by all group members and submitted to Mr. Rhoades. Your group must answer the following questions each time you meet:

- What are the major events that have happened in this section of the novel?
- Who are the major characters, and what are their roles?
- What conflicts are occurring?
- What is the biggest change you have observed from the beginning to the end of the section?
- Who is your favorite character in this section and why?
- What advice would you give to the main characters at this stage of the book?
- What grade (A, B, etc.) would you give this section of the book and why?

5 When you finish your student meetings, you will then share your responses with Mr. Rhoades. You must complete all three sessions by the March 18 deadline stated to receive two "A+" grades. Completing two sessions will earn you two "C" grades. Completing one session will earn you two "D" grades. A failure to complete any sessions will result in two "0" grades.

6 If you have any questions during this unit, please ask Mr. Rhoades at once. Also, please share with Mr. Rhoades any difficulties and successes that you may have.

1. Which of the following statements may be considered to be factual concerning the book report?

- ☐ A. "Reading a good novel can be exciting." (paragraph 1)
- ☐ B. "Finding out about the different characters and learning how the author blends each action and scene together are only some of the thrills you can have while reading." (paragraph 1)
- ☐ C. "If you read your book with a friend, then you may discuss the book together." (paragraph 1)
- ☐ D. "Have your parent/guardian sign your book permission slip." (paragraph 2)
- ☐ E. "Sometimes when you are really interested in a book, you want to read ahead." (paragraph 3)
- ☐ F. "Once a week, you and your partner will form a guided reading small discussion group." (paragraph 4)

2. **Part A**

Which of the following book genres are being assigned for the Guided Reading Book Report?

- ○ A. free choice
- ○ B. free choice fiction
- ○ C. free choice non-fiction
- ○ D. free choice biography

Part B

Which qualities are **not** generic to the genre being assigned?

- ○ A. The genre only deals with the past.
- ○ B. The genre only deals with the present.
- ○ C. The genre only deals with the future.
- ○ D. The story contains a fictional main plot, conflict, and a resolution.

3. Which of the following information does **not** need to be included "in your personal guided reading log"?

- ○ A. your reading partner's name
- ○ B. your parent/guardian's signature
- ○ C. the title and author of the book that you and your partner are reading
- ○ D. the number of books you have read so far during the marking period

4. Which of these statements is true concerning this assignment?

- ☐ A. You may not read a book that anyone else in class is already reading.
- ☐ B. A permission slip is suggested but not necessary.
- ☐ C. The deadline for the project is February 26.
- ☐ D. You must keep a reading log.
- ☐ E. You may not read ahead of the rest of the class.
- ☐ F. For each session, you must discuss with your group the conflicts in the book.

Be sure to check your answers with those on pages 218–219.

Plot, Characters, and Setting

- **Plot** is the basic story line: the major events. The plot can be either simple or complex.
- **Characters** are the "players" in the work. The most important ones are main characters. Those who aren't as important are minor characters.
- **Setting** is the location in which the action takes place. When the action shifts to another place, the setting changes.

Strategy

- The minor events in the **plot** affect the major ones.
- **Characters** often have opposite points of view and different situations. These can help you to understand the reasons (motives) for the **characters'** actions.
- The **setting** helps the author get the main message **(theme)** across. For example, if the setting's peaceful, the author may want the actions to be peaceful.

The first passage we'll look at is from L. Frank Baum's classic novel, *The Wonderful Wizard of Oz*. Even if you know the story well, you should still use the **PT** to help you make the best decisions on your test. **Be sure to:**

PREVIEW TECHNIQUE

1. Preview the questions.
2. Preview the material.
3. Read the entire passage.

The Wonderful Wizard of Oz

by L. Frank Baum

Chapter 1. The Cyclone

1 Dorothy lived in the midst of the great Kansas prairies, with Uncle Henry, who was a farmer, and Aunt Em, who was the farmer's wife. Their house was small, for the lumber to build it had to be carried by wagon many miles. There were four walls, a floor and a roof, which made one room; and this room contained a rusty looking cookstove, a cupboard for the dishes, a table, three or four chairs, and the beds. Uncle Henry and Aunt Em had a big bed in one corner, and Dorothy a little bed in another corner. There was no garret at all, and no cellar—except a small hole dug in the ground, called a cyclone cellar, where the family could go in case one of those great whirlwinds arose, mighty enough to crush any building in its path. It was reached by a trap door in the middle of the floor, from which a ladder led down into the small, dark hole.

2   When Dorothy stood in the doorway and looked around, she could see nothing but the great gray prairie on every side. Not a tree nor a house broke the broad sweep of flat country that reached to the edge of the sky in all directions. The sun had baked the plowed land into a gray mass, with little cracks running through it. Even the grass was not green, for the sun had burned the tops of the long blades until they were the same gray color to be seen everywhere. Once the house had been painted, but the sun blistered the paint and the rains washed it away, and now the house was as dull and gray as everything else. When Aunt Em came there to live she was a young, pretty wife. The sun and wind had changed her, too. They had taken the sparkle from her eyes and left them a sober gray; they had taken the red from her cheeks and lips, and they were gray also. She was thin and gaunt, and never smiled now. When Dorothy, who was an orphan, first came to her, Aunt Em had been so startled by the child's laughter that she would scream and press her hand upon her heart whenever Dorothy's merry voice reached her ears; and she still looked at the little girl with wonder that she could find anything to laugh at.

3   Uncle Henry never laughed. He worked hard from morning till night and did not know what joy was. He was gray also, from his long beard to his rough boots, and he looked stern and solemn, and rarely spoke. It was Toto that made Dorothy laugh, and saved her from growing as gray as her other surroundings. Toto was not gray; he was a little black dog, with long silky hair and small black eyes that twinkled merrily on either side of his funny, wee nose. Toto played all day long, and Dorothy played with him, and loved him dearly.

4   Today, however, they were not playing. Uncle Henry sat upon the doorstep and looked anxiously at the sky, which was even grayer than usual. Dorothy stood in the door with Toto in her arms, and looked at the sky too. Aunt Em was washing the dishes.

5   From the far north they heard a low wail of the wind, and Henry and Dorothy could see where the long grass bowed in waves before the coming

storm. There now came a sharp whistling in the air from the south, and as they turned their eyes that way they saw ripples in the grass coming from that direction also.

6 Suddenly Uncle Henry stood up. "There's a cyclone coming, Em," he called to his wife. "I'll go look after the stock." Then he ran toward the sheds where the cows and horses were kept.

7 Aunt Em dropped her work and came to the door. One glance told her of the danger close at hand. "Quick, Dorothy!" she screamed. "Run for the cellar!"

1. Which of these actions does **not** take place in this passage?

☐ A. Dorothy lived with her Uncle Henry and Aunt Em.
☐ B. Uncle Henry always laughed.
☐ C. Uncle Henry and Dorothy heard "a low wail of the wind" that came from the south.
☐ D. Aunt Em warned Dorothy to go in the cellar to protect herself from the cyclone that was coming.
☐ E. The tornado ripped through the house, destroying everything.

2. Which of these statements **best** describe Dorothy and Toto?

☐ A. Dorothy adopted Toto from a shelter, and he never left her side.
☐ B. Uncle Henry and Aunt Em gave Toto to Dorothy, and now Dorothy and Toto are always together.
☐ C. Toto always made Dorothy laugh.
☑ D. Dorothy loved Toto dearly.
☐ E. Dorothy loved Toto even more than she loved Uncle Henry and Aunt Em.

3. Select the events in the correct sequence from the order given below. Drag each one into the corresponding boxes. (Write the correct letter in the boxes.)

A. Dorothy saw "nothing but the great gray prairie on every side" of her.
B. Aunt Em warned Dorothy to "Run for the cellar!"
C. Uncle Henry sat on the doorstep and looked anxiously at the sky.
D. Uncle Henry "ran toward the sheds where the cows and horses were kept."
E. Uncle Henry said to his wife, "There's a cyclone coming, Em."

1. [   ]   3. [   ]   5. [   ]

2. [   ]   4. [   ]

4. **Part A**

The phrase "and he looked stern" is used in paragraph 3 to describe Uncle Henry. Which of the following defines the word **stern**?

- ☐ A. austere
- ☐ B. out of control
- ☐ C. filled with laughter
- ☐ D. sincere
- ☐ E. seldom amused

Part B

Which of the following details **best** relate to the answer to Part A?

- ☐ A. "There now came a sharp whistling in the air from the south…" (paragraph 5)
- ☐ B. "Uncle Henry never laughed." (paragraph 3)
- ☐ C. "Aunt Em had been so startled by the child's laughter…" (paragraph 2)
- ☐ D. "It was Toto that made Dorothy laugh…" (paragraph 3)
- ☐ E. "'Quick, Dorothy!' she screamed. 'Run for the cellar!'" (paragraph 7)
- ☐ F. "He did not know what joy was." (paragraph 3)

5. **Part A**

Read the following sentence from paragraph 1.

"There was no garret at all, and no cellar—except a small hole dug in the ground, called a cyclone cellar…"

The word **cyclone** refers to

- ○ A. a weather map.
- ○ B. a heat wave.
- ○ C. a desert breeze.
- ○ D. a storm with swirling winds.

Part B

Select the quotes from the passage that **best** relate to the answer to Part A.

- ☐ A. "…the sky, which was grayer than usual." (paragraph 4)
- ☐ B. "…she could see nothing but the great gray prairie on every side." (paragraph 2)
- ☐ C. "…a small hole dug in the ground…" (paragraph 1)
- ☐ D. "The sun had baked the plowed land into a gray mass…" (paragraph 2)
- ☐ E. "…the sun blistered the paint and the rains washed it away…" (paragraph 2)

6. Part A

Which of the following statements **best** describes the setting of the story?

- ○ A. an orphanage
- ○ B. the mountains and prairies in Kansas
- ○ C. the eastern coast of the United States
- ○ D. a farm on the prairies in Kansas

Part B

Which details from the passage **best** support the answer to Part A?

- ☐ A. "When Dorothy, who was an orphan…" (paragraph 2)
- ☐ B. "…the broad sweep of flat country that reached to the edge of the sky in all directions." (paragraph 2)
- ☐ C. "…she could see nothing but the great gray prairie on every side." (paragraph 2)
- ☐ D. "Dorothy lived in the midst of the great Kansas prairies…" (paragraph 1)
- ☐ E. "…the lumber to build it had to be carried by wagon many miles." (paragraph 1)

Be sure to check your answers with those on pages 219–221.

ANSWERING QUESTIONS BASED ON PAIRED PASSAGES—RESEARCH

Before we begin to analyze a passage that has a similar topic covered in *The Wonderful Wizard of Oz*, let's take a moment to discuss the ways informational text is organized. This information is critical for you to be successful on the PARCC since you will be asked questions about the structural patterns of selected informational texts.

Informational Text—Patterns

Chronological

The first structural pattern is a common one known as chronological. This pattern arranges facts according to the time at which they have occurred. For example, a social studies text covering the events of the Revolutionary War will often arrange battles as they occurred.

You are likely to find a timeline or chart that lists the most important events in the order in which they took place. For example, The Battle of Lexington and Concord is considered by many to be the first major battle of the Revolutionary War. Since it occurred in April 1775, it is listed before the Battle of Bunker Hill, which was fought in June 1775. A mention of the Battle of Saratoga would need to follow the Battle of Trenton since Trenton was fought in December 1776 while Saratoga was fought in October 1777. Other battles would need to be placed in the text according to the time order in which they took place.

When dealing with chronological order, common transitional phrases include *first of all*, *secondly*, *next*, *then*, *later*, and *finally*, along with any qualifying dates and times of the year.

Problem and Solution

Another method is known as problem and solution. Think of the beginning of a chapter in your math book in which you learn about key concepts. Often, your text will introduce a problem that includes the concept being taught. A step-by-step explanation will be shown that leads to the solution of the problem. When you are studying the associative property, for example, the problem will require you to use grouping. The problem asking you to solve $4(2x)$ requires that you regroup and then simplify. Therefore $4(2x)$ is regrouped to be $(4 \times 2)x$.

When the multiplication is done, then you can see that $(4 \times 2)x = 8x$. For an argumentative essay, the problem being addressed is explored and a solution is presented, along with a counter to the opposing side's strongest argument.

For problem and solution pieces, chronological order is important for each step. Common transitional phrases besides those already noted include numbered steps (*Step 1*, *Step 2…*), *therefore*, *as a result*, *nonetheless*, *also*, *furthermore*, *moreover*, and *in conclusion*.

Cause and Effect

In a cause and effect essay, a writer is often attempting to prove that certain causes have led directly to a resultant effect. Simply put, the stated result has occurred because of conditions *a*, *b*, *c*, and *d*. Text written about word events will explain causes that led up to a major event taking place. This event is the effect of the causes. For example, a paper for an environmental science assignment may focus on the causes of pollution in a community. Some of these may be a result of poor waste disposal methods, a lack of a comprehensive recycling program, excessive highway noise, and the excessive use of woodlands for commercial building projects. The effect is a harsh negative impact on the local environment. This will probably result in imbalances and maybe toxicity in the land, water, and air. There may also be a negative impact on the plant and animal life, as well as on the people living in the area. A key to writing a successful cause and effect piece is being sure to use textual evidence to support your point of view. References to the text should actually be direct quotes rather than indirect ones. The reason is simple. A reader is unlikely to miss material that is highlighted in quotations, but a text reference can easily be missed if a reader doesn't realize that the information being given is being taken directly from the text. For cause and effect pieces, common transitional phrases besides those already noted include, *since, because of the fact, for that reason, provided that, thus,* and *for this reason.*

Compare and Contrast

To create a compare and contrast essay, you must focus upon similarities and differences among two or more topics. Imagine that your English teacher has assigned you to write an essay comparing the writing styles of Ray Bradbury and John Steinbeck. You can compare the two by illustrating the passion each had for the topics that they addressed. Bradbury and Steinbeck both showed the ways that people can sometimes be a bit harsh. Both Bradbury and Steinbeck wrote of characters who were the victims of an unthinkable and at times harsh society. However, Bradbury's prose has a definite poetry in its descriptiveness although that sometimes became excessive. On the other hand, Steinbeck used a more economical and less flowery style to describe his characters and scenes.

For comparison and contrast pieces, common transitional phrases besides those already noted include *despite, nevertheless, nonetheless, on the one hand, on the other hand, similarly, in contrast,* and *in similar fashion.*

Description

When writing an essay using description, your major task is to paint a clear word picture.

You must give the details in such a way that those who have little experience in the area can still understand your point clearly. Let's say that your teacher has assigned you a descriptive essay. You decide to describe the general rules of baseball. You decide that including the major areas of the game: pitching, hitting, fielding, throwing, base running, and strategy is too daunting a task. Therefore, you concentrate on hitting. You must consider the selection of a bat, the grip of the bat, the stance, the swing, and strategy. To do so effectively, you decide to take each area and explain it in detail so even someone who is not familiar with baseball can understand your points. Effective description will allow you to do this.

For description pieces, common transitional phrases besides those already noted include *in front of, behind, next to, across, over,* and *on top of.*

Paired Passages

Now that you have practiced with a single passage, let's move to the second one called a paired passage. *The Wonderful Wizard of Oz* is a novel that features the weather phenomena known as cyclones, or tornadoes. On the PARCC, you will be asked questions that are similar to the ones that you have just completed. However, another passage will be introduced. This passage will be similar to the previous one since it will contain material that somehow relates to the first passage. In this case, tornadoes are a plot device in the first work while they are the main topic in the second. Please read this second passage and then answer the questions that follow.

Tornadoes—The Facts

What exactly are tornadoes?

1 They are defined as violently spinning columns of air that both extend between and make contact with a cloud and the earth's surface. The winds of the most powerful tornadoes have been known to reach speeds of 200 miles an hour. Surprisingly, the winds of some tornadoes have even been measured at more than 250 miles an hour.

2 It is interesting to note that the speeds which a tornado's winds achieve are not measured during the weather event. Rather, they are determined once the tornado has moved on. The determining factor for figuring these speeds is the amount of damage that has been produced. Furthermore, a scale is used to determine the strength of each tornado. This scale is known as the Enhanced Fujita Scale. It uses a number progression from one to five to categorize the tornado's power. A rating of zero is assigned to the weakest tornadoes while a rating of five is assigned to those with the most intense power. According to the National Oceanic and Atmospheric Administration (NOAA), tornadoes cause about 70 deaths and 1,500 injuries each year.

3 Tornadoes are often mistakenly referred to as cyclones, as L. Frank Baum did in *The Wonderful Wizard of Oz*. It should be noted that Baum made this meteorological error by calling the tornado in the story a cyclone. Actually, a cyclone is a hurricane and not a tornado.

Is there a pattern that tornadoes follow?

4 Tornadoes are quite unpredictable. It seems that they can touch down in an area one at a time. However, they can also travel in clusters. When they

do so, their potential to wreak havoc and cause devastation to homes, farms, buildings, and any edifice and area in their paths increases greatly. Generally, the pattern that tornadoes follow is variable and somewhat unpredictable. They are capable of leveling an area as small as less than 100 yards wide and as large as more than a mile or two wide. In fact, some tornadoes can travel on the ground for more than 50 miles.

Can a person see through tornadoes?

5   At first, tornadoes may be almost transparent. However, as they travel, they gather up a collection of dust and debris. As these begin to accumulate inside the tunnels of the tornadoes, the transparency lessens considerably. It is interesting to note that tornadoes tend to move from the southwest to the northeast, but they have been seen moving in any direction.

Where are tornadoes most common?

6   Unfortunately for Americans, the United States reports the highest incidence of tornadoes. Even though fewer than 25 or so tornadoes may be reported by the media during the year, over 1,000 tornadoes devastate some part of the country during a typical year. It seems that there are certain geographical factors that make this possible. For instance, Canada to the north sends down its air from the North Pole. The Gulf of Mexico supplies warm, moist air. The Southwest region is also a factor by supplying very dry air. Whenever these three fronts combine, the potential for both thunderstorms and tornadoes rises dramatically.

Is there a section of the U.S. where tornadoes are the most common?

7   In the United States, the state of Texas has the highest incidence of tornadoes with an average of almost 140 tornadoes each year. The next highest state on average is Oklahoma with 57 every year. Kansas and Florida are tied for third place with an average of 55 a year.

8   The United States has the highest incidence of tornadoes worldwide, with more than 1,000 occurring every year. This is due to the unique geography that brings together polar air from Canada, tropical air from the Gulf of Mexico, and dry air from the Southwest to clash in the middle of the country, producing thunderstorms and the tornadoes they spawn.

9   What should people do if they hear that a tornado warning has been issued? First of all, note that a tornado watch is issued when severe stormy

weather is predicted within the upcoming hours. At this time, it is wise to take shelter. Listen to the local radio and TV reports to stay current with the weather situation. Find a safe, solid shelter and go there if you have time. Do not open your windows to alleviate the pressure from the tornado because you may be injured by flying glass while you are opening the windows. Besides, there is no advantage gained by opening the windows.

If a tornado is coming in your direction, what should you do?

10 If you see a tornado approaching, run in the opposite direction of its path. Your main concern is your own safety and that of your family. The best course of action is to leave the area of the storm before it becomes visible. Forget about your possessions. Those can be replaced. You and your family cannot.

In *The Wonderful Wizard of Oz*, L. Frank Baum wrote that a "cyclone" swept up Dorothy and Toto. Doesn't "cyclone" refer to a hurricane and not a tornado?

11 When L. Frank Baum wrote his novel, he actually misused the term "cyclone." It does indeed refer to a hurricane, but the twister that Dorothy experienced was a tornado. A hurricane generally has strong, blowing winds, but those winds are not necessarily swirling. Therefore, Baum's "cyclone" was actually a tornado. For the following questions, we shall use the term "tornado" and "cyclone" interchangeably to reflect Baum's intent.

1. Which of the following **two** facts mentioned in the second passage are **not** supported in *The Wonderful Wizard of Oz*?

   - ☐ A. Tornadoes have the potential to be dangerous.
   - ☐ B. The winds of the most powerful tornadoes have been known to reach speeds of 200 miles an hour.
   - ☐ C. Tornadoes are not common in Kansas.
   - ☐ D. The United States has the highest incidence of tornadoes.
   - ☐ E. Some tornadoes have been known to travel along the ground for 50 miles.

2. When comparing *The Wonderful Wizard of Oz* with "Tornadoes—The Facts," select the **two** answers that are correct.

   ☐ A. *The Wonderful Wizard of Oz* is written to inform and "Tornadoes—The Facts" is written to entertain.

   ☐ B. *The Wonderful Wizard of Oz* gives advice for anyone who sees a cyclone approaching and "Tornadoes—The Facts" does not.

   ☐ C. *The Wonderful Wizard of Oz* refers to the weather phenomenon as a cyclone while "Tornadoes—The Facts" refers to the weather phenomenon as a tornado.

   ☐ D. *The Wonderful Wizard of Oz* portrays a set of fictional characters who are dealing with a cyclone and "Tornadoes—The Facts" contains advice but no characters.

   ☐ E. *The Wonderful Wizard of Oz* is non-fictional, and "Tornadoes—The Facts" is fictional.

3. What information from "Tornadoes—The Facts" is important to include in a summary? Choose **three** facts from the list below and arrange them in the correct order to create a short summary.

   A. Tornadoes make contact with a cloud and the surface of the earth over which they are traveling.

   B. *The Wonderful Wizard of Oz* is set in Kansas and features a cyclone, which is another name for a blizzard.

   C. Some people have been known to follow tornadoes while recording these "twisters" on cameras.

   D. More tornadoes occur in the United States than they do in any other part of the world.

   E. People should turn off their radios and TV sets during a tornado to conserve electricity.

   F. Even though tornadoes generally move from the southwest to the northeast, they have been known to travel in every direction.

4. Which of the following **two** facts does "Tornadoes—The Facts" present to support the idea that tornadoes can be very dangerous?

   ☐ A. Every tornado is almost completely transparent as it travels across the ground.
   ☐ B. The winds of a tornado are seldom more than 125 miles per hour.
   ☐ C. The pattern of a tornado is at times unpredictable and variable.
   ☐ D. The Enhanced Fujita Scale, used to measure the strength of tornadoes, assigns a rating of five to the most powerful tornadoes.
   ☐ E. Opening your windows during a tornado will help to equalize the pressure in your house and thereby help to keep it safe.
   ☐ F. When a tornado watch is announced, it is wise to take shelter.

5. What is the pattern in which this text is arranged?
   ○ A. cause and effect
   ○ B. compare and contrast
   ○ C. description
   ○ D. problem and solution

Be sure to check your answers with those on pages 221–222.

WRITING CLEAR, THOROUGH ESSAYS BASED ON READING PASSAGES

You'll be writing essays dealing with questions relating to the themes, structures, characters, people, and/or concepts, and purposes of paired fictional and non-fictional pieces. The short answers are scored 4 (high) to 0 (low). To earn a score of 4, you must answer the question thoroughly, support your main point(s) with details from the passage, add insight (thinking beyond obvious points), and use correct grammar, spelling, and vocabulary. A 2 is average. A 0 means the response either didn't answer the question or address the topic.

The first prompt requires a literary analysis of Baum's *The Wonderful Wizard of Oz.* You are asked to write about the author's use of description in the passage. You must remember to do the following things to be successful:

- Prewrite—Think about the prompt and sketch out a plan of action for your essay. Your plan should include direct textual evidence ("quotes") from the work. When you quote directly, there is no chance that a reviewer will miss your reference. The same is not always true for an indirect quote. This step should take five minutes or less to complete.
- Restate the question.

- As you begin to write, be sure to refer to your plan. Deviate from it only if it is absolutely necessary since you are being given no more than 30 minutes to complete the full task.
- When you are halfway finished with your essay, check to see that you have enough time to complete your task. If you are running behind schedule, then you may need to combine the important points so they get covered in your essay. Also, make sure that you are staying on topic. Do not "bird walk" (go off on a tangent). Stick to the prompt.
- When you finish writing, you should have at least five more minutes to edit your work. Be sure to check your spelling, sentence structure, and grammar. Make sure that you have used commas to separate compound sentences, used words correctly, changed to a simpler word if you are not sure of the meaning, substituted "happens when," "occurs when," or "takes place when," for "is when," and avoided mistakes at the beginning and the end of your piece. Those are the worst places to make a mistake since those are the places where you can make a good or bad first and last impression.

 ## HELPFUL HINTS FOR ESSAYS

Step 1—Preview the Questions
Read the questions given for the passage before you read the passage.

Step 2—Preview the Material
Skim through the essay and look for key words and phrases.

Step 3—Read the Entire Passage
Get all the information you'll need to answer the questions.

Step 4—Address the Prompt Directly
Be sure that you restate the question and make specific text references.

Essay for Plot, Character, and Setting

The setting of *The Wonderful Wizard of Oz* is a farm in Kansas. Explain how the author uses the setting (literary analysis) to show how difficult it must be to live there. Use the details in "Tornadoes—The Facts" to support your position.

PREWRITING SECTION
Use the empty space provided to make a writing plan for your essay before you begin writing.

Write your essay here.

Be sure to check your essay against the sample responses and suggestions on pages 222–226.

Theme, Cause and Effect, and Point of View

The **theme** is the main message that the author wants you to get while you're reading the work.

Every event has at least one **cause** that results in an **effect**.

Point of view deals either with the way a character sees things or the way a story is told. It's the "voice" that tells the story. A **first person narrator** tells the story in the "I" or "we" voice. A **second person narrator** tells the story in the "you" voice. A **third person narrator** tells the story using "she," "he," "it," or "they."

Strategy

When you're looking for the **theme**, ask yourself the following questions:

- What did I learn from this novel, story, or poem?
- What has the author had the main characters do to show the theme?
- Has the author made this point easy to see, or did (s)he hide it?

Look to connect the cause with the effect that results. Phrases like "As a result" and "Therefore" help to make the connection.

A **first person narrator** is a character who tells the story in the "I" or "we" voice. This allows you, the reader to be told the story by a character. A **second person narrator** speaks directly to "you" and often teaches a lesson. A **third person narrator** tells the story from someone who isn't usually part of the story.

Details and Sequence of Events

- Reading passages always have **details**, the facts that explain the information you're reading.
- The **sequence of events** is the order in which things happen.

Strategy

When looking for **details**, concentrate on the facts and not on opinions.

When looking for the **sequence of events**:

- Look for transition words and phrases like "**first**," "**next**," and "**the final step**."
- Look for numbers or bullet points to guide you.
- Look for the abbreviations "**AM**" and "**PM**" for time sequences.

Practice

The poem that you will read is one that you may have seen before. It is "The Road Not Taken" by Robert Frost.

Read the poem thoroughly, then answer the questions. **Be sure to:**

PREVIEW TECHNIQUE

1. Preview the questions.
2. Preview the material.
3. Read the entire passage.

"The Road Not Taken"
by Robert Frost

Two roads diverged in a yellow wood,
And sorry I could not travel both
And be one traveler, long I stood
And looked down one as far as I could
(5) To where it bent in the undergrowth

Then took the other, as just as fair,
And having perhaps the better claim,
Because it was grassy and wanted wear;
Though as for that the passing there
(10) Had worn them really about the same,

And both that morning equally lay
In leaves no step had trodden black.
Oh, I kept the first for another day!
Yet knowing how way leads on to way,
(15) I doubted if I should ever come back.

I shall be telling this with a sigh
Somewhere ages and ages hence:
Two roads diverged in a wood, and I—
I took the one less traveled by,
(20) And that has made all the difference.

1. From which point of view is the poem being told?

   ○ A. first person
   ○ B. second person
   ○ C. third person
   ○ D. both A and C

2. **Part A**

   What is the main idea in the first stanza (paragraph in poetry)?

   ○ A. The traveler was lost.
   ○ B. The traveler was hungry.
   ○ C. The traveler was happy that he could travel both roads.
   ○ D. The traveler was sad that he couldn't travel both roads.

   Part B

   Which line in the poem provides the detail to support the position in Part A?

   ○ A. "Two roads diverged in a yellow wood" (line 1)
   ○ B. "And sorry I could not travel both" (line 2)
   ○ C. "To where it bent in the undergrowth" (line 5)
   ○ D. "Because it was grassy and wanted wear" (line 8)

3. The traveler hoped someday to take the road that "bent in the undergrowth," but what did he believe that the effect of his hopes would be?

   ○ A. The traveler hoped but doubted he would take the other road some day.
   ○ B. The traveler was sure he would take the other road some day.
   ○ C. The traveler was paralyzed with fear.
   ○ D. The traveler was encouraged by his friend to take the other road.
   ○ E. The traveler was addled.

4. Part A

Which of the following details do not appear in the poem?

- ☐ A. Two roads ran parallel in the woods.
- ☐ B. The narrator took the more traveled road.
- ☐ C. The narrator couldn't decide which road to travel and thus took neither.
- ☐ D. The narrator took the road that had not been traveled as much as the other road.
- ☐ E. The narrator walked down each road before he made a decision about which one to travel.
- ☐ F. Each road was used about the same amount.
- ☐ G. The narrator believes that the course he chose to take has made a significant difference in his own life.
- ☐ H. The narrator isn't sure if he'll ever return to the road he had not taken.
- ☐ I. The narrator consulted with a good friend before deciding which road to take.

Part B

Drag (Write) the **three** details that happen in the poem and drop them in the boxes below. Make sure to place them in the order in which they are mentioned.

A. Two roads ran parallel in the woods.
B. The narrator took the more traveled road.
C. The narrator couldn't decide which road to travel and thus took neither.
D. The narrator took the road that had not been traveled as much as the other road.
E. The narrator walked down each road before he made a decision about which one to travel.
F. Each road was used about the same amount.
G. The narrator believes that the course he chose to take has made a significant difference in his own life.
H. The narrator isn't sure if he'll ever return to the road he had not taken.
I. The narrator consulted with a good friend before deciding which road to take.

5. Which of these statements describes the main theme of the poem?

    ○ A. The choice of the road taken happens in a dream.
    ○ B. The choice of the road taken is no challenge.
    ○ C. The choice of the road taken changes the traveler's life.
    ○ D. The choice of the road taken frustrated the traveler.

6. What is the rhyme scheme of the second stanza of the poem?

    ○ A. aabbc
    ○ B. abcbc
    ○ C. abbba
    ○ D. abaab

Be sure to check your answers with those on pages 226–227.

Fact vs. Opinion

A **fact** is information that can be measured and proven. An **opinion** shows the way someone feels about a **fact**.

Strategy
As you are doing your reading, use these strategies.

    A fact is something that is easy to measure and prove.

- Look for measurements for proof (for example, **gallons**, **days**, and **inches**).
- Look for quotes and citations from books and newspapers.

An **opinion** is an interpretation.

- Look for key words or phrases, such as **Sometimes** or **As I see it**.

Paired Passage

How Do We Handle a Challenge?

by Philip Postrun

1 Our lives are often filled with many challenges. There are problems that we need to solve, difficult questions that we need to answer, and obstacles that we have to overcome. We can either face those challenges or give in to them. Both options, however, can lead us in different directions in our lives.

2 Take, for example, an important assignment that we have been given. This assignment will count for one-third of our grade. Our options are fairly basic: we can work with a plan, divide up our time, and proceed to complete the task both well and on time. Our other option is to proceed without a plan. We may decide that there are friends that we would like to see, movies that we would like to watch, and games we would like to play. Eventually, however, the time will come to pass when our assignment will be due.

3 If we haven't worked hard so far, then we have placed ourselves in an unenviable position. We may wish to complete our work now, but we likely have run out of enough time to do the assignment effectively. We are definitely in a bind.

4 Imagine that a friend comes by and offers to help us to complete the assignment. He says that he can have someone get him a completed assignment. It will cost us some money, and we can't ask any questions. He also promises that he will deny helping to get the assignment if there is any trouble in the future. Do we give in, knowing that there's a chance that we could get caught cheating? If we are caught, then we shall be in serious trouble both at school and at home. If we don't cheat, however, then one-third of our grade may be an "F." That will also get us in trouble.

5 What should we do? Should we take the easy way out, or should we be honest and accept the consequences of our negligence, even though there will also be consequences for our honest actions? The answer is not a simple one, but facing these challenges is something we must ultimately do ourselves.

1. Which statement contains the theme of this passage?

- ○ A. "Our lives are often filled with many challenges."
- ○ B. "There are problems that we need to solve, difficult questions that we need to answer, and obstacles that we have to overcome."
- ○ C. "We can either face those challenges or give in to them."
- ○ D. "Facing these challenges is something we must ultimately do ourselves."

2. Which **four** of these statements from the passage are opinion statements, rather than factual statements? Select each opinion.

- ☐ A. "Our lives are often filled with many challenges."
- ☐ B. "Both options, however, can lead us in different directions in our lives."
- ☐ C. "This assignment will count for one-third of our grade."
- ☐ D. "…the time will come to pass when our assignment will be due."
- ☐ E. "If we haven't worked hard so far, then we have placed ourselves in an unenviable position."
- ☐ F. "He says that he can have someone get him a completed assignment."
- ☐ G. "The answer is not a simple one…"

3. Part A

How is this passage organized?

- ○ A. cause and effect
- ○ B. compare and contrast
- ○ C. description
- ○ D. problem and solution

Part B

Select the word from the passage that is common for the organizational pattern of the piece, as selected above.

- ○ A. "often" (paragraph 1)
- ○ B. "challenges" (paragraph 1)
- ○ C. "imagine" (paragraph 4)
- ○ D. "assignment" (paragraph 4)

4. Select the phrase from "How Do We Handle a Challenge?" that reflects the main idea in "The Road Not Taken."

- ○ A. "Take, for example, an important assignment that we have been given." (paragraph 2)
- ○ B. "If we haven't worked hard so far, then we have placed ourselves in an unenviable position." (paragraph 3)
- ○ C. "Do we give in, knowing that there's a chance that we could get caught cheating?" (paragraph 4)
- ○ D. "What should we do?" (paragraph 5)

5. In the sentence, "If we haven't worked hard so far, then we have placed ourselves in an unenviable position" (paragraph 3), what does the word **unenviable** mean?

- ○ A. difficult
- ○ B. inane
- ○ C. complicated
- ○ D. advantageous

Be sure to check your answers with those on pages 227–228.

Essay for Theme, Cause and Effect, Point of View, Details, Sequence, and Fact vs. Opinion

Both Robert Frost and Philip Postrun deal with the concept of facing a challenge. Compare the way each addresses the main idea, being sure to include the impact of the text structure, the similarities and differences in the causes and effects of the challenges, the author's point of view, and the author's intended response from the reader.

PREWRITING SECTION
Use the empty space provided to make a writing plan for
your essay before you begin writing.

Write your essay here.

Be sure to check your essay against the sample response and suggestions on pages 229–230.

Conflict and Resolution and Making Predictions

Conflict

The **conflict** refers to a problem. The main conflict is the main problem being faced by one or more of the protagonists (heroes) in the work.

Resolution

The **resolution** is the solution to the conflict. When the conflict is resolved, the resolution isn't always one that the protagonist(s) may have wanted.

Making Predictions

Making predictions helps you to use the information that you've read and to predict the action that's likely to take place.

Strategy

- The **conflict** should appear early in the work. One or more main characters are going to be challenged. This challenge will be the **main conflict**. In novels, there are often **minor conflicts** that make the **major conflict** appear even worse.
- The **resolution** happens when the problem is solved. Be sure to look for hints (**foreshadowing**) the author may give you to help you to guess the resolution. As you read the following passage, *The Queen Bee*, consider how the marble horses and the absence of men **foreshadow** the fate that will come to pass upon the two older brothers.
- Whether you **make predictions** about events likely to occur in the story or after the story ends, base them only on the story's information.

Practice

The fable that you will read is *The Queen Bee* by the Brothers Grimm. It deals with the struggles faced by three brothers. Answer the questions based on this passage.
Be sure to:

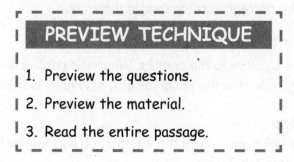

PREVIEW TECHNIQUE

1. Preview the questions.
2. Preview the material.
3. Read the entire passage.

The Queen Bee
by The Brothers Grimm

1   Two kings' sons once upon a time went into the world to seek their fortunes; but they soon fell into a wasteful foolish way of living, so that they could not return home again. Then their brother, who was a little insignificant dwarf, went out to seek for his brothers: but when he had found them they only laughed at him, to think that he, who was so young and simple, should try to travel through the world, when they, who were so much wiser, had been unable to get on. However, they all set out on their journey together, and came at last to an ant hill. The two elder brothers would have pulled it down, in order to see how the poor ants in their fright would run about and carry off their eggs. But the little dwarf said, "Let the poor things enjoy themselves; I will not suffer you to trouble them."

2   So on they went, and came to a lake where many ducks were swimming about. The two brothers wanted to catch two, and roast them. But the dwarf said, "Let the poor things enjoy themselves; you shall not kill them." Next they came to a bees nest in a hollow tree, and there was so much honey that it ran down the trunk; and the two brothers wanted to light a fire under the tree and kill the bees so they could get their honey. But the dwarf held them back and said, 'Let the pretty insects enjoy themselves; I cannot let you burn them."

3   At length the three brothers came to a castle: and as they passed by the stables they saw fine horses standing there, but all were of marble, and no man was to be seen.

4   Then they went through all the rooms, until they came to a door on which were three locks: but in the middle of the door was a wicket, so that they could look into the next room. There they saw a little grey old man sitting at a table; and they called to him once or twice, but he did not hear: however, they called a third time, and then he rose and came out to them.

5   He said nothing, but took hold of them and led them to a beautiful table covered with all sorts of good things; and when they had eaten and drunk, he showed each of them to a bed-chamber.

6   The next morning he came to the eldest and took him to a marble table, where there were three tablets, containing an account of the means by which the castle might be disenchanted. The first tablet said: "In the wood, under the moss, lie the thousand pearls belonging to the king's daughter; they must all be found: and if one be missing by set of sun, he who seeks them will be turned into marble."

7   The eldest brother set out, and sought for the pearls the whole day: but the evening came, and he had not found the first hundred: so he was turned into stone as the tablet had foretold.

8   The next day the second brother undertook the task; but he succeeded no better than the first; for he could only find the second hundred of the pearls; and therefore he too was turned into stone.

9   At last came the little dwarf's turn; and he looked in the moss; but it was so hard to find the pearls, and the job was so tiresome!—so he sat down upon a stone and cried. And as he sat there, the king of the ants (whose life he had saved) came to help him, with five thousand ants; and it was not long before they had found all the pearls and laid them in a heap.

10   The second tablet said: "The key of the princess's bed-chamber must be fished up out of the lake." And as the dwarf came to the brink of it, he saw the two ducks whose lives he had saved swimming about; and they dived down and soon brought in the key from the bottom.

11   The third task was the hardest. It was to choose the youngest and the best of the king's three daughters. Now they were all beautiful, and all exactly alike: but he was told that the eldest had eaten a piece of sugar, the next some sweet syrup, and the youngest a spoonful of honey; so he was to guess which it was that had eaten the honey.

12   Then came the queen of the bees, who had been saved by the little dwarf from the fire, and she tried the lips of all three; but at last she sat upon the lips of the one that had eaten the honey: and so the dwarf knew which was the youngest. Thus the spell was broken, and all who had been turned into stones awoke, and took their proper forms. And the dwarf married the youngest and the best of the princesses, and was king after her father's death; but his two brothers married the other two sisters.

1. Which of the brothers seems to shy away from conflict?

    ○ A. the youngest (the dwarf)
    ○ B. second oldest
    ○ C. oldest
    ○ D. all of the above

2. Part A

When the king's youngest son is referred to as "a little insignificant dwarf" (paragraph 1), the word **insignificant** means

    ○ A. unimportant.
    ○ B. important.
    ○ C. wealthy.
    ○ D. precocious.

Part B

Select the **two** phrases/sentences that refer to the opposite of the king's younger son's insignificance.

    ☐ A. "…they soon fell into a wasteful foolish way of living."
    ☐ B. "when he had found them they only laughed at him."
    ☐ C. "Let the pretty insects enjoy themselves; I cannot let you burn them."
    ☐ D. "they saw fine horses standing there, but all were of marble."
    ☐ E. "he could only find the second hundred of the pearls."
    ☐ F. "the dwarf married the youngest and the best of the princesses."

3. What conflict does the old man give the oldest brother to resolve?

    ○ A. find the first hundred pearls or be turned into marble
    ○ B. find all the missing pearls or be turned into marble
    ○ C. find the dwarf or be turned into stone
    ○ D. find the princess or be turned into stone

4. In paragraph 8, when "The next day the second brother undertook the task," he

    ○ A. ran away.
    ○ B. locked the old man in a prison and escaped with his brothers.
    ○ C. accepted the challenge and succeeded.
    ○ D. accepted the challenge and failed, also getting turned into marble.

5. Because the little brother (dwarf) had shown kindness to the ants, ducks, and bees, you can predict that

    ○ A. they would attack him because he's a dwarf.
    ○ B. they would pay him money.
    ○ C. they would run away because they're afraid of dwarfs.
    ○ D. they would help him later in the story.

Be sure to check your answers with those on pages 230–231.

"Friends, Romans, countrymen, lend me your ears"

William Shakespeare

Taken from *Julius Caesar* and spoken by Marc Antony (Act 3, Scene 2)

Friends, Romans, countrymen, lend me your ears;
I come to bury Caesar, not to praise him.
The evil that men do lives after them;
The good is oft interred with their bones;
(5) So let it be with Caesar. The noble Brutus
Hath told you Caesar was ambitious:
If it were so, it was a grievous fault,
And grievously hath Caesar answer'd it.
Here, under leave of Brutus and the rest—
(10) For Brutus is an honourable man;
So are they all, all honourable men—
Come I to speak in Caesar's funeral.
He was my friend, faithful and just to me:
But Brutus says he was ambitious;
(15) And Brutus is an honourable man.
He hath brought many captives home to Rome
Whose ransoms did the general coffers fill:
Did this in Caesar seem ambitious?

When that the poor have cried, Caesar hath wept:

(20) Ambition should be made of sterner stuff:

Yet Brutus says he was ambitious;

And Brutus is an honourable man.

You all did see that on the Lupercal

I thrice presented him a kingly crown,

(25) Which he did thrice refuse: was this ambition?

Yet Brutus says he was ambitious;

And, sure, he is an honourable man.

I speak not to disprove what Brutus spoke,

But here I am to speak what I do know.

(30) You all did love him once, not without cause:

What cause withholds you then, to mourn for him?

O judgment! thou art fled to brutish beasts,

And men have lost their reason. Bear with me;

My heart is in the coffin there with Caesar,

(35) And I must pause till it come back to me.

1. Part A

The word **ambitious** means

- ○ A. nervous.
- ○ B. uncaring.
- ○ C. somewhat dishonest.
- ○ D. having a strong desire or determination to succeed.

Part B

Marc Antony's purpose in this speech is to demonstrate that

- ○ A. there was a conflict between Caesar and Brutus caused by Brutus's ambition.
- ○ B. there was a conflict between Caesar and Brutus caused by Antony's ambition.
- ○ C. there was a conflict between Caesar and Brutus caused by Caesar's ambition.
- ○ D. the implied conflict is between Caesar and Antony.

2. **Part A**

When looking only at the opening two lines of Marc Antony's speech, "Friends, Romans, countrymen, lend me your ears; I come to bury Caesar, not to praise him," one could infer that

- ○ A. Marc Antony wished to portray Caesar as a hero.
- ○ B. Marc Antony was not liked by the citizens of Rome.
- ○ C. Marc Antony disliked Caesar.
- ○ D. Marc Antony was related to Caesar.

Part B

When Marc Antony says, "When that the poor have cried, Caesar hath wept: Ambition should be made of sterner stuff: Yet Brutus says he was ambitious; And Brutus is an honourable man," Marc Antony is actually saying

- ○ A. Caesar was overly emotional, and stress had caused his death.
- ○ B. Brutus was honorable, and Caesar was not.
- ○ C. Caesar was a poor man when he died.
- ○ D. Caesar was honorable, and Brutus was not.

3. **Part A**

What does the word **sterner** mean when Marc Antony says, "Ambition should be made of sterner stuff" (line 20)?

- ○ A. more serious
- ○ B. more intelligent
- ○ C. more imaginative
- ○ D. more creative

Part B

At this point in the speech, it can be concluded that the statement from Part A, "Ambition should be made of sterner stuff," means

- ○ A. Marc Antony is falsely accusing Brutus of stealing gold from Caesar's treasury.
- ○ B. Marc Antony says that Brutus's accusation that Caesar was "ambitious" is false.
- ○ C. Marc Antony is glad that Caesar has been killed so he (Antony) can ascend to the throne.
- ○ D. Marc Antony is angry that he has not received any praise for killing Caesar.

Be sure to check your answers with those on page 231.

Essay for Conflict and Resolution and Making Predictions

Both the dwarf in *The Queen Bee* and Marc Antony in his speech from Shakespeare's *Julius Caesar* were faced with a conflict that was not easy to resolve. Compare and contrast the challenge that each of these two individuals faced. Explain how the paths that led each one to the resolution of his problem were developed by the authors. You are encouraged to acknowledge the use of the literary devices used by the authors.

PREWRITING SECTION
Use the empty space provided to make a writing plan for your essay before you begin writing.

Write your essay here.

Be sure to check your essay against the sample responses and suggestions on pages 232–234.

Mood and Tone

Mood

Mood is the general feeling "in the air" in a work. The mood could be gloomy, realistic, hopeful, or even romantic.

Tone

Tone is the attitude or way the speaker presents himself/herself. The tone could be serious, angry, happy, sad, or formal.

Strategy

- When reading, pretend that the narrator and main character(s) are speaking directly to you. As you listen to their words, consider how the situation feels to you. Is it hopeful? Are things dark and depressing? To find the mood, just listen to the way the story's being told. It may help you to understand mood if you place yourself directly into a situation that has occurred in your favorite story, novel, movie, TV show, or even song. Next, examine the feelings that you are experiencing. If there is hope for a brighter future, then the mood would likely be positive and uplifting. On the other hand, a feeling of hopelessness would set a quite somber mood.

- You can find the tone in a similar way. What emotions are the narrator and main character(s) feeling? Are they discussing serious issues, yelling during a fight, smiling, or speaking formally? What types of words are they using? Are these words supportive ("I'll help you right away," for example) or are these words displaying displeasure ("You'll never be able to steal from me again, you horrible thief!")? These emotions reflect the tone of the text.

> It is important for you to be able to analyze the mood and tone of a piece. Many of the concepts being tested, including author's intent, motivation, irony, and foreshadowing can be impacted by both mood and tone.

Practice

In the poem "The Children's Hour," Henry Wadsworth Longfellow shares the narrator's thoughts about an evening spent while playing with his children, to whom he was very devoted.

Read the poem thoroughly, then answer the questions. **Be sure to:**

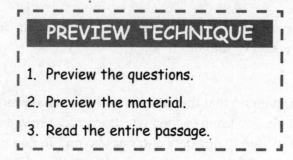

"The Children's Hour"

by Henry Wadsworth Longfellow

(1) Between the dark and the daylight,
When the night is beginning to lower,
Comes a pause in the day's occupations,
That is known as the Children's Hour.

(5) I hear in the chamber above me
The patter of little feet,
The sound of a door that is opened,
And voices soft and sweet.

From my study I see in the lamplight,
(10) Descending the broad hall stair,
Grave Alice, and laughing Allegra,
And Edith with golden hair.

A whisper, and then a silence:
Yet I know by their merry eyes
(15) They are plotting and planning together
To take me by surprise.

A sudden rush from the stairway,
A sudden raid from the hall!
By three doors left unguarded
(20)   They enter my castle wall!

They climb up into my turret
O'er the arms and back of my chair;
If I try to escape, they surround me;
They seem to be everywhere.

(25)   They almost devour me with kisses,
Their arms about me entwine,
Till I think of the Bishop of Bingen
In his Mouse-Tower on the Rhine!

Do you think, o blue-eyed banditti,
(30)   Because you have scaled the wall,
Such an old mustache as I am
Is not a match for you all!

I have you fast in my fortress,
And will not let you depart,
(35)   But put you down into the dungeon
In the round-tower of my heart.

And there will I keep you forever,
Yes, forever and a day,
Till the walls shall crumble to ruin,
(40)   And moulder in dust away!

1. What is the rhyme scheme used by Longfellow in his poem?

   - ○ A. aaab
   - ○ B. aabb
   - ○ C. aaba
   - ○ D. abcb

2. Which **two** of the following are **not** possible tones of the poem's first four lines "Between the dark and the daylight, when the night is beginning to lower, comes a pause in the day's occupations, that is known as the Children's Hour"?

   - ☐ A. formal
   - ☐ B. clear
   - ☐ C. realistic
   - ☐ D. gloomy
   - ☐ E. insincere

3. What word describes the tone of lines 13–16, "A whisper, and then a silence: Yet I know by their merry eyes—they are plotting and planning together—to take me by surprise"?

   - ○ A. nasty
   - ○ B. playful
   - ○ C. angry
   - ○ D. sad

4. **Part A**

   In line 21, Longfellow uses the word **turret**. Select the **two** choices that are correct definitions.

   - ☐ A. a small tower
   - ☐ B. bookcase
   - ☐ C. a tank missile
   - ☐ D. stairway
   - ☐ E. lap
   - ☐ F. a gunner's enclosure

Part B
Which four words from lines 21–24 connect with the term **turret** from Part A?

- ☐ A. climb
- ☐ B. arms
- ☐ C. back
- ☐ D. escape
- ☐ E. surround
- ☐ F. everywhere

5. Choose the tone of lines 29–32, "Do you think, o blue-eyed banditti, because you have scaled the wall, Such an old mustache as I am is not a match for you all!"

- ○ A. angry
- ○ B. pompous
- ○ C. sad
- ○ D. challenging

6. What is the mood of the narrator in lines 33–40, "I have you fast in my fortress, and will not let you depart, ...till the walls shall crumble to ruin, and moulder in dust away!"?

- ○ A. worried
- ○ B. sad
- ○ C. serious
- ○ D. playful

Be sure to check your answers with those on pages 234–235.

"We Shall Fight on the Beaches"

by Winston Churchill

Excerpts from a speech presented to the House of Commons on June 4, 1940

1   We are told that Herr Hitler has a plan for invading the British Isles. This has often been thought of before. When Napoleon lay at Boulogne for a year with his flat-bottomed boats and his Grand Army, he was told by someone. "There are bitter weeds in England." There are certainly a great many more of them since the British Expeditionary Force returned.

2   We have found it necessary to take measures of increasing stringency, not only against enemy aliens and suspicious characters of other nationalities, but also against British subjects who may become a danger or a nuisance should the war be transported to the United Kingdom. I know there are a great many people affected by the orders which we have made who are the passionate enemies of Nazi Germany. I am very sorry for them, but we cannot, at the present time and under the present stress, draw all the distinctions which we should like to do. If parachute landings were attempted and fierce fighting attendant upon them followed, these unfortunate people would be far better out of the way, for their own sakes as well as for ours. There is, however, another class, for which I feel not the slightest sympathy. Parliament has given us the powers to put down Fifth Column activities with a strong hand, and we shall use those powers subject to the supervision and correction of the House, without the slightest hesitation until we are satisfied, and more than satisfied, that this malignancy in our midst has been effectively stamped out.

3   Turning once again, and this time more generally, to the question of invasion, I would observe that there has never been a period in all these long centuries of which we boast when an absolute guarantee against invasion, still less against serious raids, could have been given to our people. In the days of Napoleon the same wind which would have carried his transports across the Channel might have driven away the blockading fleet. There was always the chance, and it is that chance which has excited and befooled the imaginations of many Continental tyrants. Many are the tales that are told. We are assured that novel methods will be adopted, and when we see the originality of malice, the ingenuity of aggression, which our enemy displays, we may certainly prepare ourselves for every kind of novel stratagem and every kind of brutal and treacherous maneuver. I think that no idea is so outlandish that it should not be considered and viewed with a searching, but at the same time, I hope, with a steady eye. We must never forget the solid assurances of sea power and those which belong to air power if it can be locally exercised.

4 I have, myself, full confidence that if all do their duty, if nothing is neglected, and if the best arrangements are made, as they are being made, we shall prove ourselves once again able to defend our Island home, to ride out the storm of war, and to outlive the menace of tyranny, if necessary for years, if necessary alone. At any rate, that is what we are going to try to do. That is the resolve of His Majesty's Government—every man of them. That is the will of Parliament and the nation. The British Empire and the French Republic, linked together in their cause and in their need, will defend to the death their native soil, aiding each other like good comrades to the utmost of their strength. Even though large tracts of Europe and many old and famous States have fallen or may fall into the grip of the Gestapo and all the odious apparatus of Nazi rule, we shall not flag or fail. We shall go on to the end, we shall fight in France, we shall fight on the seas and oceans, we shall fight with growing confidence and growing strength in the air, we shall defend our Island, whatever the cost may be, we shall fight on the beaches, we shall fight on the landing grounds, we shall fight in the fields and in the streets, we shall fight in the hills; we shall never surrender, and even if, which I do not for a moment believe, this Island or a large part of it were subjugated and starving, then our Empire beyond the seas, armed and guarded by the British Fleet, would carry on the struggle, until, in God's good time, the New World, with all its power and might, steps forth to the rescue and the liberation of the old.

1. **Part A**

   Winston Churchill states that when Napoleon had prepared to invade England, he was told by someone that "There are bitter weeds in England." Select the **two** answers that correctly define the phrase **bitter weeds**. (paragraph 1)

   ☐ A. England could not defend itself.
   ☐ B. England was in the midst of a drought.
   ☐ C. England was a country known for its farms.
   ☐ D. England would not be an easy target for any invaders.
   ☐ E. England was prepared to defend itself, but would prefer a peaceful solution.
   ☐ F. England was prepared to defend itself aggressively as it had done in the past.

   Part B

   When Winston Churchill uses the phrase, "There are bitter weeds in England" from Part A, his tone is

   ○ A. timid.
   ○ B. inconsistent.
   ○ C. determined.
   ○ D. light-hearted.

2. Winston Churchill states that "We have found it necessary to take measures of increasing stringency." What does the word **stringency** mean?

   ○ A. rigor
   ○ B. exhaustion
   ○ C. mildness
   ○ D. creativity

3. **Part A**

   Winston Churchill uses the term **Fifth Column activities**. Choose the two answers that refer to the term.

   ☐ A. patriotism
   ☐ B. loyalty
   ☐ C. espionage
   ☐ D. oratory
   ☐ E. faith-based
   ☐ F. sabotage

Part B

Winston Churchill asserts, "We shall use those powers... until we are satisfied... that this malignancy in our midst has been effectively stamped out." To **whom** or to **what group** is he referring?

- ○ A. Napoleon's army
- ○ B. the British Expeditionary Force
- ○ C. British subjects
- ○ D. Fifth columnists

4. **Part A**

Which **two** words **best** describe the mood at the beginning of this excerpt?

- ☐ A. reassuring
- ☐ B. insensitive
- ☐ C. vengeful
- ☐ D. aggressive
- ☐ E. hopeful

Part B

Which **two** words **best** describe the mood at the conclusion of the excerpt?

- ☐ A. timid
- ☐ B. inconsistent
- ☐ C. determined
- ☐ D. light-hearted
- ☐ E. antagonistic
- ☐ F. uplifting

5. When Winston Churchill keeps saying the phrase, "We shall fight...," what literary term does he use?

- ○ A. simile
- ○ B. metaphor
- ○ C. personification
- ○ D. repetition for effect

Be sure to check your answers with those on pages 235–236.

Essay for Mood and Tone

Winston Churchill's excerpted speech deals with an invasion, as does Henry Wadsworth Longfellow's poem. Each has a particular purpose in mind. State each author's purpose and tell how each writer used the idea of a battle. Consider the intent of both authors, as well as the literary devices each uses to craft his piece.

Briefly explain what the tone of the poem is in the first four stanzas (paragraphs in poetry). Is Longfellow angry, serious, or sad? Is he formal, suspicious, or witty (clever)? Is the tone different from the choices mentioned?

PREWRITING SECTION
Use the empty space provided to make a writing plan for your essay before you begin writing.

Write your essay here.

Be sure to check your essay against the sample responses and suggestions on pages 236–238.

Poetic Devices—Metaphor, Simile, Personification, Rhyme Scheme, and Alliteration

Metaphor

A metaphor shows how two objects or ideas are similar, even though they're usually not similar. For example, "The cloud is a soft pillow."

An extended metaphor "connects" two objects or ideas. Moreover, it's used throughout the work instead of in just one section.

Simile

A simile also shows how two objects or ideas are similar, even though they're usually not similar. However, a simile uses "like" or "as" to make the comparison. A metaphor doesn't. For example, "The cloud is as soft as a pillow" or "She runs like a jaguar in the jungle."

Personification

Personification gives human or living qualities to non-human or non-living things. For example, "The river sang a peaceful song of hope to the weary travelers."

Rhyme Scheme

Rhyme scheme is the pattern of words that sound alike in two or more lines of a stanza (poetry paragraph). Look at the last word in the line to find the rhyme. In the following example, notice that lines one and three rhyme.

Example:
I went to the park
To play baseball.
When it became dark
I went home.

Alliteration (Specifically Assonance and Consonance)

Alliteration repeats the beginning sounds (often consonants) of words that are close by. When vowels are repeated, this form of alliteration is known as assonance. When consonants are repeated, this from is known as consonance.

First example (assonance):
All the animals are alive.
Anyone can achieve an "A" in astronomy class.

Second example (consonance):
Many more military men will receive medals this morning.
Most of the militia will be mentioned.

Strategy

Metaphors and similes add vivid description to literature.

- They provide vivid descriptions. For example, "The cloud is (as soft as) a pillow."
- They use the traits of the object or idea in the comparison. For example, "She was as stubborn as a forged bar of steel" suggests that the girl's will power is very strong.
- Metaphors and similes help you to see clearly the writer's images.

Personification adds life to descriptions. For example, "The ocean scolded the fishermen by slapping their boats with its powerful waves and roaring disapproval."

Practice

As you read Joyce Kilmer's poem, "Trees," notice Kilmer's use of metaphor, simile, and personification. Also, look for an extended metaphor.

Read the poem thoroughly, then answer the questions. **Be sure to:**

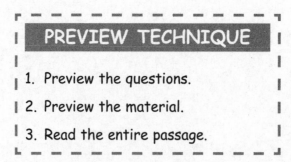

PREVIEW TECHNIQUE

1. Preview the questions.
2. Preview the material.
3. Read the entire passage.

"Trees"
By Joyce Kilmer

I think that I shall never see
A poem lovely as a tree.

A tree whose hungry mouth is prest (pressed)
Against the earth's sweet flowing breast;

(5) A tree that looks at God all day,
And lifts her leafy arms to pray;

A tree that may in Summer wear
A nest of robins in her hair;

Upon whose bosom snow has lain;
(10) Who intimately lives with rain.

Poems are made by fools like me,
But only God can make a tree.

1. The simile used in line 2 of the poem compares the poem to what object?

   O A. a tree
   O B. grass
   O C. a mouth
   O D. robins

2. In line 3 of the poem, what is the tree's "hungry mouth" doing?

   O A. speaking
   O B. crying
   O C. getting nourishment
   O D. yawning

3. **Part A**

   In line 6 of the poem, "And lifts her leafy arms to pray," what are the **three** literary devices being used?

   ☐ A. simile
   ☐ B. metaphor
   ☐ C. personification
   ☐ D. alliteration
   ☐ E. rhyme scheme

   Part B

   Which word relates to the image from Part A?

   ○ A. practical
   ○ B. romanticizing
   ○ C. neutral
   ○ D. imaginary

4. Lines 7 and 8 of the poem state, "A tree that may in Summer wear /
   A nest of robins in her hair." Choose the answer that explains the way the author is portraying the tree.

   ○ A. a hungry predator
   ○ B. a living form of shelter
   ○ C. a fashion model
   ○ D. the poet

5. Select **two** statements that would accurately portray Joyce Kilmer's feelings about trees as expressed in the poem.

   ☐ A. Trees exhaust all the nutrients from the earth.
   ☐ B. Trees are nice until they have to be cut down.
   ☐ C. Trees are a beautiful part of nature.
   ☐ D. Trees are a beautiful part of nature, but they can be dangerous for birds.
   ☐ E. Trees like the snow, but they don't enjoy the rain because it washes away the soil.
   ☐ F. Trees think that Joyce Kilmer is foolish.
   ☐ G. Trees can figuratively pray.

Be sure to check your answers with those on page 239.

Forest Trees of Wisconsin: How to Know Them

(Published by the Department of Natural Resources—
Madison, Wisconsin—Division of Forestry)

—Excerpted http://dnr.wi.gov/files/PDF/pubs/fr/FR0053.pdf

Introduction

1   Trees, like all living things, grow and mature and die while the forest, which is a community of trees, may live indefinitely because the trees reproduce before they die.

Vegetative Reproduction

2   Many trees reproduce vegetatively under certain conditions; for example, most of the broad leaf trees will sprout if cut when small, while some like basswood will sprout regardless of age. Others like the quaking aspen and black locust will send up shoots from the roots at considerable distance from the parent tree.

3   The only American conifer (cone-bearing tree) which sprouts is the redwood, but we have one conifer in Wisconsin which often reproduces vegetatively, but by a method other than sprouting. Lower limbs of black spruce often touch the ground and, where moss grows over the limb back of the tips, roots develop, and finally the tip of the branch becomes a new tree.

4   Man uses the ability of some trees to reproduce vegetatively. Cuttings from small branches of willow or eastern cottonwood bearing several buds can be set in the ground to grow, because they will develop roots. Other methods like budding and grafting are used to propagate horticultural varieties. We cannot grow Baldwin apple trees from seed, but must graft a twig from a Baldwin tree onto a seedling apple tree.

Reproduction by Seed

5   However, most of our forest trees grow from seed and the way the seeds are produced is the basis for classifying plants. For example, white pine seeds grow in pairs on the inner surface of the cone scales, while the hickory seed is enclosed in a nut. This really is the difference between the conifers or evergreens, and the broadleaf trees. In this bulletin the word "fruit" is used

in the botanical sense, meaning the seeds and seed bearing part, therefore, the acorn and its cup together constitute a fruit.

The Formation of Seed

6   Some seed is produced from "perfect" flowers, like the cherries where both stamens and pistils are found in the same tree. This is best illustrated with the corn plant, where the tassel or staminate flower produces the pollen which must fertilize the grains in the ear. You have all seen ears of corn where some of the kernels did not develop because they were not fertilized by pollen.

7   With some species like the ashes and the poplars, some trees have only staminate flowers and others only pistillate flowers, so that the female trees will not bear seed unless there are staminate trees in the vicinity. The Lombardy poplar which is a horticultural variety of the European poplar never bears seed because the variety was developed as a mutation and there are no Lombardy poplars bearing staminate flowers. Therefore, it is always reproduced vegetatively; that is, by cutting or sprouts.

Distribution of Seed

8   Since some trees mature their seed in spring while others ripen later, seeds developed several methods of scattering or planting themselves. Seeds from the aspens are very light and so perishable that they must come in contact with moist mineral soil within a few hours. As they are covered with cottony down they are carried by the wind. These two characteristics have enabled the aspen to reforest many of the burned over areas. Pin cherry also comes in on areas after forest fires because birds eat the cherries and may drop the seed far from the parent tree.

9   Seeds of pine, maple and basswood have wings so that they are carried farther by wind, while the heavy nuts and acorns are often buried by squirrels and then forgotten. Seeds of trees which grow along the stream banks are carried by the water.

10   Jack pine is especially interesting because it protects its seeds from fire. While most of the cones will open the first autumn, a few will remain closed, sometimes for many years. Then following a forest fire, these cones will open from the heat and drop seeds on the denuded land. In this way jack pine predominates on lands which originally carried mostly Norway or white

pine. If jack pine grows in your vicinity look for some of these unopened cones and place one on a hot stove and watch the scales open.

How Trees Grow

11 The growth of new wood in any year forms a complete layer over the entire tree. That is why we can determine the age of a tree from the number of rings on the stump. Height growth occurs only in the new wood of any one year. If a nail is driven into the trunk of a ten foot tree at five feet from the ground, it will still be five feet from the ground when the tree is a hundred feet tall.

12 The form of trees depends on the growing space. A close spacing between trees, shades the tree stems by restricting sunlight and causes side branches to die and fall off, leaving tall straight clean stems which are valuable for timber. Shade trees which have room to spread out have a large crown with spreading limbs and a short stem. Notice the trees at the edge of a forest, they have branches on the side towards the open while the other side is free of branches.

Variations in Trees

13 Since form and size or color and character of bark vary with size and growing conditions, too much importance should not be placed on them in identifying trees. The leaves from the lower branches of a tree may have a very different outline than those from the tip of the tree, while leaves on the sprouts from a tree which was cut may be excessively large and of unusual shape. Notice the difference between the twigs and needles of balsam trees when one has had full sunlight and the other grew in the shade.

14 An effort has been made to point out several distinguishing characteristics in describing each tree. After you have identified the trees, they can be recognized as you recognize your friends on the street even though you cannot describe them so that a stranger will recognize them.

1. **Part A**

   Select the **two** statements that are true from the "Introduction."

   ☐ A. Trees and forests are both communities.
   ☐ B. Neither trees nor forests are communities.
   ☐ C. Trees are communities, and forests are not.
   ☐ D. Forests are communities, and trees are not.
   ☐ E. Trees and forests have the same life span.
   ☐ F. Trees and forests have different life spans.

   Part B

   Which one of the following statements best supports the answer to Part A and explains the way in which the "Introduction" is structured?

   ○ A. chronological
   ○ B. sequence of events
   ○ C. cause and effect
   ○ D. compare and contrast

2. Select the **two** statements that are true about vegetative reproduction.

   ☐ A. Seeds or nuts from the trees are used in vegetative reproduction.
   ☐ B. Cuttings are used in vegetative reproduction.
   ☐ C. All conifers reproduce vegetatively by sprouting.
   ☐ D. Regardless of age, most conifers reproduce vegetatively by sprouting.
   ☐ E. Baldwin apple trees can grow from seeds and not from grafting.
   ☐ F. Most trees in the forest grow from seeds, not vegetative reproduction.

3. Choose the **two** statements that are true about forest trees that grow from seed.

   ☐ A. The acorn is considered to be a botanical fruit.
   ☐ B. The corn plant reproduces vegetatively, not by seed.
   ☐ C. For trees like the ashes and the poplars, "the female trees will not bear seed" unless there are pistillate trees "in the vicinity."
   ☐ D. The Lombardy poplar bears no staminate flowers since it was developed as a mutation.
   ☐ E. The Lombardy poplar can reproduce both vegetatively and through the formation of seed.

4. In the sentence from paragraph 10, "In this way jack pine predominates on lands which originally carried mostly Norway or white pine," what does the word **predominates** mean?

   ○ A. grows
   ○ B. simplifies
   ○ C. explores
   ○ D. prevails

5. Select the statements that you think are true.

   □ A. Since seeds from the aspen "are very light and so perishable" and their "cottony down covers" make them easy to be "carried by the wind," they are able to reforest any area that is not "burned over."

   □ B. After birds eat pin cherries, they "may drop the seed far from the parent tree" and thereby help to reforest areas "after forest fires."

   □ C. "Seeds of pine, maple and basswood have wings so that they are carried farther by wind," thereby hindering in the reproduction process.

   □ D. Since the jack pine "protects its seeds from fire," it is a good reforestation tree "following a forest fire."

   □ E. The "growing space" for trees has a direct effect on the "form of trees" growing in the space.

   □ F. When looking at "the trees at the edge of a forest," notice that the side that is "towards the open" part of the forest "is free of branches."

Be sure to check your answers with those on pages 239–241.

Poetic Devices—Metaphor, Simile, Personification, Rhyme Scheme, and Alliteration

Joyce Kilmer and The Wisconsin Division of Forestry had a different purpose in mind when writing about trees. Compare and contrast the pieces and focus on the genre they used, the way they created their imagery, and the method of explaining their topic. Also consider how the style and structure influenced their writing.

PREWRITING SECTION
**Use the empty space provided to make a writing plan for
your essay before you begin writing.**

Write your essay here.

Be sure to check your essay against the sample responses and suggestions on pages 241–243.

Reading: Informational (Everyday) Text

WHAT IS EVERYDAY READING?

In English class, you read many poems, stories, novels, grammar exercises, and more. In other classes and outside of school, you may be reading newspapers, magazines, e-mails, IM's (Instant Messages), **text messages**, and other printed material. This is **informational (everyday) reading**.

> Text messages are casual forms of writing that do not necessarily follow the rules of grammar and spelling. Therefore, text message form should not be used when you write any of your responses on the exam.

Reading every day will help you to be a better reader. It is important to keep practicing and keep up your skills.

Strategy

To answer questions for this unit, part of unit 1 of PARCC, you must read the passages carefully. Before you do so, continue to use the **PT (Preview Technique) Strategy**.

PREVIEW TECHNIQUE

1. Preview the questions you actually need to answer.

2. Preview the material.

3. Read the entire passage to find key lines or phrases that relate to the questions.

81

ANSWERING QUESTIONS BASED ON INFORMATIONAL TEXT

This section of the test will give you reading selections found in textbooks, magazines, reference books, or other sources. Even though you may find a topic or person that you don't know a lot about, read the entire passage carefully since the questions are based on the passage.

Details and Sequence of Events

- Reading passages always have **details**, the facts that explain the information you're reading.
- The **sequence of events** is the order in which things happen.

Strategy

When looking for **details**, concentrate on the facts and **not** on opinions.

When looking for the **sequence of events**:

- Look for transition words and phrases, such as, "**first**," "**next**," and "**the final step**."
- Look for numbers or bullet points to guide you.
- Look for the abbreviations "**AM**" and "**PM**" for time sequences.

SAMPLE PASSAGES

This passage is entitled "Things Had Really Changed!" It deals with a young boy who doesn't start out being happy on the first day of school. Use only facts from the passage to answer the questions that follow.

Things Had Really Changed!

1   When Jonathan walked into his 7th grade homeroom on the last day of class, he wasn't as happy as he thought he would be. Yes, he loved the freedom in the summer. He wouldn't have to follow a schedule every day. On the first day of school in September, Jonathan had quickly written a note in his planner as he sat down at his desk. The note said, "Only 179 more days to go until summer comes back!" He never expected that he might actually enjoy school this year.

2   Jonathan's previous years in school had not been that bad, but they also weren't great. He got into trouble sometimes, but he had never been suspended. He always knew when to stop his fooling around with his friends.

3   He didn't think that he would like any of his classes this year, but he was actually wrong. He found that he liked Miss Rumson's English class the best. She had encouraged him to write when he was in central detention with her last year. She had looked at some of his writing and even laughed at his story about falling off his bike while showing off to his friends.

4   Things would get even better in Miss Rumson's class. After he had handed in his first assignment, she told him that he has a lot of writing talent. A lot of teachers had said that to Jonathan before, but this was different somehow. Miss Rumson seemed to take a personal interest in Jonathan's writing.

5   For the first month of school, Miss Rumson tried to get Jonathan to join the school newspaper. He resisted at first, but Miss Rumson was persistent. Finally, he agreed and was assigned to cover the school's wrestling matches. Jonathan had never gone to a school event before because his friends would think he wasn't "cool." That's why he didn't tell his friends that he was going.

6   When he was at the first match, he noticed that the head cheerleader, Katie, smiled at him. He smiled back, but he didn't think anything about it. When his story came out about the school team's first win of the year,

Jonathan knew that his friends would make fun of him. Actually, that didn't happen because the captain of the team was also the brother of one of his good friends.

7 School really began to change for Jonathan. He started to take his books home every night. Sometimes he went out with his friends instead of studying, but there were times when he actually did study. After one of those times when he studied, he received the second highest grade on Miss Rumson's test. Who had received the top grade? Katie earned a perfect score, of course.

8 His friends teased Jonathan a little more for his high score on the test, but he didn't get as upset about it as he had thought he would. In fact, something good happened. Katie asked him if he would study with her for the next test. Jonathan was shocked, but he was also very pleased.

9 Jonathan believed that no one had ever thought that he was a good student. He remembered that his fourth grade teacher had told him he could be a very good student if he would just work a little harder. He hadn't listened because most of his friends didn't study. Jonathan hadn't wanted to lose his friends.

10 Things were different now. Jonathan was on the school newspaper. The older brother of one of his friends was on the team so Jonathan wouldn't be teased for covering the wrestlers for the school newspaper. More importantly, the head cheerleader, Katie, wanted to study with him.

11 Two weeks later, Jonathan had become a little uneasy. When he had arrived home after school, his mom mentioned that Miss Rumson had called. Even though he didn't remember doing anything wrong in school, he was ready to apologize. He figured that he must have done something wrong. Why else would the teacher be calling?

12 Well, things couldn't have been better for Jonathan. He learned that he had received the highest grade in the class on the last test. His grade was actually one point higher than Katie's. He also learned that Miss Rumson liked his reporting skills so much that she had contacted the local newspaper. The editor said that he would be willing to take Jonathan's reports about the school wrestling team and place them in the paper.

13 Jonathan had not been very happy when the school year had started. Now, he looked at things completely differently. The next day, Jonathan wrote in his planner that 7th grade wasn't so bad.

1. **Part A**
   Starting with Jonathan's first day in 7th grade, which event is out of sequence?

   ○ A. First, "Jonathan had quickly written a note in his planner as he sat down at his desk."
   ○ B. Second, Jonathan "was assigned to cover the school's wrestling matches."
   ○ C. Third, Jonathan "had received the highest grade in the class on the last test."
   ○ D. All events are listed in sequence.

   Part B
   Choose the words below that mean the same as **sequence**.

   ☐ A. randomness
   ☐ B. logical order
   ☐ C. inductive reasoning
   ☐ D. particular arrangement
   ☐ E. cohesion

2. **Part A**
   Why didn't Jonathan tell his friends that he was covering the wrestling team?

   ○ A. His best friend had been thrown off the team.
   ○ B. He thought his friends wouldn't think he was "cool."
   ○ C. He thought Katie wouldn't think he was "cool."
   ○ D. He thought his teachers wouldn't think he was "cool."

   Part B
   Jonathan's reason for **not** telling his friends that he was covering the wrestling team is an example of

   ○ A. implying.
   ○ B. investigating.
   ○ C. attempting not to lose his friends.
   ○ D. showing Katie he was better than she.
   ○ E. both B. and D.

3. **Part A**

For what group did Jonathan cover the wrestling team?

- ○ A.   the principal's newsletter
- ○ B.   the parent-teacher group's newsletter
- ○ C.   the class newspaper
- ○ D.   the school newspaper

Part B

Which of the following words are antonyms for the word **cover** as it is used in Part A?

- ○ A.   disregard
- ○ B.   incorporate
- ○ C.   report on
- ○ D.   instigate

Be sure to check your answers with those on page 243.

Essay for Details and Sequence of Events

Explain how "school really began to change for Jonathan." Next, relate how you have dealt successfully with a change that you have faced.

PREWRITING SECTION
Use the empty space provided to make a writing plan for your essay before you begin writing.

Write your essay here.

Be sure to check your essay against the suggestions on page 244.

Central Idea or Theme

The **theme** of a passage is different from the **main idea**. The theme states the main purpose of the message and is what Robert Frost referred to as "so what?" The theme is the reason a passage has been written. It refers to the general message that is conveyed or the lesson that is taught (which is seen often in fables and parables). Theme is also known as "the thesis," an idea that the author is trying to prove or disprove. The main idea, however, refers to the overall idea of a passage: what it is about. For example, the main idea of Aesop's fable "The Fox and the Grapes" is the struggle and subsequent failure of the fox to reach the grapes that are above him. The theme, however, is the lesson of the fable: "Sometimes people will give the impression that they don't care about something when they can't get it for themselves."

Please note: *Standardized tests often confuse the main idea and the theme. Therefore, be very careful when you answer this type of question. Look over your choices to make sure that the theme and the main idea are not being confused, and answer with the choice or choices that best seem to fit the question.*

Strategy

As you are reading a chapter in your textbook, an article on the Internet, or a story about a famous person, try these strategies to help you to find the **central idea** or **theme**.

- Look at the title since it may often contain the **central idea** or **theme**.

- Look at the first sentence in the first paragraph. It may either contain the theme or be leading you directly to it.

- Look for a summary or a closing comment at the end of the passage, as well.

Practice

You will read an article entitled "Vacation." It is about the different places you can go on a vacation right in your own country.

Read the passage thoroughly, then answer the questions. **Be sure to:**

PREVIEW TECHNIQUE

1. Preview the questions.
2. Preview the material.
3. Read the entire passage.

Vacation

1 Many of us travel long distances to take our vacations. Even though it's nice to travel, did you know that you could take a vacation right in your own country? Whether you like the mountains, the ocean, shopping, or sightseeing, there are many interesting attractions to see throughout your own country. Every state has great vacation spots.

2 If the mountains interest you, then visit the Delaware Water Gap in the northwest section of the state of New Jersey. They have hiking trails, boating, fishing, beautiful scenery, and more. If you head to the Skylands area in the northwest, be sure to visit in the winter. You'll find many skiing, snowboarding, and sledding areas where you can burn off some of that extra energy. Don't forget the reservoirs throughout the state that provide some of the same activities as the ones you can find in the Delaware Water Gap and the Skylands.

3 On a hot summer day, head for the shores of North Carolina. Explore miles and miles of sandy beaches where you can swim or get a tan. Get a few friends and ride your boogie board. Take a walk and enjoy the shops, the saltwater taffy, the Italian ice treats, and the amusements on the nearby boardwalks.

4 If you're into sports, New York has Madison Square Garden. This is the home of various professional sports teams. Baseball fans can take in a game at either Yankee Stadium or Citifield. Some of the teams that play there include the Yankees and the Mets. If you like auto racing, visit one of the auto racetracks that sponsor NASCAR and NHRA races in states like Alabama, Florida, and even Michigan. Throughout this country, there are many public parks for you to enjoy too!

5 Your own state may provide a lot of variety for your vacations, and you never have to leave. Depending on where you live, whether you're looking for amusement rides, majestic mountains, sandy beaches, sports, or history, you can find them in your own home state.

1. **Part A**

   Which of the following is the theme of "Vacation"?

   - ○ A. You should take a vacation.
   - ○ B. Vacations are overrated.
   - ○ C. When you take a vacation, you should look outside of your state.
   - ○ D. When you take a vacation, you should look to your own country first.

   Part B

   The main idea of the second paragraph of "Vacation" is

   - ○ A. mountains are dangerous.
   - ○ B. mountains in the Delaware Water Gap are dangerous.
   - ○ C. mountains in New Jersey are not as much fun as those elsewhere.
   - ○ D. mountains in the Delaware Water Gap can be fun for a vacation if they interest you.

2. **Part A**

   What is the main point of the third paragraph?

   - ○ A. It's hot at the seashore.
   - ○ B. The North Carolina seashore has swimming, shopping, food, and more.
   - ○ C. All of the historic areas are located at the seashore.
   - ○ D. The seashore doesn't get many visitors in the winter.

   Part B

   Which of the following words best describe the correct answer to Part A?

   - ☐ A. eclectic
   - ☐ B. diverse
   - ☐ C. implausible
   - ☐ D. isolated
   - ☐ E. sweltering
   - ☐ F. uniform

3. Which one of these statements is a detail that does **not** support the main idea in the fourth paragraph?

    ○ A. Madison Square Garden is the home of various professional sports teams.

    ○ B. There are eight different professional league parks for baseball.

    ○ C. There are swimming pools in many towns.

    ○ D. There are auto racetracks that sponsor NASCAR and NHRA races.

4. Which one of these statements is a detail that supports the main idea in the last paragraph?

    ○ A. Your own state may be the best place to take a vacation.

    ○ B. You can find beaches, shopping, and history elsewhere.

    ○ C. The entire country has great vacation spots.

    ○ D. The best places to vacation have mountains.

Be sure to check your answers with those on pages 244–245.

Essay for Main Idea or Theme

State the **main idea** or **theme** of the entire article. Be sure to use specific examples to explain your answer.

PREWRITING SECTION
Use the empty space provided to make a writing plan for your essay before you begin writing.

Write your essay here.

Be sure to check your essay against the suggestions on page 245.

Questioning, Clarifying, and Predicting

Questioning is the effective use of questions to gather information. **Clarifying** is the way to find out further information about a topic. **Predicting** is making educated guesses based on both the information that you have already found out and information that you already know.

Strategy

As you are doing your reading, use these strategies.

- [ ] For effective **questioning**, make sure that your questions are designed to bring you the information that you seek. Be specific.

- [ ] Use specific questions when you need help **clarifying** information.

- [ ] When you are **predicting**, make sure that your predictions are based on logic and common sense.

Practice

The excerpt that you will read is about two girls' friendship the last day of school.

Read the excerpt thoroughly, then answer the questions. **Be sure to:**

> ### PREVIEW TECHNIQUE
>
> 1. Preview the questions.
> 2. Preview the material.
> 3. Read the entire passage.

The Parting of the Ways
by Marjorie Dean

1   What am I going to do without you, Marjorie?" Mary Raymond's blue eyes looked suspiciously misty as she solemnly regarded her chum.

2   "What am I going to do without *you*, you mean," corrected Marjorie Dean, with a wistful smile. "Please, please don't let's talk of it. I simply can't bear it."

3   "One, two—only two more weeks now," sighed Mary. "You'll surely write to me, Marjorie?"

4 "Of course, silly girl," returned Marjorie, patting her friend's arm affectionately. "I'll write at least once a week."

5 Marjorie Dean's merry face looked unusually sober as she walked down the corridor beside Mary and into the locker room of the Franklin High School. The two friends put on their wraps almost in silence. The majority of the girl students of the big city high school had passed out some little time before. Marjorie had lingered for a last talk with Miss Fielding, who taught English and was the idol of the school, while Mary had hung about outside the classroom to wait for her chum. It seemed to Mary that the greatest sorrow of her sixteen years had come. Marjorie, her sworn ally and confidante, was going away for good and all.

6 When, six years before, a brown-eyed little girl of nine, with long golden-brown curls, had moved into the house next door to the Raymonds, Mary had lost no time in making her acquaintance. They had begun with shy little nods and smiles, which soon developed into doorstep confidences. Within two weeks Mary, whose eyes were very blue, and whose short yellow curls reminded one of the golden petals of a daffodil, had become Marjorie's adorer and slave. She it was who had escorted Marjorie to the Lincoln Grammar School and seen her triumphantly through her first week there. She was thrilled with unselfish pride to see how quickly the other little girls of the school had succumbed to Marjorie's charm. She had felt a most delightful sense of pardonable vanity when, as the year progressed, Marjorie had preferred her above all the others. She had clung to Mary, even though Alice Lawton, who rode to school every day in a shining limousine, had tried her utmost to be best friends with the brown-eyed little girl whose pretty face and lovable personality had soon made her the pet of the school.

7 Year after year Mary and Marjorie had lived side by side and kept their childish faith. But now, here they were, just beginning their freshman year in Franklin High School, to which they had so long looked forward, and about to be separated; for Marjorie's father had been made manager of the northern branch of his employer's business and Marjorie was going to live in the little city of Sanford. Instead of being a freshman in dear old Franklin, she was to enter the freshman class in Sanford High School, where she didn't know a solitary girl, and where she was sure she would be too unhappy for words.

1. **Part A.**

   In the phrase "she solemnly regarded her chum" (paragraph 1), the word **chum** means

   - ○ A. bait.
   - ○ B. relative.
   - ○ C. frenemy.
   - ○ D. friend.

   Part B

   What **two** words may be used as synonyms for **chum** as the word is used in Part A?

   - ☐ A. lure
   - ☐ B. hook
   - ☐ C. cousin
   - ☐ D. pal
   - ☐ E. graduate
   - ☐ F. rival
   - ☐ G. buddy

2. In the sentence "The two friends put on their wraps almost in silence" (paragraph 5), which of the following answers is the **most likely** reason why Mary Raymond and Marjorie Dean are not continuing their conversation?

   - ○ A. Mary is suspicious of Marjorie.
   - ○ B. Mary and Marjorie are beginning to realize that they will not be seeing each other regularly anymore.
   - ○ C. Marjorie is jealous of Mary.
   - ○ D. Mary and Marjorie had grown tired of each other.

3. Which of the following reasons might Marjorie likely have had for lingering "for a last talk with Miss Fielding"?

   - ☐ A. Marjorie wanted to ask Miss Fielding about her final grade.
   - ☐ B. Miss Fielding, a popular teacher, would be missed by Marjorie.
   - ☐ C. Marjorie was hoping to get a recommendation for her future college applications.
   - ☐ D. Marjorie was hoping that Mary would decide not to wait for her and therefore leave.
   - ☐ E. Marjorie and Mary had been rivals from the first day that Mary had moved in next to Marjorie.
   - ☐ F. Marjorie was trying to avoid having to leave school and soon afterwards, Mary.

4. **Part A**

In the sentence "She was thrilled with unselfish pride to see how quickly the other little girls of the school had succumbed to Marjorie's charm," the word **succumbed** means

- ○ A. triumphed.
- ○ B. overwhelmed.
- ○ C. submitted.
- ○ D. became inspired.

Part B

Which of the following words are antonyms for **succumbed** mentioned in Part A?

- ☐ A. capitulate
- ☐ B. conquer
- ☐ C. accede
- ☐ D. defend
- ☐ E. demise
- ☐ F. extant

5. Which of the following titles would be suitable ones to substitute for the original title?

- ☐ A. A Painful Move
- ☐ B. You're Finally Leaving
- ☐ C. Even Best Friends Keep Secrets From Each Other
- ☐ D. High School Adventures
- ☐ E. Friendship Can Sometimes Be Challenging
- ☐ F. Deception

Be sure to check your answers with those on pages 245–246.

Essay for Questioning, Clarifying, and Predicting

Predict how the summer is expected to go for Marjorie and Mary. Use information from the essay to support your predictions.

PREWRITING SECTION
Use the empty space provided to make a writing plan for your essay before you begin writing.

Write your essay here.

Be sure to check your essay against the suggestions on page 246.

Fact vs. Opinion

A **fact** is information that can be measured and proven. An **opinion** shows the way someone feels about a **fact**.

Strategy

As you are doing your reading, use these strategies.

A **fact** is something that is easy to measure and prove.

☐ Look for measurements for proof (for example, **gallons**, **days**, and **inches**).

☐ Look for quotes and citations from books and newspapers.

An opinion is an interpretation.

☐ Look for key words or phrases, such as **Sometimes** or **As I see it**.

Practice

The passage that you will read is a 7th-grade student's letter to the mayor of her town.

Read the passage thoroughly, then answer the questions that follow. **Be sure to:**

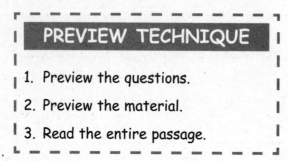

PREVIEW TECHNIQUE

1. Preview the questions.
2. Preview the material.
3. Read the entire passage.

A Letter to the Mayor

14 Pleasant Avenue
Springtown, NJ 09151

March 25, 2007

Dear Mayor Patel,

1   I believe that we should have a place in town where all the kids can get together. The park near the river used to have a building where we could play games or just sit with our friends and talk. There was even some blacktop where we used to roller skate or ride our skateboards. Now, the building is closed because there's no one to take care of it. Mr. Ross used to volunteer his time on the weekends to make sure the building was kept up for us kids, but he retired and moved to Florida.

2   A meeting place for us kids is a great idea for our town. Right now, we have no place to go where we can be with our friends. When we go to the movies, the security guards are mean to us. They're always chasing us away. Sometimes, they even holler at us for laughing too loudly. How can we help it if something's funny? Don't you laugh out loud sometimes, too?

3   Every time we ask for a meeting place for us teens, we're told that large groups of teens cause trouble. Why do people say this to us? We don't look for trouble. Now, I know that some kids can cause problems, but that's why there are adults to watch us. If you put a large group of adults together, don't you think that some of them would get in trouble too? If you don't believe me, just look at the police records for the past month. Are teens the only ones causing trouble?

4   Last month when we came to a town council meeting to ask for a teen center, you became upset with us. You told us that there were too many kids hanging out in the Maple Grove Shopping Center parking lot behind the movie theater. You told us that you were concerned that nine teenagers had been arrested for fighting during the last month. That may be so, but those kids don't represent all of us in town who really want a place to go at night. If you gave us a teen center, there wouldn't be any more trouble in town because we'd be off the streets. We'd all want to be with our friends.

5   Please reconsider my request for a teen center in town. It's a place we really need. Without it, we'll probably just keep having trouble in town.

Sincerely,

Victoria Martinez

1. **Part A**
   Which of the following statements is a fact?

     ○ A. Victoria Martinez wrote the letter to Mayor Patel.
     ○ B. Victoria Martinez wrote the letter to her friends.
     ○ C. Mayor Patel wrote the letter to Victoria Martinez and her friends.
     ○ D. Mayor Patel wrote the letter to Victoria Martinez.

   Part B
   Which **two** words also mean **fact** from Part A?

     ☐ A. versatility
     ☐ B. authenticity
     ☐ C. palpability
     ☐ D. precluding
     ☐ E. presiding
     ☐ F. abject

2. Choose the statement that is **not** a fact?

     ○ A. "I believe that we should have a place in town…"
     ○ B. "…the building is closed."
     ○ C. "Mr. Ross used to volunteer his time on the weekends."
     ○ D. Mr. Ross "retired and moved to Florida."

3. Which of these statements is a **fact**?

     ○ A. The security guards are "always chasing us away."
     ○ B. "…the security guards are mean to us."
     ○ C. "…we go to the movies."
     ○ D. "…large groups of teens cause trouble."

4. **Part A**

Which of these statements is an **opinion**?

- ○ A. "...we came to a town council meeting."
- ○ B. "...there were too many kids hanging out in the Maple Grove Shopping Center parking lot."
- ○ C. We asked "for a teen center."
- ○ D. "...nine teenagers had been arrested for fighting during the last month."

Part B

Which of the following words also means **opinion** as used in Part A?

- ☐ A. sentiment
- ☐ B. certainty
- ☐ C. credibility
- ☐ D. conscientious
- ☐ E. foreboding
- ☐ F. conjecture

Be sure to check your answers with those on pages 246–247.

Essay for Fact vs. Opinion

Victoria asks for a meeting place where she and her friends can go. She says, "If you (Mayor Patel) gave us a teen center, there wouldn't be any more trouble in town because we'd be off the streets. We'd all want to be with our friends." Is this an example of **fact** or **opinion**? Please explain in detail.

PREWRITING SECTION
Use the empty space provided to make a writing plan for
your essay before you begin writing.

Write your essay here.

Be sure to check your essay against the suggestions on page 241.

Be sure to check your essay against the suggestions on page 247.

Following Directions

To do something well, we should make sure that we follow directions carefully. These are our guides for success.

Strategy

As you are doing your reading, use these strategies.

Directions are given in order. We must follow the order to get the desired result.

☐ Look for key words and phrases—for example, "**first**," "**next**," and "**after**" completing *Step 1*.

☐ Look for warning phrases—for example, "**before continuing**" and "**be sure to.**"

☐ Only use the directions that are given to write your essay. Do not wander from the topic.

Practice

The passage that you will read contains the guidelines to a Guided Book Report.

Read the passage thoroughly, then answer the questions. **Be sure to:**

```
┌─────────────────────────────────────┐
│   PREVIEW TECHNIQUE                  │
│                                      │
│  1. Preview the questions.           │
│  2. Preview the material.            │
│  3. Read the entire passage.         │
└─────────────────────────────────────┘
```

Guided Reading Book Report—Guidelines
Free Choice Fiction

1 Reading a good novel can be exciting. Finding out about the different characters and learning how the author blends each action and scene together are only some of the thrills you can have while reading. This experience can be a good one. If you read your book with a friend, you can discuss the book together. That means that it's OK to pick out a book to read with a friend, read the book together, and then discuss it too.

2 Once you select your book, you will need to follow these steps.

1. Find a friend who also wants to read the same book.
2. Have your parent/guardian sign your book permission slip.
3. Return your slip to Mr. Rhoades by February 26.
4. Write down the following information in your personal guided reading log:

    a. Your name.
    b. Your reading partner's name.
    c. The title and author of the book that you and your partner are reading.

5. Divide your book into three sections. Enter the page numbers into your reading log.
6. Write down the dates that you plan to discuss each section of your book. Be sure to schedule a meeting at least once a week so you and your partner can complete the assignment no later than March 18.

3 You will be expected to finish reading the book and complete all the discussions with your partner. If you wish to read more quickly than the rest of the class, you may do so without worrying about discussing sections that you were not yet assigned to read. Sometimes when you are really interested in a book, you want to read ahead. This unit has been designed to encourage you to do that.

4 Once a week, you and your partner will form a guided reading small discussion group. You will meet for no more than 20 minutes with another pair of students who are reading a different book. One of you will serve as a group facilitator who will keep the discussion "on track." You will also select a recorder who will take notes that will be signed by all group members and

submitted to Mr. Rhoades. Your group must answer the following questions each time you meet:

- What are the major events that have happened in this section of the novel?
- Who are the major characters, and what are their roles?
- What conflicts are occurring?
- What is the biggest change you have observed from the beginning to the end of the section?
- Who is your favorite character in this section and why?
- What advice would you give to the main characters at this stage of the book?
- What grade (A, B, etc.) would you give this section of the book and why?

5 When you finish your student meetings, you will then share your responses with Mr. Rhoades. You must complete all three sessions by the March 18 deadline stated to receive two "A+" grades. Completing two sessions will earn you two "C" grades. Completing one session will earn you two "D" grades. A failure to complete any sessions will result in two "0" grades.

6 If you have any questions during this unit, please ask Mr. Rhoades at once. Also, please share with Mr. Rhoades any difficulties and successes that you may have.

1. What type of book is being assigned for the Guided Reading Book Report?

   - ○ A. free choice
   - ○ B. free choice fiction
   - ○ C. free choice non-fiction
   - ○ D. free choice biography

2. Select the next step the passage states after "Have your parent/guardian sign your book permission slip." Highlight the step below.

A.	Find a friend who also wants to read the same book.
B.	Ask a parent/guardian to help you select a book.
C.	Have your partner sign your book permission slip.
D.	Return your book permission slip to Mr. Rhoades by February 26.

3. Part A

Which of the following information does **not** need to be included "in your personal guided reading log"?

- ○ A. your name
- ○ B. your reading partner's name
- ○ C. your parent/guardian's signature
- ○ D. the title and author of the book that you and your partner are reading

Part B

Which of the following words mean the same as **unnecessary**?

- ☐ A. essential
- ☐ B. imperative
- ☐ C. requisite
- ☐ D. superfluous
- ☐ E. extraneous
- ☐ F. fundamental

4. Which of these grades will a student earn by completing two guided reading sessions?

- ○ A. two "A+" grades
- ○ B. two "C+" grades
- ○ C. two "C" grades
- ○ D. two "D" grades

Be sure to check your answers with those on pages 247–248.

Essay for Following Directions

Describe the steps needed to form a guided reading small discussion group. You do not need to discuss the questions that will be asked.

PREWRITING SECTION
Use the empty space provided to make a writing plan for your essay before you begin writing.

Write your essay here.

Be sure to check your essay against the suggestions on page 248.

Recognizing Literary Forms and Information Sources

There are many types of literary forms including novels, short stories, and poetry. There are also many information sources such as books, magazines, and Internet sites.

Strategy

As you read literature:

- Always look for the theme, the main character(s), the setting, and the conflict/ resolution. These have been covered in the previous chapter.

As you read information sources:

- Always look for the main idea and supporting details.

Practice

Read the passage thoroughly, then answer the questions. **Be sure to:**

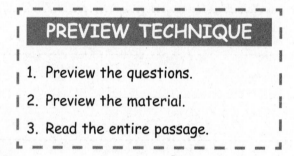

PREVIEW TECHNIQUE

1. Preview the questions.
2. Preview the material.
3. Read the entire passage.

Professional Sports Broadcasting—My Dream Job

by Philip Cheung

1   I've always wanted to be a professional sports broadcaster. That's all I've ever wanted to be. While my friends talk about their dreams of becoming movie stars, hip hop artists, fashion designers, or chefs, I just smile. While all of those career choices might be exciting, they don't get me personally excited. If the conversation happened to turn to sports broadcasting, however, then I would join right in and tell everybody about my plans.

2   You see, I've never wanted to do anything else. Becoming a professional sports broadcaster is my dream job. Whenever my friends and I would play ball, I would think about what it would be like to be sitting in a booth with the TV cameras pointed directly at me. I would talk about my team's record, our recent successes and failures, and our strategy for winning today's game. Then I would call over my friend Karl and interview him about the great

Be sure to check your essay against the suggestions on page 114.

catches he's been making all year. If there was time, I would interview a player from the opposing team to discuss their recent progress.

3   Most people might say that I wouldn't be able to play the game and announce it at the same time. I disagree. I plan to introduce a whole new way to broadcast a game. Sometimes the manager of a team is "hooked up" to a microphone during a game. I've even seen this done with certain star players. Why couldn't I do the same thing? I could describe the game and give my commentary right from the playing field. Who would be better to describe the game than somebody who's right in the middle of the game? Yes, that "somebody" would be me.

4   Now I know that I have to go to school "to learn my trade," as my dad is always telling me. That's not a problem. I'm willing to work hard to realize this dream. I won't give up until I make it.

5   I'm already reading a lot of books about famous sports broadcasters. Right now, I'm reading books about Mel Allen, Red Barber, Howard Cosell, Jon Miller, and Jim McKay. I've written a short story for my English class. It involves my meeting with Phil Rizzuto, the Hall of Fame player and former broadcaster. I've even written a song about becoming a sports broadcaster. It's called "My Search for Air Time." I played it during our school's talent show, and I won third place.

6   My favorite sports poem is "Casey at the Bat." The main character, Casey, had a lot of confidence. He probably had too much because he didn't even swing at the first two strikes. What a great interview I could have with Casey. I would run over to him and ask him about his decision not to swing at the first two pitches. I'd also ask him if he felt that he tried his best to hit the last pitch. Then I would probably have to stop the interview because Casey might be angry with me.

7   I'm only in seventh grade now, but it's not too early to start preparing for my dream career. I've already joined the school newspaper to help me with my writing skills. I've volunteered to be a helper at the broadcasts of our high school's soccer games, as long as I'm not playing a game myself that day. I've also called our local cable television station and asked if I could maybe have a tour of the studio. If I'm lucky and my dream comes true, maybe I'll be a famous broadcaster and some seventh graders will call my station to ask for a tour. I'll gladly show him or her around.

1. **Part A**
   What is the main idea of Philip's essay?

   - ○ A. Phil's dream to go to college
   - ○ B. Phil's dream to be a professional sports manager
   - ○ C. Phil's dream to be a professional sports broadcaster
   - ○ D. Phil's dream to be a hip hop artist

   Part B
   As **dream** is being used in the passage, what words mean the same?

   - ☐ A. nightmare
   - ☐ B. aspiration
   - ☐ C. conscience
   - ☐ D. reciprocity
   - ☐ E. inveigle
   - ☐ F. ambition

2. Philip's piece deals directly with his own life. What type of essay would it be?

   - ○ A. autobiographical
   - ○ B. biographical
   - ○ C. fictional
   - ○ D. poetic

3. **Part A**
   Which of these statements would most likely **not** be true about books that feature famous sportscasters?

   - ○ A. The books feature sportscasters who enjoy sports.
   - ○ B. The sportscasters received training before they began to broadcast.
   - ○ C. The sportscasters enjoy working with people.
   - ○ D. The books feature sportscasters who never cared about playing the game.

   Part B
   Which of the following words are antonyms for the word **true**?

   - ☐ A. bona fide
   - ☐ B. counterfeit
   - ☐ C. veracity
   - ☐ D. genuine
   - ☐ E. fraudulent
   - ☐ F. authentic

4. If Philip's piece were to be published, in which type of publication would it most likely be found?

    ○ A. a professional broadcasting magazine

    ○ B. a school literary magazine

    ○ C. a university literary magazine

    ○ D. a national weekly sports magazine

Be sure to check your answers with those on pages 248–249.

Essay for Recognizing Literary Forms and Information Sources

Describe how this student's written work would be different if it were written as a short story.

PREWRITING SECTION
Use the empty space provided to make a writing plan for
your essay before you begin writing.

Write you essay here.

Be sure to check your essay against the suggestions on page 249.

Finding Information and Answering with Prior Knowledge

Whenever you are reading textbooks, magazines, or other information sources, the material that you may be learning is blended with the material that you already know. For example, the guidelines that you are given to write a science report are combined with your prior knowledge about writing effective reports.

Strategy

As you read:

☐ Always find the main idea(s).

☐ Follow all the directions that you are given.

☐ Use the knowledge that you know to make your efforts even more effective.

Practice

Read the passage thoroughly, then answer the questions. **Be sure to:**

```
┌─────────────────────────────────────┐
│  ┌──────────────────────────────┐   │
│  │     PREVIEW TECHNIQUE        │   │
│  └──────────────────────────────┘   │
│                                      │
│  1. Preview the questions.           │
│                                      │
│  2. Preview the material.            │
│                                      │
│  3. Read the entire passage.         │
└─────────────────────────────────────┘
```

Guidelines for Making a Class Presentation
by Miss Ostrovsky

Your major assignment for this marking period is a five-minute presentation to the class. You will select any of the major topics that we have covered in our class and then re-teach that material to the other students in our class. You will be graded for your coverage of the material, your use of media, your platform (presenting) skills, and your professionalism. Remember that your information and the way you present it are both important. You will be graded on both areas.

Let's look at each of the categories on which you will be graded.

Coverage of Material

You must select a major concept from our unit dealing with verbs. Please choose one of the following main divisions.

For Transitive Verbs:

☐ Direct Objects
☐ Indirect Objects

For Intransitive and Linking Verbs:

☐ Predicate Complements
☐ Predicate Nouns (and pronouns)
☐ Predicate Adjectives

For Subject/Verb Agreement:

☐ Singular
☐ Plural

For Helping (Auxiliary) Verbs:

☐ Part of a Verb Phrase
☐ Part of a Contraction

For Verb Modifiers:

☐ Adverbs
☐ Adverb Phrases

You must provide the following information:

- Definitions
- Rules
- Examples
- Exceptions (if any)

Your Use of Media

Choose at least two of the following media options.

For Computer Slide Show:

- ☐ Laptop Computer
- ☐ LCD Projector

For Flip Chart and Easel:

- ☐ White Board
- ☐ Posters

Follow our Classroom Guidelines for Graphics.

- Clarity
- Legibility
- Color
- Size
- Shapes

Give your media a test run a day or more before you present the lesson.

Your Platform (Presenting) Skills

Please speak effectively. Watch your:

- Volume
- Pace
- Inflection

Use some gestures appropriately.

Stand up straight.

Make good eye contact.

Your Professionalism

- Stay in control at all times.
- Don't laugh or act silly with your friends.

1. **Part A**

   Which of the following is **not** a major verb division for Miss Ostrovsky's class?

   ○ A. transitive verbs
   ○ B. intransitive and linking verbs
   ○ C. helping (auxiliary) verbs
   ○ D. conjugating verbs

   Part B

   Which of the following words are synonyms for the word **division** as used in Part A?

   ☐ A. category
   ☐ B. assignment
   ☐ C. preposition
   ☐ D. class
   ☐ E. diagram
   ☐ F. conjunction

2. Besides using a laptop computer and an LCD projector for a computer slide show, what other piece of equipment would be the **most** useful?

   ○ A. audio headset
   ○ B. movie screen
   ○ C. spiral notebook
   ○ D. chalk eraser

3. Choose the likely result for a student who does **not** follow the "Classroom Guidelines for Graphics."

   ○ A. No one will notice because the information is the most important part of the presentation.
   ○ B. Miss Ostrovsky will give the student one more chance to do better.
   ○ C. The student will receive a lower grade.
   ○ D. The student will receive a detention.

4. **Part A**

What would be the **most** unlikely reason for Miss Ostrovsky to assign this project?

- ○ A. She just bought a new computer.
- ○ B. She's punishing the students for misbehaving.
- ○ C. She's going on maternity leave.
- ○ D. She understands that teaching with media helps to improve learning.

Part B

Which of the following words are antonyms for the word **unlikely** as used in Part A?

- ☐ A. probable
- ☐ B. feasible
- ☐ C. incomprehensible
- ☐ D. implausible
- ☐ E. insincere
- ☐ F. inconceivable

Be sure to check your answers with those on pages 249–250.

Essay for Finding Information and Answering with Prior Knowledge

When Miss Ostrovsky's students give their lessons about verbs, they must provide four different types of information. Explain why this information is important.

PREWRITING SECTION
Use the empty space provided to make a writing plan for
your essay before you begin writing.

Write your essay here.

Be sure to check your essay against the suggestions on page 250.

Notice that the name of the task is "The Research Simulation Task." It is part of Unit 2 of PARCC. You are not being asked to conduct research in a lab. That would be impossible in the time frame allotted for this test. You are being asked, however, to think. Many prompts of this type ask you, the test-taker, to examine two written pieces and a video. Another possibility might be two written pieces followed by a third written piece that contains a different method of displaying information. While two passages may have their facts presented mostly through text, for example, a third might supplement the writing with a combination of charts, graphs, and illustrations.

Typically, there will be one set of questions for the first passage and another set of questions for the second passage. The questions often have two parts. The second part requires accurate information from the first part. Please note that you will receive half credit for a question when you answer the first part correctly and not the second. However, you will receive no credit for the second part of the question if you answer the first part incorrectly. The reason given by the test designers is that the second part of a question is based directly on you, the test-taker having the proper knowledge to have answered the first part correctly. If you have missed the first part of a question but answered the second part correctly, the test designers presume that you have guessed at the second answer. It is also important to note that you must mark each answer carefully since your chance to receive any credit for a question relies on an accurate answer to the first part.

Some of the research simulation task essays ask you to analyze the passages and possible video by comparing and contrasting the structure the author used to produce the piece. Typically, there are five major structures. Let's look at these one at a time.

 HELPFUL HINTS FOR ESSAYS

Using a Venn diagram or T-chart can best help you while you read passages and organize information from a video.

FIVE MAJOR STRUCTURES OF RESEARCH

Structure #1—Description

Description is the structure that has details about characters and occurrences. It tells the "story" of that which is being described. An example of description is: *A carpenter is a master of a variety of skills. Besides having good dexterity, (s)he must also be strong and able to visualize a completed project even before it has begun.* Effective graphic organizers for description include spider webs and story maps. Key words may include *for instance, consists of,* and *the components include.*

Structure #2—Cause and Effect

This structure takes a look at a situation or occurrence, determines the cause, and then addresses the effects of the cause. The key concept is "Why?" An example of cause and effect is: *Hard work does indeed pay off with success. In class last year, we studied a variety of strategies so we could perform well on our State tests. Every one in the study group I had organized completed all homework, paid attention in class, and asked mindful questions when we needed an answer. As a result, our study group scored higher than those who chose not to join our group.* Effective graphic organizers for cause and effect include tree charts and flow charts. Key words may include *as a result, therefore,* and *since.*

Structure #3—Sequence

This structure places items in a time sequence. It tells what happened first, second, third, and so on. The sequence rather than problem and solution is the major focus. An example of chronological order is: *For our field trip to the historical museum tomorrow, we are being asked to arrive at school at 8:30 A.M. instead of 7:55 A.M. We shall meet in the cafeteria to review the rules and take attendance. Then, we shall proceed to our assigned seats on the buses.* Effective graphic organizers for chronological order are flow chart, menus, and bulleted lists. Key words may include *first of all, next, at the same time, then,* and *finally.*

Structure #4—Problem and Solution

This structure is used to focus on a given problem and then follow the steps that best lead to a viable solution. The key concept here is solving a problem by following a series of steps. An example of problem and solution is: *Last month there was a* problem with some students in our school leaving their trash on the playground after lunch was over. Our student council representatives decided to call a special meeting to address this issue. After a lengthy discussion during the regularly-scheduled student council meeting, the officers decided simply to ask the students to be more conscientious. On the first day of the announcement, more than half the trash was picked up and thrown away by the students. Effective graphic organizers include tree charts and flow charts. Key words may include *the problem is, if…then,* and *therefore.*

Structure #5—Comparison and Contrast

This structure is used to find similarities and differences. As the title says, we compare and we contrast. An example of comparison and contrast is: *Basketball and soccer are the two favorite sports in my school. Both sports provide an element of excitement. Each requires good physical fitness, and competition is always rigorous. However, there are also some differences. While basketball is often played both indoors and outdoors, soccer is mainly played outdoors. Basketball is played on a paved court while soccer is played in a field.* Key words may include *in contrast, however,* and *either…or.*

SAMPLE PASSAGES

Directions: Look at each short passage and determine which type of text structure is being used. Select the correct one from the five text structures previously discussed and write it inside the box below the passage.

Passage 1

1   When you're a serious underdog in sports and there seems to be no way for your team to win, how can you beat the odds and secure a victory? Winning is possible if you have the right plan and you follow it step by step. On this day, Ralph Badger found that plan and executed it to perfection.

2   The Township Tigers trailed the City Warriors by three points. The Tigers had the ball with a little more than a minute to play. It was third down, and everyone sensed that fullback Oscar Carrion would be given the ball to drive for the first down that would end the game. There seemed to be little chance for the Warriors to lose.

3   The first thing Coach Whitfield did was to rally his team on the sidelines. His star defensive player and captain Alan Papi had been hurt on the

previous play and taken to the locker room for medical treatment. However, he was approached by Ralph Badger who told the coach that he (Badger) had a plan that he was certain would be successful. Whitfield agreed to listen.

4 To start, Badger asked Coach Whitfield for permission to address the team, and the coach agreed. Next, Badger rallied the team together and implored them to "Win this one for Papi!" Knowing that the Warriors quarterback would be handing the ball off to Carrion to seal the win, Badger then called for every defensive player to go after Carrion and get the ball. He said, "I know they're not going to pass. Carrion has been good for a least five yards a carry all game. They're not going to give the ball to anyone but Carrion." The coach agreed as he sent his players back onto the field.

5 The result was better than anyone might have expected. Carrion took the handoff as all had expected and smashed directly into the line. Badger met him with a fierce tackle that jarred the ball loose from Carrion's arms. As players from both teams scrambled to recover the fumble, Badger managed to scramble to his feet, pick up the ball, and rumble 55 yards for a game-winning touchdown.

Passage 2

1 Every winter when the flu epidemic breaks out, there are many people who blame the fact that many are not dressing properly. They cite a direct correlation between the decrease in the temperature outside and an increase in the number of people who do not dress appropriately to keep sufficiently warm. They dismiss the fact that germs and not temperature cause infection. Not dressing warmly will not help to keep us healthy. Neither will it strengthen our immune systems. Nonetheless, we must never discount the fact that it is the exposure to germs that leads to illness. In fact, we should avoid shaking hands and we should wash our hands often to reduce our exposure to germs, the root cause of infections.

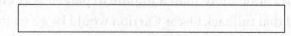

Passage 3

1 The garden that my dad grows in our backyard every summer is known as "The Green Grocery Store" throughout my entire neighborhood. He began tending to a garden when he was a little boy. With my Grandpa Alex, he would grow the healthiest and most fruitful tomato vines in the entire neighborhood. The variety of tomatoes they grew would include big boys, plum, and cherry.

2   Today, my dad continues to grow outstanding tomatoes. In addition, he grows many other plants. The cucumbers are always green and fresh. Sometimes, he picks the cucumbers before they mature and at the time when they are still very tender. These are known as gherkins. His green bean plants grow so tall that he has to contain them inside support cages, just as he does with his tomato plants. His carrots are always a deep orange with a flavor that is incredibly sweet.

Passage 4

1   One of the common questions when deciding on the location to take a summer vacation is: "Should I go to the beach or the mountains?"

2   The beach and the mountains can both provide a haven from the sweltering heat. At the beach the temperature may be higher than it is inland, but the cooling breezes and the rolling surf help to cool the air. In the mountains, the temperature is usually somewhat cooler. No breeze is necessary to allow this condition to occur. Obviously, there is no rolling surf since the mountains may have lakes rather than oceans as part of their landscape.

3   The sport of fishing can be enjoyed in both locales, but the type of fishing differs. At the beach and in the mountains, it is possible to fish from the land and from a boat. However, the mountain lakes and rivers are fresh water ones while the oceans at the beaches consist of saltwater. Thus, the species of fish living in each type of water differs.

4   Recreation options can be different, too. Surfing tends to be more popular and practical at the beach since the rolling waves are fun to ride. In the calmer waters of the mountains, on the other hand, popular forms of recreation often include canoeing and rafting.

Passage 5

1 Congratulations! You have been selected to participate in The Pride Run, the annual 5K marathon race sponsored by the scouting organizations representing the Tri-County Chapter.

2 To ensure that the race is facilitated in the most efficient manner possible, the following timelines will be strictly adhered to.

- 7:30 A.M.—All runners are expected to be in the registration line located at the west entrance to Anthem Park. It is suggested that all runners plan to arrive at least 20 minutes early in case there are unexpected delays. (Please note: This line is only for runners. Those who are attending to watch the race will not be admitted until 8:30 A.M. The entrance for those viewing the race is located at the northeast gate.)

- 8:20 A.M.—A brief overview of the course will be given. Rules and expectations will be reviewed. All runners are expected to have read these rules and expectations prior to the day of the race. A brief question and answer period will follow.

- 9:00 A.M.—All runners will proceed to the starting line and begin to line up for the race.

- 9:10 A.M.—The National Anthem will be played, a very brief greeting will be given by Mayor Arkin, and the race will begin.

3 The awarding of the medals for the top three finishers will take place at the conclusion of the race.

Answers

Passage 1: Problem and Solution
Passage 2: Cause and Effect
Passage 3: Description
Passage 4: Comparison and Contrast
Passage 5: Sequence

Compare and Contrast Texts

Read, analyze, and answer questions. Read the following passages and then respond to the questions that follow.

Steps to Resolve Problems with Purchases

by Fiona Quimby

1   Imagine saving your money over a period of a few months because you are hoping to make a special purchase. That purchase may be as expensive as a new computer for school or a complete set of specialized protective athletic gear. That purchase may also be something less expensive such as a new sweater or a protective case for a cell phone. That purchase may also be for a service such as taking private lessons from a tutor or coach. When you have finally saved enough money, you make the purchase. However, you are soon disappointed with either the quality or the performance of that which you have purchased. What can be done? Is the situation hopeless, or can you possibly get some satisfaction from either the manufacturer of the product or the person or the store from which you have made the purchase?

2   Don't despair. There is actually hope. You must make sure that the product or service you have purchased is indeed not performing the way it was promised to perform. To help you to make this decision, try following these steps.

Step #1

3   Did you read the product description? Often, the product description includes terms such as "durable" and "convenient" to describe the it. Services use terms such as "improvement" or "a better way" to promote their service. These are terms designed to "sell" the product as a desirable one. There may also be statistics that state that the company has a customer satisfaction rate of more than 90%. This figure may be closer to 90% (90.2%, for example) than it is to 100%. Moreover, this statistic does not guarantee that you are not one of the less than 10% of customers who are dissatisfied.

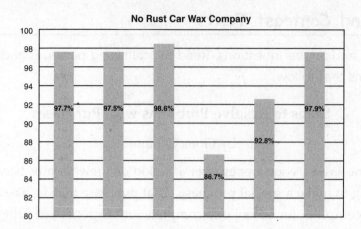

4 Companies make it a point to maintain a high level of customer satisfaction. Your satisfaction is important to them, and they have trained personnel ready to help you to resolve all reasonable complaints. Companies take pride in maintaining a high percentage of satisfied customers.

5 Notice in the chart that the No Rust Car Wax Company had a high percentage of customer satisfaction for many years. When they decided to change their formula in a move to cut their cost of materials, the performance of their product was found to be less satisfactory by their customers. Hence, customer satisfaction dropped 15%. When the original formula was reintroduced along with a sales campaign designed to reacquire former customers, the rate of customer satisfaction rose again. After three years, it almost regained all of its lost percentage in the area of customer satisfaction. Rodney Fairview, the president of No Rust Car Wax, stated, "The people have spoken, and we have listened. Thank you to everyone who has made No Rust Car Wax the best choice on the market."

Step #2

6 Is there a broken "promise" by the company? If the company has made a claim that their product or service is guaranteed to perform a certain way and it does not, then you have grounds for seeking redress. For example, you may have purchased a backpack that guaranteed that you will have no more shoulder pain when you wear it. If you are experiencing shoulder pain while you wear your backpack that is filled with an amount of weight that does not exceed the suggested amount, then you are justified in making a complaint. However, if you have filled your backpack beyond capacity and you are experiencing shoulder pain caused by the overfilled backpack, then the cause of the problem is not the fault of the company. Rather, the cause of the problem is your fault for not following directions.

Step #3

7   Have you followed the directions for using the product or service? Before using any product, you should read the directions first. Before using a service, you should read the contract first. Make sure to follow the directions as instructed. If you don't understand these directions, then consider reaching out to the help line that most companies provide. If it is not possible to contact the help line because it is either after hours or closed for a holiday, then simply make your contact as soon as the help line reopens.

8   Have you done anything that was not included in the directions? Did you think that you could just try to solve the problem yourself? If you have done something that was not recommended by the company in their set of instructions, you may have voided any warranties that accompanied your product or service. Should this be the case, then you are not going to receive a replacement product or refund from the company.

Step #4

9   If there is any assembly or special procedure to follow concerning your product or service, then it may be wise to take the following steps. Have the product (or contract with a service) with you when you make contact with the help line. Many companies provide "live" help lines to assist you in "real" time. Be patient as you go through this process since the associate helping you is also helping a small number of others at the same time. These associates are trained to handle a number of cases simultaneously. Be patient.

Step #5

10   Take notes when you receive advice on a help line. While the associate is telling you what to do (or not to do), keep a note pad or an open note-taking file nearby. Some people prefer to type up and print out the conversation they had with the associate to use for reference once the help line session has concluded. There is no shame in having notes to which you may refer. This practice is similar to the one you use in school when you are taking notes during a lesson.

Step #6

11 If you continue to be dissatisfied with your purchase, then you should write a letter to the customer service department. In this letter, you should list as much information as possible about the steps you have taken so far. These steps should include your research about the product or service, your prior history (if any) with both the product or service and the company, the specific areas of concern that are causing you the problem, your interaction with the help line associate, and your desire to reach a practical solution. It's important for you also extend your thanks in advance to the receiver of your letter. This gesture emphasizes the point that you are a reasonable individual who wishes to resolve this problem in a reasonable manner.

12 Whenever you purchase a product for which assembly is required or a service that requires special conditions, be sure to follow the appropriate instructions for set-up and/or use. In addition, reach out to the company if you find that you are either dissatisfied or are having a problem with the performance of the product or service. Finally, do not do anything to compromise the warranty that accompanies the product. By following these steps, you should be able to resolve any problem that might arise with the product or service.

Step #7

13 If the first six steps do not result in your receiving customer satisfaction, then you should consider legal action. Before you do so, however, consider filing a complaint with the **Better Business Bureau**. This organization keeps a record of complaints filed against a company. Before making a major purchase, you may actually wish to check this list to learn whether or not the company producing the product has a number of complaints that have been filed. It may also be wise to visit the U.S. Government's Website to learn your rights under the law. They even supply you with a sample complaint letter. The URL is: *https://www.usa.gov/consumer-complaints*.

14 Finally, if all these attempts have failed, you may then wish to contact a lawyer if you have not received satisfaction through other avenues. Please understand that fees must be paid to a lawyer for the professional expertise and efforts on your behalf.

1. **Part A**

   Which text organization pattern is used in the article "Steps to Resolve Store and Online Purchases"?

   ○ A. description
   ○ B. cause and effect
   ○ C. sequence
   ○ D. problem and solution

   Part B

   Which **two** phrases would you expect to see in the text organization pattern used for "Steps to Resolve Problems with Purchases"?

   ☐ A. on the other hand
   ☐ B. consists of
   ☐ C. therefore
   ☐ D. first of all
   ☐ E. if…then
   ☐ F. in conclusion

2. **Part A**

   Which of the following words describe Ms. Quimby's piece?

   ○ A. confrontational
   ○ B. moralistic
   ○ C. creative
   ○ D. instructional

   Part B

   Which of the following words express the purpose of Ms. Quimby's piece?

   ○ A. mandatory
   ○ B. misappropriated
   ○ C. ad hoc
   ○ D. advisory

3. Which of these titles could be used correctly for Ms. Quimby's article?

   ○ A. How Not to Get Scammed by Companies
   ○ B. Follow This Plan When You Make a Customer Complaint to a Company
   ○ C. Getting Your Money Back from a Company
   ○ D. An Insider's Look at Getting Satisfaction for a Faulty Product or Service

4. Which **two** sentences in the passage relate directly to the concept that the customer might "get some satisfaction from either the manufacturer of the product or the service from which s(he) has made the purchase?"

☐ A. "Imagine saving your money over a period of a few months because you are hoping to make a special purchase."

☐ B. "Often, the product description includes terms such as "durable" and "convenient" to describe the product."

☐ C. "If you are experiencing shoulder pain while you wear your backpack that is filled with an amount of weight that does not exceed the suggested amount, then you are justified in making a complaint."

☐ D. "Rather, the cause of the problem is your fault for not following directions."

☐ E. "If there is any assembly or special procedure to follow concerning your product or service, then it may be wise to take the following steps."

☐ F. "This gesture emphasizes the point that you are a reasonable individual who wishes to solve this problem in a reasonable manner."

5. Which of the following statements contains the main idea of Ms. Quimby's article?

○ A. Companies are often taking advantage of their customers.

○ B. Only aggressive customers get satisfaction when dealing with companies.

○ C. Reasonable customers sometimes get help from companies, but not often.

○ D. Customers should carefully examine a number of steps to resolve a problem with a company.

6. Where might you find this article? (Select all that are correct.)

☐ A. a business journal

☐ B. a newspaper

☐ C. an almanac

☐ D. a numismatist journal

☐ E. a blog

☐ F. an instructional manual

Be sure to check your answers with those on pages 251–252.

Steps to File a Complaint Against a Company

After you buy an item or service, you may experience problems with your purchase. If this happens, you have the right to complain. Use these steps to get started:

- **Gather supporting documents**, such as sales receipts, warranties, contracts, and work orders from the purchase. Also, print out e-mails or logs of any contact you've had with the seller about the purchase.

- **Contact the seller**, preferably in writing. You may be able to solve the problem by contacting a salesperson or customer service representative. If this doesn't work, contact a supervisor or manager. If this still fails, try going higher up to the national headquarters. Use this sample complaint letter as an example.

Your Address
Your City, State, Zip Code
(Your e-mail if sending via e-mail)

Date

Name of Contact Person (if available)
Title (if available)
Company Name
Consumer Complaint Division (if you have no specific contact)
Street Address
City, State, Zip Code

Dear (Contact Person or Organization Name):

Re: (account number, if applicable)

On (date), I (bought, leased, rented, or had repaired) a (name of the product, with serial or model number or service performed) at (location, date and other important details of the transaction).

Unfortunately, your product (or service) has not performed well (or the service was inadequate) because (state the problem). I am disappointed because (explain the problem: for example, the product does not work properly, the service was not performed correctly, I was billed the wrong amount, something was not disclosed clearly or was misrepresented, etc.).

To resolve the problem, I would appreciate your (state the specific action you want—money back, charge card credit, repair, exchange, etc.) Enclosed are copies (do not send originals) of my records (include receipts, guarantees, warranties, canceled checks, contracts, model and serial numbers, and any other documents).

I look forward to your reply and a resolution to my problem and will wait until (set a time limit) before seeking help from a consumer protection agency or Better Business Bureau. Please contact me at the above address or by phone at (home and/or office numbers with area code).

Sincerely,

Your name

Enclosure(s)

- **Contact third parties** if the seller fails to fix your problem. File a complaint with your local consumer protection offices or the state regulatory agency or licensing board that has jurisdiction over the seller. Notify the Better Business Bureau (BBB) in your area about your problem. The BBB tries to resolve complaints against companies. Contact an appropriate federal agency. While these agencies may not resolve your problem, your complaint helps them investigate fraud. If the purchase was made online across international borders, you may also file a complaint with econsumer.gov.

- **Seek legal help.** If none of these options work, you may seek to resolve your problem through the legal system or through an alternative dispute program, such as arbitration, conciliation, or mediation.

Source: *https://www.usa.gov/consumer-complaints*

7. Which of the following statements **best** summarize the claim made by the author of this passage? Select all that are correct.

- ☐ A. When you have a complaint, always go right to the top to get satisfaction.
- ☐ B. Don't complain unless you really have no other way to resolve your problem.
- ☐ C. It is your right and duty under the U.S. Constitution to complain.
- ☐ D. When you have a complaint, you should contact the company.
- ☐ E. You should gather supporting documents before you contact a company.
- ☐ F. You don't really need to gather supporting documents before you contact a company.

8. In the phrase "logs of any contact you've had," (bullet 2) which **two** words mean the same as the word **logs** as it is used here?

- ☐ A. business ledgers
- ☐ B. newspapers
- ☐ C. pieces of firewood
- ☐ D. anecdotal notes of phone calls
- ☐ E. previous correspondence
- ☐ F. product advertisements

9. Part A

Which of the following would be another title for this article?

- ○ A. Get Your Money Back!
- ○ B. How to Get the Best Prices
- ○ C. Tips about Getting Customer Satisfaction
- ○ D. Making a Profit

Part B

Which **two** terms would be the **best** for an Internet search to find this article?

- ☐ A. consumers, price wars, justice system
- ☐ B. consumers, complaints, redress
- ☐ C. consumers, the law, the courts
- ☐ D. consumers, complaints, lawyers
- ☐ E. consumers, complaints, resolution
- ☐ F. consumers, the law, the Supreme Court

10. **Part A**

In the phrase "Consumer Complaint Division," what does the word **Division** mean?

○ A. a math process

○ B. a sector

○ C. a sports team

○ D. a treaty

Part B

Which of these terms also means the same as **Division**?

☐ A. a math process

☐ B. the addition of integers and fractions

☐ C. associative properties

☐ D. finances

☐ E. branch

☐ F. group

Be sure to check your answers with those on pages 252–253.

ESSAY FOR THE RESEARCH SIMULATION TASK

Directions: Think about the content, the structure, and the intention of each text. You have read an article and a letter on how to fix consumer issues. Write an essay in which you compare the article by Fiona Quimby, "Steps to Resolve Problems with Purchases," with the U.S. Government piece entitled "Steps to File a Complaint Against a Company." You may wish to use the Venn diagram provided or a similar graphic organizer to help you arrange your ideas efficiently.

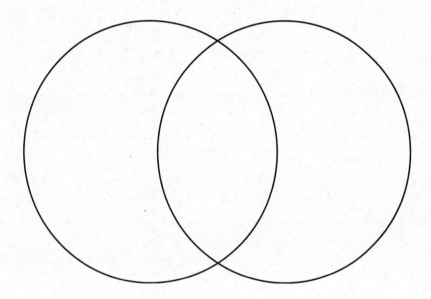

Write your essay here.

Be sure to check your essay against the sample response and suggestions on pages 254–256.

The Narrative Writing Task

CHAPTER 4

WHAT IS THE NARRATIVE WRITING TASK?

The Narrative Writing Task, which is Unit 3 of PARCC, requires you to create a story or scenario (a brief scene) from a few details given in the test directions. When writing a narrative, a good imagination comes in handy. First, you will need a good idea to begin writing your story. Your story should focus around a conflict with a resolution. Then, you will need to give enough details so your reader understands your story. Finally, bring your story to a logical conclusion and always make sure to use correct grammar and spelling.

What will I have to write about?

You will be given a brief description of a situation. Then, you will be asked to think about what you feel might happen as the situation develops. In other words, you'll be asked to write a story from the details you're given. For example, if you're given a situation in which a youngster has wandered too far from home, you might be asked to tell the story of the things that happen next. Possibly, you may decide to write about the youngster's challenge to find his/her way home.

What should I include in my story?

You should write your story in a way the reader knows exactly what is happening. Make sure it makes sense. Write your story to answer the question you're being asked. In other words, don't write about an adventure in an amusement park if your question deals with a lost child trying to return home. Catch your reader's attention in the opening paragraph by using a solid **compositional risk**. A compositional risk is a technique used by a writer to grab the attention of the reader. Link your story. Don't change the details. Begin your writing where the first one left off, if possible. Then make a clear connection to the story that preceded yours. Make sure that your risk sets a tone. For example, avoid using a startling statement for a story with a comforting mood. Moreover, be sure to use a higher level (academic) vocabulary that uses words such as "microscopic" instead of "tiny."

Should I pre-write (make notes to plan my writing) before I actually begin?

You should always pre-write before you begin writing. By doing so, you will organize your thoughts, create your plan for writing, and actually warm up your brain to prepare yourself for a good writing session. Moreover, the majority of current research has found that your chances for writing successfully increase when you carefully pre-write before you begin composing.

CREATING A STORY PLAN

My Writing Plan

Writing a story for the narrative writing portion of most ELA standardized tests in literacy is different from writing other pieces.

To write an effective story, you need a new plan. For the narrative writing task, you're going to use your imagination to help describe what might happen in a certain situation. You will be addressing the main question, "What do you think is happening?"

Time to Practice

Imagine that you have a Chihuahua puppy. Your Chihuahua puppy is a very excitable dog that always seems to have a lot of energy. Today, you hear your dog barking more loudly than usual. Think about what might be causing your dog to be so excited.

Once you decide upon the cause of your Chihuahua's barking, create a story and fill in the details of that story. Remember, your story should be based on events that most people would understand. Otherwise, you may not make a connection with the picture prompt.

Please remember that our practice throughout this book is meant to be completed at a slower pace than you will have when you take the actual test. By practicing in the book, you should be able to gain the skills needed to work at a much faster pace.

TEN-STEP STRATEGIC PLAN FOR SUCCESS

Follow these ten steps to help you write a narrative essay successfully.

Step 1—Create the Realistic Main Conflict

The first thing we need to do is to think about possible situations (story lines or plots) for this story. These will each be created from a main conflict (problem). For this exercise, we will use the following scenario: Your best friend hears the sounds of a puppy barking in the kitchen excitedly. For the conflict, let's imagine that the puppy smells smoke that is coming from the oven because the breakfast muffins are burning.

Second, think about the reason why the puppy might be discovering the beginning of a major problem. Consider not only the loss of one of the muffins for breakfast, but more importantly the safety hazard that might occur. These actions would be rising actions, which are events that authors use to strengthen a reader's interest in the plot. In the space given below, write down both what you think the main conflict is and the reason why the muffins burning could be a problem.

Conflict and Reason

A possible response may be that the muffins that are baking in the oven have started to smoke and will soon catch fire. The smoke has just started and hasn't yet reached the detector. Even so, this situation is dangerous because your friend's mom is in the backyard and doesn't see that the muffins are starting to burn. Your friend has just awakened and is getting out of bed upstairs. The puppy has noticed the smoke, and it begins to bark while running back and forth in front of the stove.

Meanwhile, if the muffins catch fire, then the entire kitchen might also catch fire. That would be terrible.

Consider now what the main conflict is. Is it…

- Your friend not realizing that the puppy's barking is really a warning of a possible fire in the house?
- The muffins smoking and being close to catching fire?

The main problem is the possible fire in the house. Even so, this situation has become a problem because your friend does not realize that the muffins are starting to burn. Your friend being awakened when (s)he hears the puppy barking and scurrying around is a good starting point for the story.

Step 2—Create the Plot (Plan of Action)

The next step is to create a plot line. You may use the plot line as a plan of action in your story. You will focus on "setting the stage" by identifying the problem (conflict), creating the action (rising action), and then solving the problem (resolution or falling action). Use the questions below to start building your plan of action.

1. What is the reason for the puppy barking and running around so much?

   ----

2. Does your friend investigate immediately the reason why the puppy is excited, or does (s)he wait a few moments? Why? (Remember, this is the beginning of the rising action.)

   ----

3. When the muffins catch fire, what happens next? (This is the main event leading to the climax.)

----

4. How does your friend deal with the fire? Was anything badly damaged? (This is the resolution, also known as the falling action.)

Step 3—Create the Setting

Think about the setting of your story. When you write your story for the test, be sure to include details. This makes your story seem realistic. Be sure to paint a thorough word picture to give your reader a clear view of your scenes. Also, be sure to include a compositional risk in your opening to grab your reader's attention.

As an exercise, write down one detail to describe your friend's room. If you practice this technique, you'll train your mind to begin to think of these details automatically. On the actual test, you won't have much time to improve your story. You will need to jot down details quickly. The amount of detail that you will be able to include and the length of your story will depend on the amount of time it takes you to write an effective story. Remember, this is a timed test. Once the time runs out, you cannot return to the test to finish an item. Practice writing down some details.

Detail

Next, do the same for your friend's kitchen.

Detail

Here is a possible detail for your room.

- Detail— There is an old clock radio that wakes your friend up in the morning.

Here is a possible detail for your friend's kitchen.

- Detail—The window shade was blocking the sun from shining directly on the door leading into the kitchen.

Step 4—Give Each Main Character a Personality

Now it's time to jot down a brief outline of the facts of the story so far. Fill in the information next to each section.

Two (or more) personality traits and a name for each main character

Friend

Trait 1

When does your friend show this trait?

Trait 2 ....

When does your friend show this trait?

Name ....

Puppy

Trait 1 ....

When does the dog show this trait?

Trait 2 ....

When does the dog show this trait?

Name ....

Here are some possible responses:

Friend

- Name—JJ Wilburn
- Gender—Female
- Trait 1— Reliable
- When does your friend show this trait? (S)he always helps out in an emergency. (S)he fed the dog belonging to Mr. Barnes, a neighbor, every day last summer until he returned from the hospital.
- Trait 2—Quick to take action
- When does your friend show this trait? When another student was being bullied at school, your friend stepped in and told the others to stop. (S)he didn't hesitate at all.

Dog

- Name—Frisky
- Gender—Male
- Trait 1—Full of Energy
- When does the dog show this trait? Like most puppies, this one seems to have an unlimited supply of energy. One day, the puppy ran around the house almost non-stop for ten minutes. One minute later, the puppy was gobbling down its food. Ten minutes later, the puppy was sleeping to rest up for the next dash around the house.
- Trait 2— Loyal
- When does the dog show this trait? The puppy appreciates the love he receives in the Wilburn house. JJ is always taking him for walks and play sessions outside. Mrs. Wilburn lets the dog sit in her lap after JJ goes to sleep. While Mrs. Wilburn watches her favorite program, Frisky falls asleep too.

Step 5—Develop the Story (Plot Line)

The next step is to create a plot line. You may use the plot line as a plan for the action in your story. You will focus on "setting the stage," identifying the problem (conflict), creating the action (rising action), and then solving the problem (resolution).

Action

Think about the action taking place. After waking up and getting out of bed, your friend hears the new puppy barking and scurrying around the kitchen. Consider these questions as you prepare to write your story.

1. What does your friend think is the reason for the puppy barking and running around so much?

    ----

2. Does your friend investigate immediately the reason why the puppy is excited, or does (s)he wait a few moments? Why?

    ----

3. When the muffins catch fire, what happens next?

    ----

4. How does your friend deal with the fire? Was anything badly damaged?

    ----

5. What is the lesson that your friend and her mom learn from this experience?

Here are some possible responses to the questions that were just asked.

1. What does your friend think is the reason for the puppy barking and running around so much?

    Your friend might think that the puppy is just excited about one of his toys or maybe a bird that has flown by.

2. Does your friend investigate immediately the reason why the puppy is excited, or does (s)he wait a few moments? Why?

    Your friend might yawn, stretch a little, and then walk downstairs to try to find out the reason why the puppy is barking so much.

3. When the muffins were smoking and almost ready to catch fire, what happens next?

    Your friend might start to fill up a bucket with water to throw on the flames. However, (s)he might remember the previous conversation with Uncle Ralph, the firefighter, about throwing water on a fire. You friend may also realize that there may be an exposed electrical wire, and water could also be dangerous in that situation. Therefore, before the fire gets too large to manage, your friend opens a box of salt and throws it on the fire to douse it.

Step 6—Write the Solution for the Problem (Resolve the Conflict)

This is the point where your story begins to wrap up. The events have developed, and the solution lies just ahead.

Here are some questions for you to consider for this step.

1. How does your friend deal with the fire? Was anything badly damaged?

    Luckily, your friend thought clearly and was able to put out the fire.

2. What is the lesson that your friend and her/his mom learn from this experience?

The lesson might be, "When you are cooking or baking, don't ever leave the stove unattended."

> Please note that the second question is requiring you to be introspective. The PARCC evaluators are looking for writing that demonstrates how a writer has thought about the situation at hand.

Step 7—Give Your Story a Working Title

When you write a story, you must always give it a title. This title should relate to the events of your story. It should, in fact, reflect the main conflict in some way. Also, it should make the reader want to read your story because the title sounds exciting.

Which of these titles do you think fits your story the best?

1. **My New Puppy**

2. **My Friend JJ's Noisy Puppy**

3. **My Friend Hates to Wake Up**

The first title "My New Puppy" would be better for a story about a friend getting a new puppy. The second title is a better one because it relates somewhat to the action of the story. The third one isn't good because it sounds like the story deals with your friend's dislike for waking up.

Even though the second title is not a great one, it's the best one of the bunch. Let's use it for now until you actually write the story. Once you're done, the title may be easier to write.

Using the information that you have gathered from our guided pre-write, please write a draft of your speculative story. Be sure to get all your ideas down on paper before you even begin to think about editing. Make sure that you do the following as you write:

Start with a realistic situation.

- Consider writing about things you know.
- Keep your ideas realistic, or at least clear and precise.
- Make your situation one that could actually occur in real life. The situation may even be one that has happened to you or something that you have witnessed.

Grab your audience's attention in the same way that a good author or public speaker captures the audience's attention: use a compositional risk to *grab* that audience's attention.

Introduce your main conflict. Tell about:

- The problem that seems to be happening.
- The reason that the situation being described is a problem.

Pay attention to the plot of your story.

- Write your story so it relates directly to your plot.
- Be sure that your story makes sense so the adults who will be scoring your test can understand it.

Give each of your characters a personality. Let your reader get close to your characters by:

- Describing the way they look.
- Showing their traits.

Create the setting by:

- "Painting a word picture" that describes the characters and places in the scene.
- Making sure that your scene "fits" your story and is not "out of place" or confusing.

Develop the plot by:

- Writing your story so the events follow a regular pattern.
- Making sure that the events relate directly to your main conflict.

Decide what the resolution will be.

- Heroic action (an action taken by someone who disregards personal comfort and safety to ease another's burden).
- Unlikely happening (the difference between that which is expected and that which actually occurs).

Give your story a working title. You may change it after the story is written. For now, however, it will give your story a point you can use to focus it.

Consider whether or not a lesson was learned by the main character(s).

- If so, does the lesson make sense from the story you have written?
- If not, does the story come to a definite conclusion?

Step 8—Write Your First Draft

Title: _____

Here's a possible essay draft.

My Friend JJ's Noisy Puppy

As the sun came up, JJ heard her alarm clock go off. She was asleep when some noise woke her up. The noise was from downstairs, and it was loud. She figured her mom would take care of business, but she didn't. How much louder could the noise become?

JJ always helped people. She stopped some bullies at school one time. She took care of a neighbor's dog.

As she walks out of her room, she was able to tell that the noise was being made buy Frisky. Frisky sounded excited, but JJ figured that her puppy was acting the way it always did. This puppy would run around for almost ten minutes at a time. The barking was probably just Frisky's way of being psyched.

When JJ got downstairs, however, she noticed that something was berning. JJ called to her mom to ask if nothing was wrong, but her mom didn't answer. JJ called again, but she still didn't get an answer.

As JJ opened the door to the kitchen; the sun that would usually be in JJ's eyes was blocked since her mom had pulled down the shade. At once, JJ noticed that Frisky was barking and running around in circles. Before she tried to calm down her puppy, JJ noticed smoke. JJ had to act quick.

She started to fill up a bucket with water, but JJ remembered a conversation last week with her Uncle Ralph. JJ asked him if you throw water on a fire. He told her to do so if the fire isn't a grease or electrical fire. For those, he said to open a box of salt and throw the salt on the fire.

JJ was able to take a box of salt in case she needed to use it to put out the fire, make sure the fire hadn't started, open the door, and take out the muffins. JJ's mom raced into the kitchen.

JJ's mom asked her what had happened. JJ told her that Frisky woke her up, and she came down to turn off the oven. JJ thought that Frisky was now a hero.

Her mom thought JJ was a hero too because JJ may have saved their lives. JJ did ask her mom to promise not to go outside again if the oven was on. JJ's mom agreed.

Step 9—Add Dialogue

Now that you have written your draft, consider adding dialogue to make your story sound more realistic. This dialogue will also help your reader to hear directly the thoughts of those who are speaking.

Notice that when you write dialogue, you change the paragraph every time you change the speaker. Also, make sure that the dialogue fits the character who is speaking. A child on the playground will not sound like a college professor. At the same time, a parent should not be using language common to second graders.

JJ was worried. (S)he didn't know what to do. (S)he had never had to put out a fire before.

Suddenly, JJ remembered a conversation (s)he had had with her/his Uncle Ralph, a fireman, at dinner last week.

JJ asked, "Should you throw water on a fire?"

Uncle Ralph replied, "Not if the fire is a grease fire—you know, like the ones in a kitchen."

Now that you have found some places in your story where you can include dialogue, proofread your work for mistakes. Also, look for places where you can add more detail.

> Remember: When you write dialogue, you change the paragraph every time you change the speaker.

Step 10—Edit and Submit Your Essay Writing

10. (A) Check Your Grammar and Spelling

Always check for grammar and spelling mistakes. By correcting these, you can give yourself a good chance of getting a higher score. An essay with good ideas but a lot of spelling and grammar mistakes will not receive a good score.

The first mistake is contained in the fourth sentence of the first paragraph. Instead of saying "She figured her mom would take care of business," the writer should say "She figured her mom would solve the problem." Slang phrases should always be avoided in formal writing, especially on a test.

The next mistake is contained in the first sentence of the third paragraph: "As she walks out of her room, she was able to tell that the noise was being made buy Frisky." You should not shift tenses in a paragraph. If you are writing in the past tense, then continue to write in the past tense. The verb "walks" should be "walked" since the entire paragraph is being written in the past tense. Also the word "buy" is incorrect. It should be "by."

Did you notice the third mistake? It is also contained in the third paragraph. It actually appears in the final sentence of the paragraph: "The barking was probably just Frisky's way of being psyched." The word "psyched" is slang. A better word to use would be the word "excited."

The next three mistakes are in the fourth paragraph. The first mistake in the paragraph is in the first sentence: "When JJ got downstairs, however, she noticed that something was berning." The word "berning" should be spelled "burning."

For the next mistake in the paragraph, look at the second sentence: "JJ called to her mom to ask if nothing was wrong …" Instead of the word "nothing," the word "anything" should be used. There would not be a problem if "nothing" was wrong. JJ is concerned, however, since she is unsure if "anything was wrong."

The third and final mistake in the paragraph is contained in the last sentence: "JJ had to act quick." The word "quick" needs to be changed to "quickly" since the word being modified (to act) is a verb form. Only the adverb "quickly" and not the adjective "quick" can modify a verb form.

10. (B) Check Your Content

Make sure that you also edit to improve the content of your essay. Let's return to the first paragraph of the sample essay draft. Concentrate on editing for content this time. Try to rewrite this paragraph to contain more specific detail. Think about the following questions:

1. What did JJ see when she opened her eyes?
2. What slang expression should the writer change?
3. In the last sentence, the author said, "How much louder could the noise become?" Is the noise the problem, or is there more to the situation?

Consider the first question: "What did JJ see when she opened her eyes?" Instead of saying, "JJ heard her alarm clock go off," it's more effective to say, "JJ looked at the alarm clock as she lay in bed." There's a combination of action and detail in the revised sentence.

Next, look at the second question: "What slang expression should the writer change?" The sentence "She figured her mom would take care of business, but she didn't" is weakened by the slang phrase "take care of business." This overused, stale phrase is an example of a cliché. Always avoid using clichés in your writing.

Finally, think about the quote mentioned in the third question: "How much louder could the noise become?" The loudness of the noise is not the issue in the story. Instead, the issue is Frisky's barking and scurrying, which fortunately wakes up JJ.

10. (C) Submit Your Final Draft

Now it's time to submit your final draft. Give this writing your best effort. Make sure that you concentrate on the elements that we have discussed.

- Set the scene. Let your reader get close to the characters by:

  - Describing the way they look.
  - Showing their traits.
  - "Painting a word picture" that describes the characters and places in the scene.

- Introduce your conflict. Tell about:

  - The problem that seems to be happening.
  - The reason that the situation being described is a problem.

- Decide the way in which the problem will be solved.

  - Heroic action.
  - Unexpected happening.

- Consider whether or not a lesson was learned by the main character(s).

  - If so, does the lesson make sense from the story you have written?
  - If not, does the story come to a definite conclusion?

- Think of a title that truly relates to your story. Be as specific as possible.

Essay Final Draft

Title: _____

Be sure to check the sample response on pages 257–259 against your narrative writing task.

Don't Forget to Follow the Guidelines

Remember, when you write a story, always be sure to follow these guidelines.

1. Create the realistic main conflict.
2. Create the plot (plan of action).
3. Create the setting.
4. Give each main character a personality.
5. Develop the story (plot line).
6. Write the solution for the problem (resolve the conflict).
7. Give your story a working title.
8. Write your first draft and include a compositional risk (and some insight, if appropriate).
9. Add dialogue.
10. Edit and submit your final draft.

    (A) Check your grammar and spelling.
    (B) Check your content.
    (C) Submit your final draft.

NARRATIVE WRITING PRACTICE

Now that you have followed the entire writing process from beginning to end, it's time to practice your essay writing skills. Use the space provided to write a narrative on the topic below.

When you finish, check the **Suggested Main Points** listed on page 259. Your points may be just as good, if not better than the ones given.

Writing Topic

You are walking along the street when you notice there is a large box wrapped in birthday wrapping. The tag on the box has a name written on it, but it's hard to read since it is a little smeared.

Think about the box that you have found. Now create a story and fill in the details of that story. Remember, your story should be based on events that most people would understand.

Do **not** simply describe what you see in your mind. Instead, make up a story about what is going on. You may wish to include some details that have happened even before the picture was taken.

Essay

Title: _____

Grammar the Write Way

GRAMMAR GUIDE: USING GRAMMAR CORRECTLY IN YOUR WRITING

As we have already mentioned, the grammar that you use in your writing on the PARCC Grade 7 ELA/Literacy Test must be correct. The score for your essays uses grammar as one of the elements being graded. That's the reason why you must write sentences that do not have grammar mistakes.

Strategy

When you write for any standardized test like the PARCC, you always need to proofread your work. Checking the content of the essays that you write is important. It is also important to check your grammar.

Be sure to:

1. Read each essay to yourself. Make sure that your sentences sound right.
2. Be sure that you have not broken any of the grammar rules that we are going to review together.

Let's discuss and do some practice exercises so we can improve your chances of doing well on this test. Let's concentrate on some of the most common areas that can cause you major problems with your grammar.

PRACTICE

Agreement—Number, Case, and Gender

There are three major points of agreement in your sentences.

1. Number—Singular or Plural
2. Case—Subject or Object
3. Gender—Masculine, Feminine, or Neuter (Neither Masculine nor Feminine)

Please note that when considering case, the noun may be the simplest one to deal with.

For pronouns, which by definition take the place of nouns, there are actually three cases. The first is the subjective (nominative) case, which applies when a noun is either used as a subject or as the complement of a linking (copulative) verb. For example, the sentence "She is the president" may also be written as "The president is she" since the linking verb "**is**" allows the subject "She" and the predicate complement "**president**" to change places without changing the meaning of the sentence.

The second case is possessive (genitive), and the same explanation for nouns applies to pronouns as well since pronouns act as noun replacements. For example, consider the sentence: "**The actor in the play gave his soliloquy at the end of the first act.**" The pronoun "**his**" reflects the fact that the soliloquy is the actor's and not someone else's.

The third type of case is objective (accusative). Consider these sentences: "**Concerning my sister Alisha, I saw her at the beach yesterday with her boyfriend. When Alisha saw me walking home later that day, she gave me a ride. Since it began to rain soon after I got into Alisha's car, I was very grateful that she gave a ride to me.**" In the first sentence, "**her**" is a direct object (I saw whom? I saw "**her.**"). In the second sentence, "**me**" is an indirect object (Alisha gave a ride to whom? Alisha gave a ride to "**me.**"). In the third sentence, "**me**" is an object of the preposition in the phrase "**to me.**" Remember, an object of a preposition is always in the objective (accusative) case.

Number

1. Make sure that your subjects agree in number with your verbs.

    a. When a noun is singular, the verb should also be singular.
    b. When a noun is plural, then the verb should also be plural.
    c. When there is more than one noun, then the verb is automatically plural.

2. Remember that singular verbs may end in "s" but plural verbs do not. This rule is the opposite of the one for nouns: "Use '-s' or '-es' at the end of many plural nouns."

Practice

Read the paragraph below. Underline the three verbs that are incorrect. Write the correct form of the verb above the incorrect ones. Review the correct answers on page 260.

My Friend and I Is Going to the Video Game Store

After school today, my friend Sam and I don't plan to go straight home. Instead, we plans to go to the video game store. We is going to walk down Main Street and then turn right on Maple Avenue. There are three new games being released today, and we're going to be at the store to try them out with our friends.

1. Select the statement(s) that contain a subject-verb agreement mistake.

   ☐ A. "My Friend and I Is Going to the Video Game Store."
   ☐ B. "After school today, my friend Sam and I don't plan to go straight home."
   ☐ C. "Instead, we plans to go to the video game store."
   ☐ D. "We is going to walk down Main Street and then turn right on Maple Avenue."
   ☐ E. "There are three new games being released today, and we're going to be at the store to try them out with our friends."

2. Which of the pronouns are in the genitive case?

   ☐ A. My
   ☐ B. I
   ☐ C. We
   ☐ D. We're
   ☐ E. Our

Answers

1. The correct answers are **A. My Friend and I Is Going to the Video Game Store**, and **C. "Instead, we plans to go to the video game store,"** and **D. We is going to walk down Main Street and then turn right on Maple Avenue**. Remember that you are looking to find the sentences that have subject-verb agreement mistakes and not the ones that do not.

Be sure to check your answers for the incorrect verbs with those on page 260.

2. The correct answers are **A. My** and **E. Our**. These two pronouns are in the genitive (possessive) case. Answers **B. I**, **C. We**, and **D. We're (We are)** are all in the nominative case.

Case

Make sure that your sentences use the right case.

1. There are two ways to use Subject Pronouns.

   a. Subject of the sentence; for example, "*I* am the president."
   b. Predicate Complement; for example, "The president is *I*."

2. There are three ways to use Object Pronouns.

   a. Direct Object (answers "Whom" or "What" is receiving the action of the verb); for example, "Mom will take *me* to the skate park."
   b. Indirect Object (answers "To whom?" "To what?" "For whom?" or "For what?" the action of the verb is being done); for example, "Dad will make *us* dinner later."
   c. Object of the Preposition (the noun or pronoun that ends the prepositional phrase); for example, "Give your ticket to *her*."

Practice

Read the following paragraph. Then, select the pronouns that are used incorrectly and list them in the space(s) provided. (For practice, write the correct form of the pronoun above the incorrect one.)

Our Test Review Was a Game!

(1) Mr. Bogosian tried something new in class today: he played a review game to give we a chance to get ready for ours test. (2) Us kids actually had fun playing the game with him. (3) Francisco answered the most questions so we clapped for he. (4) Even so, we were the real winners since more than half of us earned ours best test score of the year.

Sentence 1

Sentence 2

Sentence 3

Sentence 4

Answers

Our Test Review Was a Game!

Mr. Bogosian tried something new in class today: he played a review game to
1. *us*   1. *our*   2. *We*
give **we** a chance to get ready for ours test. **Us** kids actually had fun playing the
3. *him*
game. Francisco answered the most questions so we clapped for **he**. Even so, we
4. *our*
were the real winners since more than half of us earned ours best test score of

the year.

Explanation
1. The object pronoun "**us**" is correct since it is the indirect object.
2. The subject pronoun "**We**" is correct since it is used in the subject position.
3. The object pronoun "**him**" is correct since it is the object of the preposition "**for.**"

Gender
When your subjects are pronouns, make sure they agree in gender with your verbs.

1. Masculine (Male), Feminine (Female), and Neuter (neither Masculine nor Feminine) pronouns need the same gender for the nouns they are replacing.

    a. Masculine—Man ⇒ *He*, *Him*, and *His*.
    b. Feminine—Female ⇒ *She*, *Her*, and *Hers*.
    c. Neuter—neither Masculine nor Feminine ⇒ *It* and *Its*

2. Gender only matters with third person singular pronouns.
3. Don't forget this important fact: whenever you refer to yourself **and** one or more other people, you always mention yourself last. That is polite. For example, "Please meet my friend and me at the mall tomorrow after school" is correct. However, "Please meet me and my friend" is incorrect since you always come last if you are being referred to with one or more others.

Practice

Part A
For the following sentences, underline the correct answers.

1. Mrs. Cairo asked Mary to pick up (her, its) books.

2. Jackson took (his, its) brother to the movies.

3. The table can hold (her, its) own weight.

Be sure to check your answers with those on page 260.

Part B
For the following paragraph, list the pronouns in each sentence on the blank lines below. For the ones that are used incorrectly, change them to the correct pronoun and write them next to the incorrect ones.

(1) On a cool day in November, Mary saw her best friend Kemisha walking down her street. (2) Before she could get to the door to wave to she, the phone rang. (3) Its seems that Mary's Aunt Belinda was calling to tell hers some good news. (4) Mary's brother Carlos was going to be coming home from college next week, and him and his friend were going to stay at Aunt Belinda's house for a day. (5) When asked if Mary would like to visit also, Mary asked, "Would it be okay if me and my best friend Kemisha both came to visit?" (6) As long as her and her mom talked first, Aunt Belinda would have no problem with Mary bringing Kemisha too.

Sentence 1

Sentence 2

Sentence 3

Sentence 4

Sentence 5

Sentence 6

Answers

Part B

In Sentence 1, "**her (best)**" and "**her (street)**" are both used correctly. In Sentence 2, "**she (could)**" is used correctly but "**(wave to) she**" should be "**(wave to) her**" since the second "**her**"—**(wave to) her**—is the object of the preposition "**to.**" In Sentence 3, "**Its seems**" should be "**It seems**" since "**Its**" is a possessive. Also, "**(to tell) hers**" should be "**(to tell) her**" since a personal pronoun rather than a possessive pronoun is needed here. In Sentence 4, the two pronouns are "**him**" and "**his.**" The phrase should read "**he (and) his (friend)**" since "**he**" is part of a compound subject and therefore needs to be a subject pronoun. In Sentence 5, the two pronouns are "**me (and) my (best friend).**" The phrase should read "**my best friend Kemisha and I**" since the speaker always goes last in a series. In Sentence 6, the pronouns are "**her**" and "**her (mom).**" The phrase should read, "**As long as she and her mom talked first.**" This substitution can easily be checked by simply substituting "**she**" for "**her.**"

Structure—Sentence Types (4 Major)

1. Simple Sentence

The major elements of a simple sentence are the subject and the verb.

Here's an example of a simple sentence:

In the woods, the bear (subject) slept (verb) *in a cave.*

2. Compound Sentence

Major Elements of a Compound Sentence—Simple Sentence (Independent Clause) + Simple Sentence (Independent Clause) connected by one of the FANBOYS ("For," "And," "Nor," "But," "Or," "Yet," and "So")

Here's an example of a Compound Sentence.

- I (Subject) wished (Verb) for a warm day last Saturday, yet my sister (Subject) wished (Verb) for a cold day.

3. Complex Sentence

Major Elements of a Complex Sentence—Simple Sentence (Independent Clause) + Subordinating Conjunction ("While," "Throughout," and "Whenever," for example) + Simple Sentence (Dependent Clause)

Here's an example of a Complex Sentence.

I studied for my test on Monday since my game was cancelled because of the heavy rain.

> Please note: It is the Subordinating Conjunction (in this case, "since") that causes the Independent Clause to become a Dependent Clause. The Subordinating Conjunction ("Because," "Despite," or "While," for example) attaches on to the Simple Sentence and thereby prevents it from standing alone as an Independent Clause. It can also appear at the front of the sentence and do the same work. For example, "Since my game was cancelled because of the heavy rain, I studied for my test on Monday" is also a Complex Sentence.

4. Compound-Complex Sentence

Major Elements of a Compound-Complex Sentence—Simple Sentence (Independent Clause) + Simple Sentence (Independent Clause) + Subordinating Conjunction + Simple Sentence (Dependent Clause)

Here's an example of a Compound-Complex Sentence.

I came home from the park yesterday and I immediately took the dog for a walk because I had forgotten earlier.

Please note: The Subordinating Conjunction works the same way here as it does in the Complex Sentence. Furthermore, it may also appear at different places in the sentence. For example, "I came home yesterday, and since I had forgotten earlier, I immediately took the dog for a walk.

Practice

Read the following passage, then answer the questions.

When I set my alarm last night, I realized that today I would be following a different routine for the next few months. When school let out in June, I had a lot more freedom. I slept a little later, ate lunch whenever I wanted to, watched my favorite daytime television programs, and just hung out with my friends. This morning, my summer will come to an end and I shall get on the bus for school.

My mom woke me up even before my alarm rang. She told me that I had to make sure that I was awake. I couldn't go back to sleep. If I did, I would be late for the first day of school. She said, "That's not the way you want to start out your school year, is it?" I just grumbled "No" and slid out of my bed.

I found my way to the bathroom, and I jumped in the shower because it was already 7:00 AM. During the summer, I never had to take my shower before breakfast. I always made some cereal, poured a glass of juice, and settled in with my favorite television program or one of the music channels. Today, however, I am showering, drying my hair, and having a little breakfast. Oh, I couldn't do these things in slow motion. My mom kept reminding me to "Hurry up!" so I wouldn't be late. She also reminded me to wear the new outfit we had bought last week. "You should always make a good first impression, especially on the first day of school," she said. It would feel funny dressing up for breakfast after an entire summer of eating while wearing my pajamas.

Match the sentence types with the appropriate sentences by writing (clicking) an "X" on the correct labeled box.

1. When school let out in June, I had a lot more freedom.

Simple	Compound	Complex	Compound-Complex

2. I slept a little later, ate lunch whenever I wanted to, watched my favorite daytime television programs, and just hung out with my friends.

Simple	Compound	Complex	Compound-Complex

3. This morning, my summer will end and I shall get on the bus for school.

Simple	Compound	Complex	Compound-Complex

4. My mom woke me up even before my alarm rang.

Simple	Compound	Complex	Compound-Complex

5. I just grumbled "No" and slid out of my bed.

Simple	Compound	Complex	Compound-Complex

6. I found my way to the bathroom, and I jumped in the shower because it was already 7:00 A.M.

Simple	Compound	Complex	Compound-Complex

7. Today, however, I am showering, drying my hair, and having a little breakfast.

Simple	Compound	Complex	Compound-Complex

Answers

1. The correct answers for **Simple** are **2.** "**I slept a little later, ate lunch whenever I wanted to, watched my favorite daytime television programs, and just hung out with my friends,**" **5.** "**I just grumbled 'No' and slid out of my bed,**" and **7.** "**Today, however, I am showering, drying my hair, and having a little breakfast.**" In **2**, there is one subject (**I**) with four verbs (**slept**, **ate**, **watched**, and **hung [out]**). This is an example of a simple subject with a compound (more than one) predicate. Also, the helping verb **could** is unstated for the other three verbs. In **5**, the simple subject **I** has two verbs: **grumbled** and **slid**. In **7**, the subject **I** has three verbs: **am showering**, **drying**, and **having**. Similar to **5**, the helping verb **am** is unstated for the other two verbs. The correct answer for **Compound** is **3.** "**This morning, my summer will end, and I shall get on the bus for school.**" The two simple sentences (independent clauses) "**This morning, my summer will end**" and "**I shall get on the bus for school**" are joined by a comma preceding the coordinating conjunction **and**. The correct answers for **Complex** are **1.** "**When school let out in June, I had a lot more freedom**" and **4.** "**My mom woke me up even before my alarm rang.**" In **1**, **I had a lot more freedom** is the simple sentence (independent clause) preceded by the phrase (dependent or subordinate clause) **When school let out in June**. The dependent clause cannot stand on its own as a dependent clause and is therefore subordinate to the independent clause. In **4**, the independent clause is **My mom woke me up** while the dependent clause is **even before my alarm rang**. The correct answer for **Compound-Complex** is **6.** "**I found my way to the bathroom, and I jumped in the shower because it was already 7:00 A.M.**" The two independent clauses are **I found my way to the bathroom** and **I jumped in the shower**. These two sentences are joined by a comma and the word **and**. In addition, the "complex" piece of the answer is the phrase **because it was already 7:00 A.M.** is a dependent clause that cannot stand alone.

Misplaced Modifiers

A misplaced modifier is simply one or more words that don't refer directly to the word(s) being modified. Instead, they refer to the wrong word(s). The result is confusion.

Strategy

1. Keep your word(s) next to or very close to the word(s) being modified.
2. If the meaning of your sentence is misleading, then rewrite it so it's clear.

Practice

Part A

Rewrite the following sentences correctly.

1. In her desk, Savannah found a blue lady's bracelet.

   ----

2. I once met a man with one arm named Rashawn.

   ----

3. I heard that the burglar has been captured on the evening news.

Be sure to check your answers with those on page 260.

Part B

Read the following passage. Review the sentences that have misplaced modifiers. Then, rewrite the sentences correctly on the lines after the passage. If no correction is needed, simply do not write an answer on the line corresponding to the sentence.

(1) When I woke up this morning, I heard my silly dog Sparky barking at the traffic near my refrigerator. (2) It seems that the traffic somehow gets more congested as soon as Sparky prepares to take his morning nap beside my bed. (3) I try to calm Sparky down, but sometimes I'm just not able to do so. (4) Sometimes I'll walk Sparky to my neighbor's house to visit with their pet dog Ruffian. (5) Distracted by Ruffian, the time seems to pass quickly. (6) Soon, Sparky isn't angry anymore.

Sentence 1

Sentence 2

Sentence 3

Sentence 4

Sentence 5

Sentence 6

Answers

Part B

1. When I woke up this morning, I heard my silly dog barking at the traffic while she was sitting next to my refrigerator. (The "**traffic**" was not near the refrigerator.)

2. It seems that the traffic somehow gets more congested as soon as Sparky prepares to take his morning nap beside my bed. (The "**morning**" is not near the bed.)

3. (Leave this line blank.)

4. (Leave this line blank.)

5. The time seems to pass quickly when Sparky is distracted by Ruffian. (The "**time**" is not being distracted by Ruffian.)

6. (Leave this line blank.)

Voice

There are two kinds of voice in all sentences.

1. **Active Voice**—The subject does the action in the sentence. *Example:* "The girls' twirling squad won the first place trophy in the county tournament."
2. **Passive Voice**—The subject does not do the action in the sentence. *Example:* "The first place trophy in the county tournament was won by the girls' twirling squad."

The active voice is preferred. Use it especially for standardized tests like the PARCC.

Strategy

1. Use the active voice to give your sentences a little more energy. Also, remember that the evaluators of standardized tests like the PARCC prefer the active voice.
2. Use the passive voice as little as you can on the test.

Practice

Part A

Read the following passage. Identify the sentences written in the passive voice. Write those sentences in the correct spaces below the passage. If the sentence is written in the active voice, then leave the space blank.

(1) Yesterday my best friend Kenny and I were planning to go to a professional soccer game. (2) We planned to see our favorite team the Smithville Screaming Hawks play the Mountain Ridge Rebels. (3) Getting tickets to the game was not an easy task. (4) A call to the Screaming Hawks was made by my Uncle Sanjay. (5) He hoped that his friend, who is an assistant coach for the team, could get us some tickets. (6) Rooting for the Hawks would be a thrill for us. (7) When my cell phone rang, Kenny and I held our breaths in anticipation. (8) The suspense was getting to be too much for us. (9) I begged my Uncle Sanjay to tell us if he was able to get the tickets. (10) The news of having sideline passes was almost too much for us. (11) We jumped up and down and made so much noise that Uncle Rajah teased us that we were going to have to become the Hawks newest cheering squad members.

Sentence 1

Sentence 2

Sentence 3

Sentence 4

Sentence 5

Sentence 6

Sentence 7

Sentence 8

Sentence 9

Sentence 10

Sentence 11

Answers

Sentences 3, 4, 6, and 10 are passive voice sentences. Sentence 3 ("**Getting tickets to the game was not an easy task**") may be rewritten as "We did not have an easy task when we wanted to get tickets to the game." Sentence 4 ("**A call to the Screaming Hawks was made by my Uncle Sanjay**") may be rewritten as "My Uncle Sanjay made a call to the Screaming Hawks." Sentence 6 ("**Rooting for the Hawks would be a thrill for us**") may be rewritten as "We would be thrilled to be rooting for the Hawks." Sentence 10 ("**The news of having sideline passes was almost too much for us**") may be rewritten as "We were overwhelmed to hear that we would be getting sideline passes, and we almost couldn't handle our excitement."

Part B

Read the following sentences and rewrite them correctly in the active voice.

1. Every desk in the library was filled with students yesterday.

   ----

2. At my favorite ice cream store, my sundae was prepared by the new owner.

   ----

3. I was scolded by my parents when I didn't do all my chores yesterday.

Be sure to check your answers with those on page 261.

Sentence Variety

When you write, your sentences should not follow the same pattern. Otherwise, they become very boring and difficult to read. The solution is to add variety when you write.

Strategy

1. Avoid starting every sentence with the subject and verb.

    a. Use a prepositional phrase or two to begin your sentence.

    Example: In the middle of the day, I usually eat my lunch.

    b. Use a prepositional phrase or two to end your sentence.

    Example: I usually eat my lunch in the middle of the day.

2. Combine two sentences to make a compound or complex sentence.

    a. Compound Sentence: Two sentences joined by adding a comma and the words "and," "or," or "but" to connect two sentences.

    Example: I went to the game, but my sister went to the park.

    b. Complex Sentence: A sentence that has one part that is a sentence and one that is not.

    Example: I went to the game while my sister went to the park.

3. Vary the length of each sentence.

    Example: I walked my dog yesterday. Because it was such a nice day, I went to my friend's house after I had my lunch.

4. Change the order of one or more adverbs, as long as the meaning stays the same.

    Example: Change "Tomorrow I will go home" to "I will go home tomorrow."

Practice

Rewrite the paragraph on the lines below. Try to include the skills that have just been covered in this section.

Getting in Trouble

I got in trouble yesterday. My friends and I cut across our neighbor's lawn. He became very upset. He yelled at us. We said we weren't hurting anything. He said that somebody stole his lawn chair as a prank. Now he's blaming us. We're innocent. I guess we shouldn't have walked on his lawn.

Be sure to check your paragraph against the sample response and explanation on page 261.

Fragments and Run-ons

A **fragment** is a piece of a sentence. It cannot stand alone as a sentence.

Example: Hassan from the school around the corner.

A **run-on** is more than one sentence that is joined incorrectly.

Example: Francesca was bored she went to the movies.

Strategy

1. Change a fragment into a full sentence.

   Example: Hassan from the school around the corner is on my soccer team.

2. Here are two ways to fix a run-on.

   a. Separate the run-on into two different sentences.

   Example: Francesca was bored. Therefore, she went to the movies.

   b. Combine the run-on into one sentence.

   Example: Since Francesca was bored, she went to the movies.

Practice—Fragments

Rewrite the following sentences correctly to eliminate fragments.

1. Through the park.

   ----

2. My best friend from Vineland.

   ----

3. Exercising every morning.

Practice—Run-ons

Rewrite the following sentences correctly to eliminate run-ons.

1. Come to my birthday party it will be fun.

----

2. I'm doing my homework now I can't talk to you

----

3. I'll take out the trash I'll walk the dog.

Be sure to check your answers with those on page 262.

Practice—Prepositional Phrases, Compound and Complex Sentences, Fragments, and Run-ons

Read the following passage. On the lines below, write the number of each sentence that contains: a prepositional phrase, a compound sentence, a complex sentence, a sentence fragment, or a run-on sentence. Once you write down the sentence number, you must also write down the answer.

(1) While I was sending a text message to my best friend, I heard a strange noise in my backyard. (2) I ignored the noise at first. (3) Since I was so busy. (4) The noise soon became louder, so I went on the porch to investigate. (5) At first, I couldn't discover the source of the noise. (6) Because I was curious, I stepped onto the patio. (7) Something came dashing across the sidewalk, I yelled for help. (8) Dumb move. (9) It was only the neighbor's dog, and it was chasing a squirrel.

Prepositional phrase(s)

Sentence numbers and phrases (listed by number and separated by a semicolon)

Compound sentence(s)

Sentence number and sentence

Complex sentence(s)

Sentence number and sentence

Sentence fragment(s)

Run-on sentence(s)

----

(1) While I was sending a text message to my best friend, I heard a strange noise in my backyard. (2) I ignored the noise at first. (3) Since I was so busy. (4) The noise soon became louder, so I went on the porch to investigate. (5) At first, I couldn't discover the source of the noise. (6) Because I was curious, I stepped onto the patio. (7) Something came dashing across the sidewalk, I yelled for help. (8) Dumb move. (9) It was only the neighbor's dog, and it was chasing a squirrel.

Answers

(1) "**While I was sending a text message** *to my best friend*, **I heard a strange noise** *in my backyard*," (2) "**I ignored the noise** *at first*," (4) "**The noise soon became louder, so I went** *on the porch* **to investigate**," (5) "**At first, I couldn't discover the source** *of the noise*," (6) "**Because I was curious, I stepped** *onto the patio*," and (7) "**Something came dashing** *across the sidewalk*, **I yelled** *for help*" contain prepositional phrases (noted with *italics*). The compound sentences are (4) "**The noise soon became louder, so I went on the porch to investigate**" and (9) "**It was only the neighbor's dog, and it was chasing a squirrel**." The coordinating conjunction in #4 is "**so**" while the coordinating conjunction in #9 is "**and**." The complex sentences are (1) "*While* **I was sending a text message to my best friend, I heard a strange noise in my backyard**" and "(6) *Because* **I was curious, I stepped onto the patio**." The subordinating conjunctions are noted in italics. The sentence fragments are (3) "**Since I was so busy**" and (8) "**Dumb move**." The run-on sentence is (7) "**Something came dashing across the sidewalk, I yelled for help**," since a coordinating conjunction such as "and," a semicolon, or a period separating the two clauses is needed.

Punctuation with Commas and End Marks

1. A **comma** has a few basic purposes in a sentence.

   a. It combines with the words "and," "or," or "but" to make a compound sentence.

      Example: I ran, but you walked.

   b. It separates more than two items in a series.

      Example: We ate, played games, and rode the rides at the amusement park.

   c. It's used when the first part of a complex sentence isn't a full sentence.

      Example: When we played video games yesterday, we had fun.

d. It separates the name of a city from the name of a state.

   Example: Linden, New Jersey.

e. It's used after greetings and closings in letters.

   Example: "Dear Moira," and "Sincerely yours,"

f. It's used after introductory words and phrases.

   Example: "Yes, I'm coming now," "During the winter, I like to ice skate," and "Nevertheless, we shall be completing our review of our homework assignment before we dismiss for recess today."

g. It's used with an appositive (a word that further explains another word).

   Example: My brother, a hard worker, was voted captain of the team.

h. It's used before a quotation.

   Example: I heard my teacher say, "Class, open your books to page 47."

2. There are four basic **end marks** used for sentences.

a. Period

   i. Declarative Sentence (Statement).

      Example: I like ice cream.

   ii. Imperative Sentence (Command or Request).

      Example: Come here.

b. Question Mark—Interrogative Sentence (Question).

   Example: Can you help me?

c. Exclamation Mark—Exclamatory Sentence (Strong Feeling or Emotion).

   Example: We won the city championship!

Strategy

1. Learn the rules.
2. Follow the rules.

Practice—Commas

Punctuate the following sentences correctly by using commas correctly.

1. I had a hamburger and you had pizza.

2. My mom asked me to go to the store mail a letter and put my dirty clothes in the wash.

3. Because I earned all "A's" and "B's" on my report card I'm getting a reward.

4. We moved to New Jersey from Springfield Ohio.

5. "Sincerely yours Allen" is the ending I used for my letter.

6. No I won't make fun of the new student in our class.

7. The winner of the fund-raising challenge was Nicole a student from my class.

Practice—Punctuating Sentences

Punctuate the following sentences by adding the correct end marks.

1. I just won a million dollars

2. Please take care of yourself

3. Did you eat the last piece of cake

4. The class project will be due on March 3

Be sure to check your answers with those on page 262.

Read the following passage. Next, circle any punctuation and end marks that are either misused or omitted. Finally, write in what each correct punctuation mark or end mark should be if it has been either misused or omitted. If no additional mark is needed in a sentence, write the sentence number and "No mark" in the margin.

(1) Neither Constantine my best friend nor I could remember the three items that my mom had told us to pick up at the supermarket. (2) We know that she was going to prepare Texas-style chili for us for dinner and we were very excited. (3) The last time she made Texas-style chili, my uncle my brother, and my older sister all complained that it was too spicy. (4) However, I like spicy foods. (5) For me Texas-style chili needs to be spicy. (6) Don't you agree?

(7) When Constantine, and I arrived at the store, we still couldn't remember all three items. (8) Constantine said "We need ground beef and cans of tomato sauce" (9) However, that's only two items. (10) I knew there had to be a third but I just couldn't remember it. (11) This was so embarrassing?

(12) Feeling a bit despondent, Constantine and I decided to return home! (13) When we arrived, we had to admit to my mom that we couldn't remember the third ingredient she had asked us to buy? (14) Imagine the looks on our faces when she took the ground beef and tomato sauce from us and asked "Where's the chili powder." (15) That was so embarrassing.

Answers

The answers are listed in order.

1. "...**Constantine, my best friend, nor I**..."—Commas are needed for the appositive.

2. "...**for dinner, and we were**..."—A comma is needed for the compound sentence.

3. "...**my uncle, my brother, and**..."—A comma is needed since there are more than two items in a series.

4. "**However, I like**..."—A comma is used after an introductory word.

5. "**For me, Texas-style**..."—See previous reason.

6. "No mark"

7. "**When Constantine and I**..."—No comma is needed after "**Constantine,**" since there are only two items in the series.

8. "**Constantine said, 'We**..."—A comma is needed before the quotation.

9. No mark

10. "...**a third, but I**..."—A comma is needed before the coordinating conjunction "**but**" in this compound sentence.

11. "**This was so embarrassing!**"—This sentence is an exclamation, not a question, and it therefore requires an exclamation mark.

12. "...**to return home.**"—This is a statement, not an exclamation.

13. "...**she had asked us to buy.**"—This is a statement, not an question.

14. "...**and asked, "Where's the chili powder?**"—The comma is needed before the quotation, and the question mark is needed for the question being posed."

15. "**That was so embarrassing!**"—The statement is an exclamation.

Homophones and Homographs

1. **Homophones** are words that sound alike and may be spelled alike or differently. Each set of homophones has the same pronunciation.

   Example: You can **pare** ("cut off") the limb of a **pear** ("fruit") tree. Then you can cut the limb into two equal pieces to make a **pair** ("set of two").

2. **Homographs** share the same spelling, but each has a different meaning.

   Example: The campers could not **bear** ("support") to think that a **bear** ("wild animal") might be wandering outside their tents.

3. **Homographs** may also have different pronunciations. For example, "**bow**" (to bend forward at the waist) and "**bow**" (the front of a ship) are pronounced differently than "**bow**" (a way to knot material like string and cloth).

Strategy

Make sure that you know the appropriate meaning of the homophones and homographs that you wish to use. Spelling and word choice do count on the test. For more examples of homophones and homographs, you can search an online dictionary or thesaurus.

Practice—Homophones

Part A

Underline the correct homophones in the following sentences.

1. I had to (so, sew) a button on my coat yesterday.

2. (Their, There, They're) not the same desserts that we had at the party last week.

3. Please hand in your homework (to, too, two) the teacher.

4. When you don't speak up, I can't (hear, here) you.

5. The petals on this lovely (flour, flower) have a pleasant aroma.

Part B

Read the following passage. Circle the misused homophones and write above them the correct answer for each.

   (1) Eye want ewe to no that I am going to fix our clock in the kitchen so it will keep the write thyme. (2) It seams that it has knot bin accurate fore the last weak. (3) That fact is not easy four me to except. (4) I wood fix the clock if aye could. (5) Even after I tried to reed the part of the instructions that explain how two repair the clock, I still was sew confused.

Answers

1. In this sentence, **"Eye"** should be **"I,"** **"ewe"** should be **"you,"** **"no"** should be **"know,"** **"write"** should be **"right,"** and **"thyme"** should be **"time."**

2. In this sentence, **"seams"** should be **"seems,"** **"knot"** should be **"not,"** **"fore"** should be **"for,"** and **"weak"** should be **"week."**

3. In this sentence, **"four"** should be **"for"** and **"except"** should be **"accept."**

4. In this sentence, **"wood"** should be **"would"** and **"aye"** should be **"I."**

5. In this sentence, **"reed"** should be **"read,"** **"two"** should be **"to,"** and **"sew"** should be **"so."**

Practice—Homographs

Part A

Choose the correct meaning of each homograph.

1. This tea was made from an exotic **bark**.

   ○ A. an animal's cry
   ○ B. the covering of a tree

2. My backpack was very **light** today.

   ○ A. not heavy
   ○ B. not dark

3. Of which local team are you a **fan**?

   ○ A. admirer
   ○ B. cooling device

4. Before you put on a bandage, be sure to clean your **wound**.

    ○ A.   turning in a circular way
    ○ B.   skin cut

5. Is this television program **live** or pre-recorded?

    ○ A.   residing in a place
    ○ B.   happening in the present time

Be sure to check your answers for Part A: Homophones and Homographs on pages 262–263.

Part B
Read the following passage. Next, note all the words that are homographs.

(1) When I went to see my favorite band playing live in concert, I was hoping to get a picture of the lead singer. (2) I couldn't believe that I would be present to listen to my favorite singer in person. (3) My sister told me that the concert promoter had arranged to record the entire show. (4) Since I had been lucky enough to win front row seats that put me very close to the stage, I was able to give my favorite lead singer a high five as she took her bow.

Answers

1. In this sentence, the homographs are "**live**" and "**lead**."

2. In this sentence, the homograph is "**present**."

3. In this sentence, the homograph is "**record**."

4. In this sentence, the homographs are "**close**" and "**bow**."

After you review the answers, be sure to go back and review any areas that gave you problems.

Grammar Demons

Unusual Order

Some sentences have an unusual order.

1. **Inverted Order** sentences have their subjects placed after the verb.

   a. Some sentences that begin with "**Here**" or "**There.**"

   Example: **Here** is the desk. **There** are the notebooks.

   b. Some declarative sentences are **Inverted Declaratives**.

   Example: In my classroom is my bag. Nearby are my shoes.

Strategy

1. Be sure that the subject and the verb agree in number in an **Inverted Order** sentence. As mentioned, look for the subject after the verb.
2. Use the same strategy for **Inverted Declaratives**.

Practice—Unusual Order

Part A

Underline the correct verbs in the following sentences.

1. Here (is, are) four tickets to the movies.

2. Upstairs (is, are) your new outfit.

3. There (is, are) a rip in the carpet.

4. In the garage (is, are) your two baseball gloves.

Be sure to check your answers for Part A with those on page 263.

Part B

Read the following paragraph. Highlight (underline) only the sentences that are written in inverted order.

(1) When I left for school this morning, everything seemed to be fine. (2) There were birds chirping in the trees as I strolled along the sidewalk. (3) When I rounded the corner, I said hello to Mrs. Gabilli as she was preparing to paint the new bird house that she had built. (4) In my hand was the set of study cards I had made last week to prepare for my art history

test today. (5) Even though there was a small cloud in the sky, I knew that it wasn't going to rain later. (6) My baseball team would be playing in our first playoff game, and I was chosen to be the starting pitcher. (7) There are many honors I could have received, but this was the most important one for me right now. (8) On my dresser was my lucky coin that I would place in my pocket whenever I would pitch. (9) I would have to make sure that I put the coin in the top pocket of my warm-up jacket for good luck.

Answers

The sentences that are written in Inverted Order are (2) "**There were birds chirping in the trees as I strolled along the sidewalk,**" (4) "**In my hand was the set of study cards I had made last week to prepare for my art history test today,**" (7) "**There are many honors I could have received, but this was the most important one for me right now,**" and (8) "**On my dresser was my lucky coin that I would place in my pocket whenever I would pitch.**"

Adjective or Adverb

Adjectives and **Adverbs** are both modifiers.

1. **Adjectives** modify nouns and pronouns.
2. **Adverbs** modify verbs, adjectives, and other adverbs.

Strategy

1. Remember that many, but **not** all adverbs end in -ly.
2. In the sentence "**You ran well**," the word "**well**" is an adverb. You cannot use the word "**good**," which is an adjective.
3. In the sentence "**You look well**," the word "**well**" is an adjective that is used instead of the adjective "**good**" because the sentence refers to health. Also, please note that you may refer to someone's appearance with the word "good": "That suit looks good on you."), but you when you tell someone that he/she looks healthy, you say, "You look well."
4. When a verb is linking the subject with a predicate complement, the complement may be an adjective but never an adverb. For example, you may say "The flowers smell nice" since nice is an adjective. You may not say "The flowers smell nicely," however, since "nicely is an adverb. Linking verbs are forms of "be" (is, am, are, was, and were) and the sensate verbs that refer to the five senses (sight, smell, taste, touch, and hear). These verbs include looks, smells, tastes, feels, and sounds. Appropriate sentences would include "I was happy," "The food on my dinner plate looks delicious," and "The cotton blanket feels very soft."

Practice—Adjective or Adverb

Part A
Underline the correct words in the following sentences.

1. That was a (good, well) meal.

2. Now that I have eaten, I feel (good, well).

3. I feel (bad, badly) about doing poorly on my science test.

4. The coach ended practice when we all performed (bad, badly).

5. I earned a (real, really) good grade on my English test.

6. My wish to be a singer someday is (real, really).

Be sure to check your answers for Part A with those on page 263.

Part B
Read the following passage. Next, circle all of the adjectives and adverbs that are misused. Then, write the correct answer above the mistakes. If there are no mistakes in a sentence, then write the number of the sentence and "No mistakes" in the margin.

(1) Last summer, my friends and I promised ourselves that we were going to have the best summer ever. (2) The previous summer had been badly for us. (3) It rained all the time, or so it seemed. (4) Anyway, we all were real excited to be getting out of school on the last day, but our friend Harry did something crazy. (5) He tried to be really cool, so he called the principal by her first name. (6) Didn't he realize that he was not acting correct? (7) The principal called his parents, and Harry had to serve detention for a full day— after school was already over!

Answers

1. In this sentence, there are no mistakes.

2. In this sentence, "**badly**" should be "**bad**."

3. In this sentence, there are no mistakes.

4. In this sentence, "**real**" should be "**really**."

5. In this sentence, there are no mistakes.

6. In this sentence, "**correct**" should be "**correctly**."

7. In this sentence, there are no mistakes.

Quotations

There are two types of **Quotations**: **Direct** and **Indirect**.

1. Direct Quotations contain the exact words that someone has said.

Example: "Bring me the newspaper, please," said my uncle.

2. Indirect Quotations give the idea behind what someone has said, rather than the exact words.

Example: My uncle asked me to bring the newspaper to him.

Strategy

1. Capitalize the first word of a **Direct Quotation**.

Example: Mom asked, "Are you coming?"

2. Separate a quotation from the rest of the sentence by using a comma.

Example: "I'm going to the video game store now," I said to my mom.

3. Do not use a comma to separate a quotation if there is an end punctuation mark (period, exclamation mark, or question mark) in the place where the comma would go.

Example: "May I go to the video game store now?" I asked my mom.

4. For a divided quotation, don't start the second part with a capital letter unless it starts a sentence.

Example: "Are you coming," Mom asked, "or are you staying home?"

Example: "I'm not coming," I answered. "My report for health class is due tomorrow."

5. For quotations that have many sentences that follow one after the other, use one set of quotation marks only.

   Example: I told Kirsten, "Don't forget to bring the sunscreen to the beach. The last time we went, you forgot to bring the sunscreen. We don't want to get sunburned."

6. Periods go inside the closing quotation marks. Question marks and exclamation marks go outside the closing quotation marks **unless** the quotation is a question or an exclamation.

   Example: My brother said, "Let's go home."

   Example: My brother yelled, "Don't go in my room!"

   Example: Did Sarah really say, "I don't care"?

7. In a dialogue, start a new paragraph each time the speaker changes.

   Example: "Can you help me with my homework?" I asked my cousin Fred.
   "I'll be happy to help you," answered Fred.
   "If we finish early, we'll go to the mall," I said.
   "That's great!" he replied.

Practice—Quotations

Add the correct capital letters and punctuation marks to the following sentences.

1. The principal said over the intercom students, please report to the cafeteria at the end of second period today

2. Write your homework assignment in your notebooks said Mrs. Hudson

3. Are we there yet said my brother after every five minutes of our trip

4. Should we go to the park said Carrie or should we go to the ball field

5. I answered we should go to the park they're having a special program there besides, all our friends will be there too

6. That's sounds great said Carrie

Be sure to check your answers with those on pages 263–264.

Underlining or Quotation Marks

Titles of works are punctuated two ways.

1. **Underlining** is used for long works including books, newspapers, magazines, movies, plays, TV series, musical compositions, art works, and certain transportation (specific planes, trains, and spacecraft). Please note that italics can be used instead of underlining when you are typing.

   Example: The Pearl, The Star-Ledger, *The Sound of Music*, and the *USS Missouri*.

2. **Quotation Marks** are used for short works including poems, short stories, articles, chapters of books, and songs.

   Example: "The Road Not Taken," "The Raven," and "Oh, Susannah."

3. Use underlines for complete works that are long. **Direct Quotation**.

   Example: Last month, we read Animal Farm in our English class.

4. Use quotations for shorter works since they may actually be a part of a larger work.

   Example: We watched "The Confrontation," which is episode three of our favorite TV show.

5. Only use italics when you are typing on the computer. Do **not** try to write in italics.

Practice—Underlining or Quotation Marks

Part A

Add the correct underlines or quotes to the following sentences.

1. My sister is reading Great Expectations, a novel by Charles Dickens.

2. In class we read Dream Deferred, a poem by Langston Hughes.

3. Before the play-off game, we stood and took off our caps as the loudspeakers played God Bless America.

4. In class today, Mr. Porter read an article from The New York Times.

Be sure to check your answers with those on page 264.

Part B

Read the following passage. When you see quotation marks, related capitalization or punctuation marks, or underlines being used incorrectly, correct the mistake on the lines provided. If there are no mistakes, then simply write "No mistakes."

(1) As the bell rang on the last day of school, I thought to myself, What am I going to do this summer? (2) Last summer, I read the Jack London classic entitled "The Call of the Wild." (3) I thought to myself, It's so hot that if I read a book about the Klondike, then I should be able to cool off. (4) Well, I didn't get any cooler, but I did especially enjoy the characters Hal, Mercedes, and Charles. (5) In fact, I've signed up this summer for a summer reading contest with The Shore Sentinel, our local newspaper. (6) I'm hoping to read Robert Frost's Stopping by the Woods on a Snowy Evening. (7) Maybe this one will help me cool off a bit.

(8) I'm finally going to be able to stay up late on occasion (with mom and dad's permission, of course) to watch my favorite team when they play the West Coast teams. (9) I'm going to re-read Alex Haley's article Thank You. (10) It tells about the importance of saying those two words, and I fully agree with him. (11) I hope to go to one of the large concert halls to listen to some live music. (12) It's always better to go to a place like the PNC Arts center to listen to a band than it is to listen to a recording. (13) The recording is great, but attending a concert is unforgettable. (14) My plans sound great, but I keep telling myself, "Don't forget to take a little time to relax.

Sentence 1

Sentence 2

Sentence 3

Sentence 4

Sentence 5

Sentence 6

Sentence 7

Sentence 8

Sentence 9

Sentence 10

Sentence 11

Sentence 12

Sentence 13

Sentence 14

Answers

1. In this sentence, it should read: **...myself, "What am...summer?"**
2. In this sentence, it should read: **...entitled <u>The Call of the Wild</u>.**
3. In this sentence, it should read: **"...myself, It's so hot...cool off."**
4. In this sentence, there are no mistakes.
5. In this sentence, there are no mistakes.
6. In this sentence, it should read: **...Frost's "Stopping by...Evening."**
7. In this sentence, there are no mistakes.
8. In this sentence, there are no mistakes.
9. In this sentence, it should read: **...article "Thank You."**
10. In this sentence, there are no mistakes.
11. In this sentence, there are no mistakes.
12. In this sentence, it should read: **...PNC Arts Center**
13. In this sentence, there are no mistakes.
14. In this sentence, it should read: **..."Don't forget...to relax."**

Spelling Demons

Definitions

There are many **spelling demons** that we have trouble spelling correctly. Even adults struggle with these words.

Strategy

1. Learn how to spell correctly as many of these **Spelling Demons** as you possibly can. Remember, spelling and word choice count on the PARCC.
2. If you are unsure of the spelling of a word while you are taking the test, use a different word that you know how to spell correctly.
3. Go on the Internet and conduct a search for misspelled words. You'll find a number of lists that you can use to help you avoid these **spelling demons**.
4. Keep a personal spelling list. Write down any words are that difficult to spell. Check your list at least once a week to review these words.

Practice—Spelling

Part A
Write the correct spelling of each misspelled word. There may be more than one misspelling.

1. If you don't bring a note to excuse your abscence from school, you'll get a detention.

   ----

2. Let's buy some baloons for hour party.

   ----

3. I am assigned the job of changing the date on the Class calender.

   ----

4. The month after January is Febuary.

   ----

5. Do we have any grammer homework tonite?

   ----

6. Oops, my shoelaces are lose.

   ----

7. Our town's parade ocurred last weakend.

   ----

8. Mom ask me to get the butter for the mashed potatos.

   ----

9. Our music Class is studying rythm and blues artists from the 1970s.

   ----

10. I used the vaccuum to pick up the dirt that spill on the rug.

Be sure to check your answers for Part A with those on page 264.

Part B

Read the following paragraph, then use the lines below to rewrite any of the italicized words that are spelled incorrectly. Please note that number three is a two-word title. You do not need to do anything for the words that are spelled correctly.

      1   2   3   4

While I was *preparing* to study for my test in my *Libary Basicks* course last *nite*,

   5   6   7   8   9

my *cell* phone started *buzzing*. I was *recieving* a *text* message from my new *friend*

  10   11   12   13   14

sandy, who had just moved here from a *foriegn* country, *Whales*. *Sandy thought* that

         15   16   17

she had left her *study* notes at her *neighbors* house when she *babysat* while they

         18   19   20   21   22

went to a local *restarant* to have *diner*. Sandy *didnt* want to *faile* the test *because*

  23   24   25   26

her *Aunt* works in a book store in her home *country*. *Luckily*, I was *abel* to take a

  27   28   29

pickture of my notes and send them as an *atachment*. *Snady* thanked me and told

        30   31   32   33   34

me that it is a *priviledge* to *know* me, which caused a *noticable blush* to *appear*

on my face.

Answers

Phrase 3 should be "**Library Basics**." The words that are incorrect should be written in the following way: 4. "**night**," 7. "**receiving**," 10. "**Sandy**," 11. "**foreign**," 12. "**Wales** (the country, not the mammal)," 16. "**neighbor's**" (singular possessive), 18. "**restaurant**," 19. "**dinner**," 20. "**didn't**," 21. "**fail**," 23. "**aunt**" (only capitalized when used either as part of a name or a substitute for a name as in "May I have your permission, Aunt, to go to the park?"), 26. "**able**," 27. "**picture**," 28. "**attachment**," 29. "**Sandy**" (Be careful not to let your brain get used to seeing the word *Sandy* spelled correctly so it automatically changes the mistake to the correct spelling while you are reading.), 30. "**privilege**," and 32. "**noticeable**."

The words that are spelled correctly (and which you were not required to write down) are as follows: 1. "**While**," 2. "**preparing**," 5. "**cell**," 6. "**buzzing**," 8. "**text**," 9. "**friend**," 13. "**Sandy**," 14. "**thought**," 15. "**study**," 17. "**babysat**," 22. "**because**," 24. "**country**," 25. "**Luckily**," 31. "**know**," 33. "**blush**," and 34. "**appear**."

Answers for Practice Exercises, Chapters 1-5

Chapter 1: Reading and the Literary Analysis Task

My First Day of School (pages 13-14)

1. The correct answer is **D.** "upset because there would be less freedom in school." This answer is supported in paragraph 1: "Since school had let out last June, I suddenly had a lot more freedom." Answer A. "happy because the summer was boring" is countered by Answer D. None of the other answers is supported in the text.

2. The correct answer is **A.** "Pat's mom would be right" since the text says in paragraph 3, "My mom told me that I would be hungry before lunch if I didn't eat a good breakfast." Yet, he didn't heed her advice. Both A and C are partially correct since C. "Pat's brother would be right" is neither supported in the text nor is a brother mentioned at all. Answer B. "Pat would be right" must be incorrect since A is the correct answer. Answer D. "Pat wanted to watch TV" is incorrect since he usually watched TV while he ate his breakfast in the summer.

3. The correct answers are **B.** "Pat's new clothes might be ruined," **C.** "Pat might get hurt and miss the first day of school," and **E.** "Pat might miss the bus." Answer A. "Pat had never ridden a skateboard before" is countered by the statement from paragraph 4: "I wonder what would happen if I took my skateboard and rode it one last time down my driveway." Answer D. "Pat might have to stay away from the class bully on the bus" has no support in the text. Since there are three correct responses, Answers F. "None of the above" and G. "All of the above" are not possible.

4. The correct answers are **B.** "eat the breakfast Pat's mother has made" (supported by paragraph 3: "My mom told me that I would be hungry before lunch if I didn't eat a good breakfast, but I just wasn't hungry") and **D.** "remember to put the completed diary assignment in the school bag" (supported by paragraph 9: "I didn't think it was fair that we were assigned a one-page journal entry in English class, but I guess I can finish by just writing about my day."). Answer A. "sleep late" is wrong since paragraph 10 begins: "Boy, I hope the weekend gets here quickly. I'm going to sleep late on Saturday." There is no text evidence to support Answers C. "send a message on social media to his girlfriend," E. "walk the dog," and F. "go to the local store and get the morning newspaper."

5. The correct answer is **D.** "have an effect." The other answers are all part of the advertising process, but they do not reflect the word influence.

A Letter to the Mayor (pages 15–16)

1. The correct answers are **B.** "Victoria Martinez wrote the letter to Mayor Patel and requested a new teen center" (paragraph 4: "Last month when we came to a town council meeting to ask for a teen center" and paragraph 5: "Please reconsider my request for a teen center in town") and **E.** "Mayor Patel believes that there is already a problem with 'too many kids hanging out in the Maple Grove Shopping Center parking lot behind the movie theater.'" (paragraph 4: "You told us that there were too many kids hanging out in the Maple Grove Shopping Center parking lot behind the movie theater"). Answer A. "Mr. Ross continues to volunteer his time so the building where the kids would skate and skateboard is 'kept up for us kids'" is incorrect since in paragraph 1 Victoria says, "Mr. Ross used to volunteer his time on the weekends to make sure the building was kept up for us kids, but he retired and moved to Florida." Answers C. "Victoria Martinez tells Mayor Patel that she has also written a letter to her friends to ask for their support" and F. "Mayor Patel once agreed to build a new teen center, but the request was not able to be realized because of a budget deficit" have no basis in the text. Answer D. "Mayor Patel is hearing for the first time this request from Victoria Martinez and her friends for a new teen center" is countered by Victoria's statement in paragraph 4 when she says "Last month when we came to a town council meeting to ask for a teen center, you became upset with us."

2. Statements **A.** "I *believe* that we should have a place in town where all the kids can get together," **D.** "A meeting place for us kids is a *great* idea for our town," **E.** "When we go to the movies, the security guards are *mean* to us," and **F.** "We don't *look for trouble*" are opinion statements with the key words in italics. Statements B. "The park near the river used to have a building where we could play games or just sit with our friends and talk" and C. "There was even some blacktop where we used to roller skate or ride our skateboards" contain facts that can be pointed to and measured. They are not opinions.

Guided Reading Book Report Guidelines (pages 18–19)

1. The correct answers are **C.** "If you read your book with a friend, then you may discuss the book together," **D.** "Have your parent/guardian sign your book permission slip," and **F.** "Once a week, you and your partner will form a guided reading small discussion group" since they reflect measurable facts. The incorrect answers that contain opinions (with the opinions in italics) are A. "Reading a good novel *can be exciting*," B. "Finding out about the different characters and learning how the author blends each action and scene together *are only some of*

the thrills you can have while reading," and E. "Sometimes when you are really interested in a book, you want to *read ahead.*"

2. Part A: The correct answer is **B.** "free choice fiction," which is noted in the title. Do not skip over the title when you read a piece, whether it is fictional or informational. The title holds key information that sets the direction of the entire piece.

   Part B: Answer **D.** "The story contains a fictional main plot, conflict, and a resolution" is the correct answer because the question asked for the "qualities that are not generic to the genre being assigned." Always read test questions thoroughly and accurately. When rushed, you could make a mistake by presuming that the information is one way while it is actually being portrayed another way.

3. Answer **D.** "the number of books you have read so far during the marking period" does not need to be included in the log. All the other information is required and supported in the text.

4. The correct answers are **D.** "You must keep a reading log" ("*Enter the page numbers into your reading log*") and **F.** "For each session, you must discuss with your group the conflicts in the book."

The Wonderful Wizard of Oz (pages 22–24)

1. The correct answers are **B.** "Uncle Henry always laughed" and **E.** "The tornado ripped through the house, destroying everything." Sentence 1 in paragraph 3 tells us "Uncle Henry never laughed." The last sentence of the passage has Aunt Em state, "Quick, Dorothy!" and then "Run for the cellar!" It does *not* mention what happened when the tornado hit. In paragraph 1, we learned that A. "Dorothy lived with her Uncle Henry and Aunt Em." In paragraph 5, C. "Uncle Henry and Dorothy heard 'a low wail of the wind' that came from the south." In the last paragraph, D. "Aunt Em warned Dorothy to go in the cellar to protect herself from the cyclone that was coming."

2. The correct answers are **C.** "Toto always made Dorothy laugh" and **D.** "Dorothy loved Toto dearly." These answers are found in paragraph 3. Answer A. "Dorothy adopted Toto from a shelter, and he never left her side." is incorrect. Although Dorothy did indeed love Toto "dearly," there is no evidence to prove that he was adopted from a shelter or that Toto never left Dorothy's side." The same reasoning can be used to find Answer B. "Uncle Henry and Aunt Em gave Toto to Dorothy, and now Dorothy and Toto are always together" to be incorrect. Answer E. "Dorothy loved Toto even more than she loved Uncle Henry and Aunt Em" is never addressed in the passage.

3. The events that are "out of sequence" are **B.** "Aunt Em warned Dorothy to 'Run for the cellar!'" and **E.** "Uncle Henry said to his wife, 'There's a cyclone coming,

Em.'" Answer B is the last action in the last paragraph, while E is mentioned in paragraph 6. Answers A. "Dorothy saw nothing but the great gray prairie on every side" found in paragraph 2, C. "Uncle Henry sat on the doorstep and looked anxiously at the sky" found in paragraph 4, and D. "Uncle Henry ran toward the sheds where the cows and horses were kept" found in paragraph 6 occur both in sequence and before Answers B and E. Please note that Uncle Henry warns his wife of the approaching tornado before he runs "toward the shed" in paragraph 6.

4. Part A: The correct answers are **A.** "austere" and **E.** "seldom amused." The first line in paragraph 3 states, "Uncle Henry never laughed." In the next sentence, the author says of Uncle Henry, "he looked stern and solemn, and rarely spoke." There is nothing in the passage to describe Uncle Henry's behavior as B. "out of control" since in paragraph 6 when "he ran toward the sheds where the cows and horses were kept," he did so with a purpose in mind. Answer C. "filled with laughter" is incorrect since the statement "It was Toto that made Dorothy laugh" is mentioned right after the first two lines in paragraph 3 to show a contrast of Dorothy's personality with that of Uncle Henry. Answer D. "sincere" has no basis in the paragraph and has nothing to do with Uncle Henry being "stern."

   Part B: The correct answers are **B.** "Uncle Henry never laughed" and **F.** "He did not know what joy was." These are the traits of someone who is "austere" and "seldom amused." All the other answers are story details that do not match the meanings of the correct answers.

5. Part A: The correct answer is **D.** "a storm with swirling winds." In paragraph 1, the "cyclone cellar" is described as the place "where the family could go in case one of those great whirlwinds arose." Answer A. "a weather map" is not a weather event. Answer B. "a heat wave" is a likely condition for a cyclone, but there may or may not be swirling winds at that time. Answer C. "a desert breeze" would not be common in Kansas, even though the ground is dry.

   Part B: The first correct answer is **A.** "...the sky, which was grayer than usual" since this grayish sky is one of the early signs of a cyclone, therefore necessitating the need for a "cyclone cellar." It is mentioned in paragraph 4. The second correct answer is **C.** "...a small hole dug in the ground..." because in paragraph 2, that is the definition the author uses to describe the "cyclone cellar." Answer B. "...she could see nothing but the great gray prairie on every side" refers to the dryness of the prairie and not the approaching cyclone. Answers D. "The sun had baked the plowed land into a gray mass..." and E. "...the sun blistered the paint and the rains washed it away..." refer to the harshness of the climate and its effects on the land and the house in the story.

6. Part A: The story setting is **D.** "a farm on the prairies in Kansas." Dorothy did originally come from A. "an orphanage," but she lived there before arriving on the farm. Answer B. "the mountains and prairies in Kansas" is only partly correct since there are no mountains mentioned. This is the type of tricky response that is typical of a standardized test. Remember, an answer is correct *only* when it is completely correct. Answer C. "the eastern coast of the United States" is wrong because Kansas is in the Midwest.

    Part B: The first correct answer is **D.** "Dorothy lived in the midst of the great Kansas prairies." The second correct answer is **E.** "…the lumber to build it had to be carried by wagon many miles" since the lumber was brought in to build Uncle Henry and Aunt Em's farm house. Answer A. "When Dorothy, who was an orphan …" refers not to the farm, but to Dorothy's background. Answers B. "…the broad sweep of flat country that reached to the edge of the sky in all directions" and C. "…she could see nothing but the great gray prairie on every side" refer to the land in general, not necessarily to a farm.

Tornadoes—The Facts (pages 29–31)

1. The first correct answer is **B.** "The winds of the most powerful tornadoes have been known to reach speeds of 200 miles an hour" is found in paragraph 1. The second correct answer is **C.** "Tornadoes are not common in Kansas" is found in paragraph 7. Answer A. "Tornadoes have the potential to be dangerous" is inaccurate since tornadoes are dangerous because they are severe storms. No mention of D. "The United States has the highest incidence of tornadoes" or E. "Some tornadoes have been known to travel along the ground for 50 miles" can be found in *The Wonderful Wizard of Oz.*

2. The first correct answer is **C.** "*The Wonderful Wizard of Oz* refers to the weather phenomenon as a cyclone while 'Tornadoes—The Facts' refers to the weather phenomenon as a tornado." The term "cyclone cellar" is used in paragraph 1 of *The Wonderful Wizard of Oz* while the term "tornado" is pluralized as part of the title of the informational piece, "Tornadoes—The Facts." The second correct answer is **D.** "*The Wonderful Wizard of Oz* portrays a set of fictional characters who are dealing with a cyclone and 'Tornadoes—The Facts' contains advice but no characters." The characters in *The Wonderful Wizard of Oz* are Uncle Henry, Aunt Em, Dorothy, and Toto. The piece 'Tornadoes—The Facts' is informational and therefore does not feature characters. Answer A. "*The Wonderful Wizard of Oz* is written to inform and 'Tornadoes—The Facts' is written to entertain" would be correct if the two titles switched places. Answer B. "*The Wonderful Wizard of Oz* gives advice for anyone who sees a cyclone approaching and 'Tornadoes—The Facts' does not" also does just the opposite. Answer E. "*The*

Wonderful Wizard of Oz is non-fictional, and 'Tornadoes—The Facts' is fictional" is also guilty of switching the facts.

3. The first correct answer is **A.** "Tornadoes make contact with a cloud and the surface of the earth over which they are traveling" is contained in paragraph 1. The second correct answer is **D.** "More tornadoes occur in the United States than they do in any other part of the world" appears in paragraph 6. The third correct answer is **F.** "Even though tornadoes generally move from the southwest to the northeast, they have been known to travel in every direction" is found in paragraph 5.

4. The first correct answer is **C.** "The pattern of a tornado is at times unpredictable and variable" is found in paragraph 4. The second correct answer is **D.** "The Enhanced Fujita Scale, used to measure the strength of tornadoes, assigns a rating of five to the most powerful tornadoes" found in paragraph 2.

5. The correct answer is **C.** "description" because in our explanation of description, we have said, "...your major task is to paint a clear word picture. You must give the details in such a way that those who have little experience in the area can still understand your point clearly." Answer A. "cause and effect" is incorrect since specific causes of tornadoes are not followed by the specific events resulting from each one. Answer B. "compare and contrast" is incorrect because we are neither comparing nor contrasting tornadoes with any other weather phenomena. Answer D. "problem and solution" is incorrect since general questions about tornadoes and strategies for dealing with them are covered. Solutions are one focus, not the main focus of "Tornadoes—The Facts."

Sample Response 1/Essay for Plot, Character, and Setting (page 33)

Severe weather can be a strong attention getter itself, but L. Frank Baum in *The Wonderful Wizard of Oz* uses the title of his first chapter "The Cyclone" not only to catch the reader's attention, but also to prepare the reader for the difficulties the characters must face.

In the second sentence, Baum establishes a depressing mood by mentioning that Dorothy lives with her Uncle Henry and Aunt Em not in a comfortable house, but rather in a "small" one. Although the term "home" would connote more of a comfortable feeling, Baum uses the term "house" to distance the characters from that feeling. The fact that the lumber "had to be carried by wagon many miles" reinforces the idea of hardship. The "one room" containing "four walls, a floor and a roof," a "rusty looking cookstove," and no evidence of anything elegant or comforting serves to reinforce a somber tone to the piece. The house lacked a garret and a cellar, but it did have "a small hole dug in the ground called a cyclone cellar, where the family could go" for protection during cyclone. In the second paragraph, Baum adds that the prairie was "gray," the land was "baked," and "Even the grass was not green." The paint on the house was "blistered" and "washed away." Unfortunately, so was the red from Aunt Em's cheeks and lips."

This ominous and depressing setting establishes Baum's intention to introduce the devastation of the approaching cyclone (which is actually "a hurricane and not a tornado" as "Tornadoes—The Facts" points out). Baum understands a cyclone's power. According to "Tornadoes—The Facts," these phenomena "have been known to reach speeds of 200 miles an hour" and can even exceed 250 miles per hour. Imagine being an orphan who moves to a simple farm house to be raised by an uncle and aunt with your only laughter coming from your pet dog Toto. When Dorothy laughed, however, Aunt Em "would scream and press her hand upon her (own) heart." As the hurricane approached, Aunt Em reacted in a similar fashion. "Quick, Dorothy!" she screamed. "Run for the cellar!"

The depressing atmosphere is further reinforced by Baum in the fourth and fifth paragraphs. In paragraph 4, Uncle Henry "sat upon the doorstep and looked anxiously at the sky, which was even grayer than usual." Dorothy wasn't laughing a child-like laugh nor was she "playing" with Toto. Rather, she was standing "in the door with Toto in her arms (while) she looked at the sky too," awaiting the storm. Baum mentioned how "the long grass bowed in waves before the coming storm" and how "There now came a sharp whistling in the air from the south" along with the "ripples in the grass." These facts build suspense before the approaching cyclone would arrive.

Aunt Em recognized that as "Tornadoes . . ." points out, a cyclone has the "potential to wreak havoc and cause devastation to homes, farms, buildings, and any edifice and area in their paths." Unwittingly, she was also heeding their advice that when a cyclone approaches, "it is wise to take shelter" and to "Find a safe, solid shelter and go there if you have time." Remember, "Tornadoes . . ." point out that Kansas and Florida have the third most tornadoes ("cyclones") with "an average of 55 a year" so this type of devastation is common to Uncle Henry and Aunt Em. Sadly, it may become common to Dorothy and Toto as well.

Dorothy dealt with a lack of laughter, drab surroundings, and two overworked and dour surrogate parents, along with an approaching cyclone. In eight short paragraphs, Baum artistically blends the playfulness of youth, the difficulty of being raised by surrogate parents, the combination of the drab existence and harsh realities of life on Uncle Henry's farm, and the inevitable havoc to be caused by an approaching cyclone to create a somber portrait of life on Uncle Henry's farm.

This essay probably earns a "4" because it:

- Begins with a compositional risk: "Severe weather can be a strong attention getter itself..."
- Addresses each question directly and thoroughly.
- Uses text-based references to both texts: "The 'one room' containing 'four walls, a floor and a roof', a 'rusty looking cookstove' in *The Wonderful Wizard of Oz* and cyclones 'have been known to reach speeds of 200 miles an hour' in 'Tornadoes—The Facts.'"
- Has great length and insight (Ex. "Although the term 'home' would connote more of a comfortable feeling, Baum uses the term 'house' to distance the characters from that feeling.")
- Uses good essay construction with varied sentence structure and length.
- Adds examples of "how difficult it must be to live" on the farm.
- Mentions the farm's physical traits and Uncle Henry, Aunt Em, and Dorothy's personalities.
- Adds insight by connecting the dullness of both the setting and the characters.
- Uses appropriate grammar, spelling, and vocabulary and academic vocabulary ("connote," "ominous," and "phenomena," for example).
- Demonstrates a strong focus and sense of unity and coherence.

Sample Response 2/Essay for Plot, Character, and Setting

L. Frank Baum in *The Wonderful Wizard of Oz* called his first Chapter The Cyclone, and it got my attention. What about you?

Uncle Henry and Aunt Em adopt Dorothy since she was an orphan. The author Baum writes some depressing things. Uncle Henry and Aunt Em live in a "small" house built by lumber that was "carried by wagon many miles." There wasn't much that was happy in this piece. The house was "one room," and they used a "rusty looking cookstove" to make their meals. Just in case a cyclone swept down on them, the family would run to the "cyclone cellar" to be safe from the storm. There were prairies, but they weren't green like they are in that Zane Grey book I read last week in the library. In *The Wonderful Wizard of Oz*, their prairie was "gray" and the land was "baked."

In the fourth paragraph, we find out that a big cyclone is headed toward the farm. We know this because the author says "the long grass bowed in waves before the coming storm" and there was "a sharp whistling in the air from the south." Even the grass had "ripples." Uncle Henry, Aunt Em, Dorothy, and Toto would be in big trouble if the storm came and they were standing around and waiting for it.

In "Tornadoes—The Facts," they have all this really cool stuff about tornadoes. They say that tornadoes can usually go about 200 miles an hour. Some can even go faster than 250 miles an hour. If Dorothy and her family knew that, then maybe they would have really been scared. They might have panicked and not gone into the "cyclone cellar" like the article says to do. They probably know what to do, however, since they live in Kansas. They have a lot of cyclones in Kansas. Well, they're really tornadoes. Baum called them cyclones by mistake. Anyway, they said in "Tornadoes—The Facts" that a cyclone can "wreak havoc and cause devastation to homes, farms" and lots of other stuff. They tell you to "take shelter . . . if you have time."

So, Dorothy had to put up with no laughs except from Toto, a dull place to live, two dull people to raise her, and a big cyclone coming her way. Wow, that L. Frank Baum sure knows how to use some details to make his audience feel sorry for Dorothy. As they said in "Tornadoes—The Facts," "take shelter . . . if you have time."

This essay probably earns a "2" because it:

- Unsuccessfully attempts to begin with a compositional risk: "L. Frank Baum in *The Wonderful Wizard of Oz* called his first Chapter The Cyclone, and it got my attention. What about you?"

- Addresses each question, but the way it does so is neither direct nor thorough.

- Uses text-based references to both texts: "The "one room" containing "four walls, a floor and a roof," a "rusty looking cookstove" in *The Wonderful Wizard of Oz* and cyclones ""wreak havoc and cause devastation to homes, farms," but the references are brief.

- Has some length, but the insight has very little academic feel to it (Ex. "So, Dorothy had to put up with no laughs except from Toto, a dull place to live, two dull people to raise her, and a big cyclone coming her way.")

- Uses simple essay construction with little variation of sentence structure and length.

- Tries to explain the difficulty of living on the farm.

- Fails to connect the farm's physical traits with Uncle Henry, Aunt Em, and Dorothy's personalities.

- Attempts to make a literary allusion ("There were prairies, but they weren't green like they are in that Zane Grey book I read last week in the library.")

- Uses simple grammar and accurate spelling.

- Uses vocabulary that lacks an academic flavor ("happy," "big," "go," and "says to do," for example).

- Demonstrates an inconsistent focus and an attempt at unity and coherence.

"The Road Not Taken" (pages 38–40)

1. The correct answer is **A.** "first person" because the author uses "I" often. Answers B. "second person" and C. "third person" are not used when "I" is used. Answer D. "both A and C" is incorrect because the poem is only written in one voice.

2. Part A: The correct answer is **D.** "The traveler was sad that he couldn't travel both roads." Sentence 2 in stanza 1 (line 2) says that the traveler was "sorry I (he) could not travel both." Answers A. "The traveler was lost" and B. "The traveler was hungry" aren't mentioned in the poem. Answer C. "The traveler was happy that he could travel both roads" is the opposite of the correct answer D.

Part B: The correct answer is **B.** "And sorry I could not travel both" (line 2). The other answers do not reflect the correct answer to Part A.

3. The correct answer is **A.** "The traveler hoped but doubted he would take the other road some day." Answer B. "The traveler was sure he would take the other road some day" is disproved by Answer A. Answers C. "The traveler was paralyzed with fear," D. "The traveler was encouraged by his friend to take the other road," and E. "The traveler was addled" do not appear in the poem.

4. Part A: The details that do not appear in the poem are **A.** "Two roads ran parallel in the woods" (since they actually "diverged"), **B.** "The narrator took the more traveled road," **C.** "The narrator couldn't decide which road to travel and thus took neither," **E.** "The narrator walked down each road before he made a decision about which one to travel," **F.** "Each road was used about the same amount," and **I.** "The narrator consulted with a good friend before deciding which road to take." Answer D. "The narrator took the road that had not been traveled as much as the other road" appears in line 19: "I took the one less traveled by." Answer G. "The narrator believes that the course he chose to take has made a significant difference in his own life" is supported by lines 19–20: "I took the one less traveled by / And that has made all the difference." Answer H. "The narrator isn't sure if he'll ever return to the road he has not taken" is supported by line 20: "I doubted if I should ever come back."

   Part B: The order of appearance in the poem is **H.** "The narrator isn't sure if he'll ever return to the road he had not taken" (line 15), **D.** "The narrator took the road that had not been traveled as much as the other road" (line 19), and **G.** "The narrator believes that the course he chose to take has made a significant difference in his own life" (line 20).

5. The correct answer is **C.** "The choice of the road taken changes the traveler's life" (line 20). The remaining answers have no basis in the text.

6. The correct answer is **D.** "abaab." In the first stanza, for example, the last words are "wood," "both," "stood," "could," and "undergrowth." Hence, lines 1, 3, and 4 (represented by A) rhyme as do lines 2 and 5 (represented by B).

How Do We Handle a Challenge? (pages 42–43)

1. The correct answer is **D.** "Facing these challenges is something we must ultimately do ourselves." Answers A. "Our lives are often filled with many challenges," B. "There are problems that we need to solve, difficult questions that we need to answer, and obstacles that we have to overcome," and C. "We can either face those challenges or give in to them" are statements that lead up to the theme.

2. Statements **A.** "Our lives are often filled with many challenges," **B.** "Both options, however, can lead us in different directions in our lives," **E.** "If we haven't worked hard so far, then we have placed ourselves in an unenviable position," and **G.** "The answer is not a simple one." These answers are all contingent upon perception, rather than fact. Statement C. "This assignment will count for one-third of our grade" is a basic statement of fact. Statement D. "...the time will come to pass when our assignment will be due" is supported by the previous statement made in paragraph 2: "proceed to complete the task both well and on time." Statement F. "He says that he can have someone get him a completed assignment" is a typically misleading type of statement that requires careful thought to be answered correctly. While the friend's statement that "he can have someone get him a completed assignment" is an opinion statement, it is embedded in the larger statement that reports that the friend "says" this. That the friend made this statement is a fact, and that is the basis for this answer.

3. Part A: The correct answer is **D.** "problem and solution" since the author is posing a problem and encouraging us to solve the problem "ourselves." Answer A. "cause and effect" is incorrect because the major focus is solving a problem, not looking at the causes of it. For Answer B. "compare and contrast" to be true, the main focus again would need to be on these techniques (comparing and contrasting different alternatives). Answer C. "description" would be correct only if the problem itself were being described in detail.
   Part B: Answer **B.** "challenges" is a word common in problem and solution essays. Answers A. "often," C. "imagine," and D. "assignment" may appear in any of the text patterns.

4. The correct answer is **D.** "What should we do?" captures the main idea of the narrator struggling with a decision he needs to make for himself. Answer A. "Take, for example, an important assignment that we have been given" would be correct only if the narrator had been given the task of making this decision. Answer B. "If we haven't worked hard so far, then we have placed ourselves in an unenviable position" presumes that someone has placed the narrator in a position of having to make his decision. Answer C. "Do we give in, knowing that there's a chance that we could get caught cheating?" is incorrect because there is no reference to cheating in the poem.

5. The word "unenviable" means **A.** "difficult." Answer B. "inane" means "senseless," Answer C. "complicated" means "complex," and Answer D. "advantageous" means "providing a favorable position."

Sample Response/Paired Passage/Essay for Theme, Cause and Effect, Point of View, Details, Sequence, and Fact vs. Opinion (page 44)

Both Robert Frost and Philip Postrun speak of making a decision. Frost takes a more personalized approach while Postrun gives advice directly. Frost doesn't seem to speak directly to everyone, which is something that Postrun does. While Postrun gives everyone a challenge by saying that everyone of us must each decide ourselfes what to do, Frost tells the story from his own eyes. Frost wants the reader to take his advice just because it's their. But Postrun says that we all have to "decide ourselves" what to do.

This essay is weak because:

- There is little to grab the reader's attention in the opening.
- The reader should restate the question somewhere in the opening, rather than saying the authors "speak of making a decision" rather than restating the phrase "deal(ing) with the concept of "facing a challenge."
- There are no direct citations from the text to expand the points being made.
- Frost's personalized approach is actually personalized to him, not the audience. That needs to be explained the way it is with Postrun giving "advice directly."
- The lack of academic vocabulary helps to keep this score low. For example, "gives" could be "presents, "what to do" could be "what action to take," "his own eyes" could be "his own point of view" or "his own perspective,"and "But" should be replaced with "However," "Nonetheless," or "In contrast."
- The spelling and grammar mistakes do not help to raise the score. "...everyone of us" needs to be "every one of us," "ourselfes" should be "ourselves," and "their" should be "there."

An essay that would receive a higher score:

- catches the reader's attention with a brief compositional risk: "Facing a challenge can be a challenge in itself, and both Robert Frost and Philip Postrun seem to realize this.:
- The question is directly stated when the passage states that the authors are dealing with "the concept of facing a challenge."
- Citations are made directly from the text: "While Frost uses the vivid imagery of 'Two roads (that) diverged in a yellow wood'" and "Postrun states very matter-of-factly that 'We can either face those challenges or give in to them'" for example.

- The main idea in Frost's piece is "And sorry I could not travel both (line 2)," as he speaks of a personal decision. In contrast, Postrun feels that when handling a challenge, "we must each decide ourselves (line 26)."
- There is good length to the essay. Two well-developed paragraphs is a reasonably good length for this type of piece.
- Academic vocabulary is evident throughout as the writer uses phrases including "vivid imagery," "significant," "personalized," and "scenario."
- Transitions including "While" and "Furthermore" are used.
- There are no grammar or spelling mistakes.

The Queen Bee (pages 50–51)

1. The correct answer is **A.** "the youngest (the dwarf)." Answers B. "second oldest" and C. "oldest" are incorrect because they wanted to tear down the anthill, kill the ducks to "roast them," and "kill the bees so they could get their honey." Answer D. "all of the above" cannot be correct since it would have to include Answers B and C.

2. Part A: The correct answer is **A.** "unimportant." Answer B. "important" is an antonym while the other definitions are simply incorrect. Please note that Answer D. "precocious" means advanced beyond one's years and is a solid academic vocabulary word.
   Part B: The correct answers are **C.** "Let the pretty insects enjoy themselves; I cannot let you burn them" and **F.** "the dwarf married the youngest and the best of the princesses." Remember, the question has asked you to find the phrases/ sentences (that) refer to the opposite of the king's younger son's insignificance, not the same. Answer B. "when he had found them they only laughed at him" indicates the son's insignificance while the other answers do not support the question.

3. The correct answer is **B.** "find all the missing pearls or be turned into marble." This is supported by a description in paragraphs 6–7: "In the wood, under the moss, lie the thousand pearls belonging to the king's daughter; they must all be found: and if one be missing by set of sun, he who seeks them will be turned into marble." The other responses have no basis in the text. Please note that Answer A. "find the first hundred pearls or be turned into marble" sounds correct since the oldest brother *did not* find even 100 pearls. If you had read the fable too quickly, you might have made this mistake. *(Let this example serve as a reminder of the importance of previewing the text and the answers before reading the text itself.)* Answers C. "find the dwarf or be turned into stone" and D. "find the princess or be turned into stone" are not accurate. Only those who were unable to complete the challenges were turned into stone.

4. The correct answer is **D.** "accepted the challenge and failed, also getting turned into marble." Answers A. "ran away" and B. "locked the old man in a prison and escaped with his brothers" do not happen in the story. Answer C. "accepted the challenge and succeeded" is true only for the little dwarf.

5. The correct answer is **D.** "they would help him later in the story." Answers A. "they would attack him because he's a dwarf," B. "they would pay him money," and C. "they would run away because they're afraid of dwarfs" have no basis in the story.

"Friends, Romans, Countrymen..." (pages 52-53)

1. Part A: The correct answer is **D.** "having a strong desire or determination to succeed." While the traits of all the other suggested definitions may in small part be related to ambitious, only Answer D is the exact definition.
    Part B: Answer **A.** "there was a conflict between Caesar and Brutus caused by Brutus's ambition" is correct since it states the main conflict of the speech. Answers B. "there was a conflict between Caesar and Brutus caused by Antony's ambition" and C. "there was a conflict between Caesar and Brutus caused by Caesar's ambition" have mixed up the roles in the conflict. Answer D. "the implied conflict is between Caesar and Antony" is illogical since Antony is speaking to defend the honor of Caesar.

2. Part A: The correct answer is **C.** "Marc Antony disliked Caesar." The two key phrases in the question are "the opening two lines" and "one could infer." At the beginning of the speech, it was Marc Antony's intent to seem as if he was coming to "bury Caesar, not to praise him." Marc Antony's true intent came later in the speech, not in the opening. This is the reason Answer A. "Marc Antony wished to portray Caesar as a hero" is incorrect. Answers B. "Marc Antony was not liked by the citizens of Rome," and D. "Marc Antony was related to Caesar," have no basis in the opening two lines.
    Part B: The correct answer is **D.** "Caesar was honorable, and Brutus was not." The quote "Ambition should be made of sterner stuff" is saying that Caesar wasn't ambitious at all. Answer B. "Brutus was honorable, and Caesar was not" is the opposite of the truth and therefore incorrect. Answers A. "Caesar was overly emotional, and stress had caused his death" and C. "Caesar was a poor man when he died" have no basis.

3. Part A: The correct answer is **A.** "more serious." Answers B. "more intelligent," C. "more imaginative," and D. "more creative" are not synonyms.
    Part B: The correct answer is **B.** "Marc Antony says that Brutus's accusation that Caesar was 'ambitious' is false." When Marc Antony says, "Ambition should be made of sterner stuff," he is using irony to show that Caesar would have needed to be much more serious about being ambitious if he were indeed ambitious at all.

Sample Response 1/Essay for Conflict and Resolution and Making Predictions (page 54)

Predictability in a story is not always an easy thing—unless one begins to act as a detective would and searches for clues. In the fable "The Queen Bee" by the Brothers Grimm and Marc Antony's speech in Shakespeare's *Julius Caesar*, the authors blend a bit of irony to achieve a purpose.

"The Queen Bee" takes the reader through a series of events in which the king's two older sons are out to "seek their fortunes" in whatever way suits them. They are willing to do that which is easy for them, even though their actions will impact negatively. Furthermore, they are not apologetic in the least. In Marc Antony's speech, however, Antony is using a bit of irony when he states, "I come to bury Caesar, not to praise him." His intention is take suspicion away from him so he can cleverly change the notion of Caesar from an enemy to a hero.

The youngest son, known as the dwarf, serves as the foil to his two older brothers in "The Queen Bee. He tells his brothers to let the ants and ducks "enjoy themselves" rather than harm them. When the older brothers later fail in their quest to find "the thousand pearls belonging to the king's daughter," the dwarf is successful because he is helped by those who received mercy through his kindness. The story instructs the reader to understand that good deeds do not go unrewarded.

Antony in *Julius Caesar* also achieves success, but his success was unforeseen by the audience he's addressing and not by Brutus's supporters. Why, he begins by addressing the audience not as enemies but as "Friends, Romans, (and countrymen)." He then proceeds cleverly to take statements Brutus had made against Caesar and ironically minimize their impact. Brutus is described as "noble" while Antony keeps repeating the phrase that Caesar is "ambitious" and then disproving the accusation. He notes that Caesar "brought many captives home to Rome," wept with the poor, and even refused "a kingly crown" three times.

Moreover, Antony ends by contrasting his own statement of "I speak not to disprove what Brutus spoke" with "You all did love him once, not without cause" so "What cause withholds you then, to mourn for him?"

The dwarf in "The Queen Bee" gained his reward as a result of his good deeds. Antony, however, faced his enemies squarely and through powerful rhetoric and irony, he used comparison and contrast to change the image of Brutus from an "honourable man" to one who was not.

In this essay

- The author catches the reader's attention with a brief compositional risk: It addresses both authors' use of making predictions and irony.

- The student wisely looks at the way the authors "Compare and contrast the challenge that each of these two individuals faced" and states this in the opening paragraph.

- The characters in "The Queen Bee" take action while Marc Antony uses irony in his speech.

- Citations are made directly from the text. For example, the two older brothers in "The Queen Bee" "are out to 'seek their fortunes' in whatever way suits them" while Marc Antony states, ""I come to bury Caesar, not to praise him." And "While Frost uses the vivid imagery of 'Two roads (that) diverged in a yellow wood'" and "Postrun states very matter-of-factly that 'We can either face those challenges or give in to them'" for example.

- There is good length to the essay. One brief and three well-developed paragraphs is an extraordinarily good length for this type of piece. Remember, length is rewarded on these standardized tests.

- Academic vocabulary is evident throughout as the writer uses phrases including "predictability," "suspicion," and "unforeseen."

- Transitions including "unless," "Furthermore," and "Moreover" are used.

- There are no grammar or spelling mistakes.

Sample Response 2/Essay for Conflict and Resolution and Making Predictions

In the story "The Queen Bee," these two brothers who are the king's son want to be on easy street so they go out to find some serious money. They have this dwarf character with them, and he's actually their younger brother. Because they wanted to pull down an ant hill as a prank and cook the ducks for food, the authors show that these guys are cruel. They show the dwarf as being much kinder, however, since he tells his brothers not to do this harmful stuff. They are complete opposites.

Marc Antony in *Julius Caesar* is an opposite too, but his opposite is Brutus. Antony tries to show up Brutus by telling all the "Friends, Romans, countrymen" that Caesar wasn't such a bad guy, but Brutus said he was ambitious and Brutus would know. You see, Antony is hinting that Brutus wasn't a good guy for killing Caesar. Caesar did good stuff like bringing back soldiers and saying three times that he didn't want to be king. Unfortunately, he got killed because Brutus said he was "ambitious." That's kind of ironic, isn't it?

This essay is weak because:

- it has no compositional risk and no restatement of the question.
- There is little if any comparison or contrast in the essay.
- The language is much too casual: "easy street," "serious money," and "stuff," for example.
- The brevity of the piece contributes to the low score attained. There need to be more thought and more examples presented.
- The Brothers Grimm's work should be referred to as a fable, not a "story."
- There are no spelling and grammar mistakes, but the use of phrases like "good stuff" are not appropriate in an academic exercise.
- The essay writer actually uses text references and the literary term "irony," but these are not properly showcased in a mindful essay.
- There are transitional phrases ("Because" and "Unfortunately," for example) used, but they need to be used in a stronger essay context.

"The Children's Hour" (pages 60–61)

1. The correct answer is **D.** "abcb." The words "lower" and "Hour" are known as near rhymes. The other answers are incorrect.
2. The correct answers are **D.** "gloomy" and **E.** "insincere." There are no signs of doom or despair, nor is there anything that could be deemed to be "insincere."
3. The correct answer is **B.** "playful" as noted in the children's "merry eyes" as they look to take Longfellow "by surprise." Answers A. "nasty, C. "angry," and D. "sad" are not typical emotions of children with "merry eyes."
4. Part A: The correct answers are **A.** "a small tower" and **F.** "a gunner's enclosure." None of the other answers fit the definition of a "turret." Answer C. "a tank missile" could be misleading if one does not read the answers carefully and hastily concludes that all of the answers with a military connection are correct.

Part B: The correct answers are **A.** "climb," **D.** "escape," **E.** "surround," and **F.** "everywhere" since they all deal with the children's playful invasion of the father's chair, which is portrayed as a turret. Answer B. "arms" is not correct since the reference in the poem is to the arms of a chair, not the arms carried by military personnel. Answer C. "back" refers to part of the chair.

5. The correct answer is **D.** "challenging." Answer A. "angry" belies the poem's playful mood. Answer B. "pompous" is wrong since the poet is not arrogant. Answer C. "sad" is the opposite of the playful tone of this poem.

6. The correct answer is **C.** "serious" since Longfellow's words are similar to those in a news report. There's no evidence to support Answers A. "worried," B. "sad," and D. "playful."

"We Shall Fight on the Beaches" (pages 64–65)

1. Part A: The correct answers are **D.** "England would not be an easy target for any invaders" and **F.** "England was prepared to defend itself aggressively as it had done in the past" since they both reflect the phrase "bitter weeds." Answer A. "England could not defend itself" is wrong because it is the opposite of the correct answer. Answers B. "England was in the midst of a drought" and C. "England was a country known for its farms" are not mentioned in the speech. Answer E. "England was prepared to defend itself, but would prefer a peaceful solution" is only partially correct since the option of a peaceful solution runs counter to the phrase "bitter weeds."
    Part B: The correct answer is **C.** "determined" since he used the phrase "bitter weeds" to show that England has been a strong force in the past and will continue to be one in the future, as well. Answer A. "timid" is wrong because it runs counter to being "determined." Answer B. "inconsistent" does the same. Answer D. "light-hearted" does not reflect a determined tone.

2. The correct answer is **A.** "rigor." Answer C. "mildness" is wrong because it has the opposite meaning. Answers B. "exhaustion" and D. "creativity" are wrong because they are not synonyms.

3. Part A: The correct answers are **C.** "espionage" and **F.** "sabotage" since they both deal with activities that look to undermine England. Answers A. "patriotism" and B. "loyalty" are traits that are not typical of fifth column actions. Answer D. "oratory" is a skill practiced by people with various beliefs, and Answer E. "faith-based" is a trait that is also held by many.
    Part B: The correct answer is **D.** "Fifth columnists" since they would look to overthrow England. Answer A. "Napolean's army" is wrong since they were involved in a different war. Answers B. "the British Expeditionary Force" and C. "British subjects (citizens)" are wrong since they all are on the side of the British.

4. Part A: The correct answers are **A.** "reassuring" and **E.** "hopeful." The British are soothed by the reference to the thwarting of Napolean's invasion that demonstrated "There are bitter weeds in England." Answers B. "insensitive," C. "vengeful," and D. "aggressive" all do not reflect the attempt by Churchill to reassure his nation that success was indeed in their future.

   Part B: The correct answers are **C.** "determined" and **F.** "uplifting." Answers A. "timid," B. "inconsistent," D. "light-hearted," and E. "antagonistic" are wrong because they reflect the wrong emotions.

5. The correct answer is **D.** "repetition for effect" since the phrase "We shall fight" is repeated by Churchill. Answers A. "simile," B. "metaphor," and C. "personification" are not used here by Churchill.

Sample Response 1/Essay for Mood and Tone (page 66)

For Winston Churchill, the British Prime Minister during WWII, a battle meant a serious encounter between his Allied forces and the Axis forces. For Henry Wadsworth Longfellow, however, he compares a battle to a playful game in which he participates with his young children.

Churchill speaks of Hitler's plan "for invading the British Isles" and Napoleon's unsuccessful invasion. Churchill states, "There are bitter weeds in England," a metaphor of the British forces' toughness. Longfellow, on the other hand, speaks of "a pause in the day's occupations (routines)" which is referred to "as the Children's Hour." Next, Longfellow describes the children's mischievous invasion by using the onomatopoeia of the "patter of little feet". In addition, the suspense created by "The sound of a door that is opened," and the contrast of this so-called invasion by children with "voices soft and sweet" emphasizes a light-hearted mood. This pleasant, yet mischievous invasion is furthered by the cute, simple rhyme of "feet" and "sweet."

The mood of Churchill's speech becomes gloomy and quite serious as he speaks of "increasing stringency," "enemy aliens and suspicious characters," and "British subjects who may become a danger or a nuisance". The alliteration in the phrases "fierce fighting" and "not the slightest sympathy" further emphasize the goal of eliminating "this malignancy in our midst," another example of alliteration. In contrast, Longfellow uses alliteration in the phrase "plotting and planning" to highlight the playfulness of the children. As the children unleash "A sudden rush from the stairway, A sudden raid from the hall!" one can almost anticipate the onrush of awaiting laughter.

Churchill contrasts the next to the last paragraph with his final one. He sees no "absolute guarantee against invasion," but states that "we shall prove ourselves once again able to defend our Island home, to ride out the storm of war, and to outlive the menace of tyranny, if necessary for years, if necessary alone." The grouping of the three actions "defend," "ride," and "outlive" add both emphasis and confidence. He ends his speech by repeating the phrase "we shall" eleven times with seven of those being "we shall fight," thus changing the serious, somber mood to one of energized hope and determination. Longfellow's battle is more playful as the children "climb up into (his) turret" and "seem to be everywhere," almost devouring him "with (playful) kisses." The literary allusion to "the Bishop of Bingen/ In his Mouse-Tower on the Rhine!" refers to a Bishop who was kept in a tower and eaten by the mice, a tale told likely to frighten little children. These threats, nonetheless, are unlike Churchill's since Longfellow vows to keep the children "fast in (his) fortress" and "in the round tower of (his) heart." The mood here is playful and mischievous, which is different than Churchill's somber mood that changes to hope.

In this essay

- The author catches the reader's attention by contrasting Winston Churchill's serious battle with Henry Wadsworth Longfellow's playful battle..
- The student methodically alternates the serious tone of Churchill with the playful one of Longfellow.
- The literary analysis reflects higher-order thinking and insight.
- The use of literary devices by both authors is mindfully included: Churchill's use of metaphor and repetition for effect and Longfellow's use of onomatopoeia and alliteration, for example.
- Citations are made directly from the text. For example, Churchill notes "There are bitter weeds in England" while Longfellow speaks of impish youngsters with "voices soft and sweet."
- There is excellent length to the essay.
- Academic vocabulary is evident throughout as the writer uses phrases including "participates," "emphasizes," and "malignancy."
- Transitions including "on the other hand," "In addition," and "In contrast" are used.
- There are grammar and spelling mistakes.

Sample Response 2/Essay for Mood and Tone

Winston Churchill gives this speech to fire up his people against Hilter's Nazi invasion while Longfellow, a poet, talks about these kids who are goofing around to try to invade his privacy.

Churchill talked about Hitler "invading the British Isles." He also talked about Napoleon, who wasn't successful with his invasion. I guess Churchill is trying to fire up his people. But Longfellow isn't. You see, he has these silly kids who are driving him crazy. He hears the kids' "patter of little feat," and "The sound of a door" opening. So you know that something's going down real soon! I guess the poet rhymes "feet" and "sweet" so this stuff sounds cute or something.

Churchill gets all serious when he talks "enemy aliens and suspicious characters." He uses some alliteration when he say "fierce fighting." But Longfellow tries alliteration when he says "plotting and planning" to attack him to play fight.

At the end of the speech, Churchill starts firing up everybody. He tells them "we shall prove ourselves once again able to defend our Island home, to ride out the storm of war, and to outlive the menace of tyranny, if necessary for years, if necessary alone." But Longfellow's invading kids "seem to be everywhere." Yeah, but he'll handle them. He'll threaten to put them "down into the dungeon." That should frighten them off.

In this essay

- There is a weak opening, and the language is a bit unfocused. Phrases such as "fire up his people" and "kids who are goofing around" can be phrased a little bit better.
- The comparison and contrast in the essay is weakened by the use of a conversational tone that sometimes includes slang.
- There are no spelling and grammar mistakes.
- The essay writer actually uses text references but no literary terms.
- There are basic transitional phrases ("also," "So," and "But," for example) used.

"Trees" (pages 71–72)

1. The correct answer is **A.** "a tree." Answer B. "grass" is neither mentioned nor hinted at. Answer C. "a mouth" is part of the personified tree, and it's mentioned in line 3 and not line 2. Answer D. "robins" is wrong because they lived in the tree. Also, they're mentioned in line 8, not line 2.

2. The correct answer is **C.** "getting nourishment." Answers A. "speaking," B. "crying," and D. "yawning" are incorrect because they're never mentioned.

3. Part A: The correct answers are **B.** "metaphor," **C.** "personification," and **D.** "alliteration" because the tree is *compared* to a person with arms (metaphor, and personification). Also, the "l" sound is repeated in the words "lifts" and "leafy." Answer A. "simile" is incorrect because the comparison does not use "like" or "as." Answer E. "rhyme scheme" is incorrect because this refers to the pattern of rhyming at the end of each poetic line.
Part B: The correct answer is **D.** "imaginary" because the reader is using literary devices to *imagine* the tree as a real person.

4. The correct answer is **B.** "a living form of shelter." Answer A. "a hungry predator" is wrong since the tree is doing the opposite of preying by giving shelter. While some high-fashion models may wear creative hats, the tree is in no way serving in that capacity so Answer C. "a fashion model" is wrong. Answer D. "the poet" is wrong since he is not the tree.

5. The correct answers are **C.** "Trees are a beautiful part of nature" and **G.** "Trees can figuratively pray." This sentiment of Answer C is reflected in the first two lines of the poem: "I think that I shall never see / A poem lovely as a tree." Answer G is reflected in lines 5 and 6: "A tree that looks at God all day, And lifts her leafy arms to pray" since Kilmer is envisioning the tree's upward branches as a sign of prayer. Answer A. "Trees exhaust all the nutrients from the earth" is incorrect since lines 3 and 4 in the poem, "A tree whose hungry mouth is prest (pressed) / Against the earth's sweet flowing breast" do not address the concept of "exhaust(ing) the nutrients." Answer B. "Trees are nice until they have to be cut down" is never addressed. Answer D. "Trees are a beautiful part of nature, but they can be dangerous for birds" runs counter to the idea that the tree wears "A nest of robins in her hair." Answer E. "Trees like the snow, but they don't enjoy the rain because it washes away the soil" is wrong since the trees live "intimately…with rain." Answer F. "Trees think that Joyce Kilmer is foolish" has no evidence in the poem to support it.

Forest Trees of Wisconsin: How to Know Them (pages 76–77)

1. Part A: The correct answers are **D.** "Forests are communities, and trees are not" and **F.** "Trees and forests have different life spans." These answers are contained in the Introduction: "Trees, like all living things, grow and mature and

die while the forest, which is a community of trees, may live indefinitely because the trees reproduce before they die." Answers A. "Trees and forests are both communities," B. "Neither trees nor forests are communities," C. "Trees are communities, and forests are not," and E. "Trees and forests have the same life span" are not supported by the text.

Part B: The correct answer is **D.** "compare and contrast" since the Introduction speaks of the differences between trees and the forest itself.

2. The statements that are true about vegetative reproduction are **B.** "Cuttings are used in vegetative reproduction" and **F.** "Most trees in the forest grow from seeds, not vegetative reproduction" are found in the second (Vegetative Reproduction) and the third (Reproduction by Seed) sections of the text. Statements A. "Seeds or nuts from the trees are used in vegetative reproduction," C. "All conifers reproduce vegetatively by sprouting," D. "Regardless of age, most conifers reproduce vegetatively by sprouting," and E. "Baldwin apple trees can grow from seeds and not from grafting" are statements that are not supported by the text: they state the opposite of the true facts.

3. The correct answers are **A.** "The acorn is considered to be a botanical fruit" and **D.** "The Lombardy poplar bears no staminate flowers since it was developed as a mutation." Answers B. "The corn plant reproduces vegetatively, not by seed" and C. "For trees like the ashes and the poplars, 'the female trees will not bear seed' unless there are pistillate trees 'in the vicinity'" are wrong because the opposite is true. Answer E. "The Lombardy poplar can reproduce both vegetatively and through the formation of seed" is wrong because it "is always reproduced vegetatively."

4. The correct answer is **D.** "prevails." Answer A. "grows" is wrong because the Norway or white pine can grow without flourishing. Answers B. "simplifies" and C. "explores" are wrong because they are not synonyms.

5. The correct answers are **B.** "After birds eat pin cherries, they 'may drop the seed far from the parent tree' and thereby help to reforest areas 'after forest fires,'" **D.** "Since the jack pine 'protects its seeds from fire,' it is a good reforestation tree 'following a forest fire,'" and **E.** "The 'growing space' for trees has a direct effect on the 'form of trees.'" The first two Answers (B. and D.) are supported in the Distribution of Seed section while Answer E is supported in the How Trees Grow section. Answer A. "Since seeds from the aspen 'are very light and so perishable' and their 'cottony down covers' make them easy to be 'carried by the wind,' they are able to reforest any area that is not 'burned over'" is incorrect since these trees are good at reforestation after a fire. Answers C. "'Seeds of pine, maple and basswood have wings so that they are carried farther by wind,' thereby hindering the reproduction process" and F. "When looking

at 'the trees at the edge of the forest,' notice that the side that is 'towards the open' part of the forest is free of branches" are wrong since the opposite is true for both responses.

Sample Response 1/Essay for Poetic Devices (page 78)

Joyce Kilmer's poem *Trees* and the informational text from the Wisconsin Division of Forestry clearly indicate the difference between poetry and prose. In *Trees*, Kilmer paints a heartfelt picture of the beauty of a tree when he mentions that it pales in comparison to a poem: "I think that I shall never see / A poem lovely as a tree." In contrast, the Wisconsin Division of Forestry makes a matter-of-fact statement about trees: "Trees, like all living things, grow and mature and die while the forest, which is a community of trees, may live indefinitely because the trees reproduce before they die." The soft, pleasant tone in Kilmer's piece is replaced by the naturally unemotional tone of "textbook" prose in the Division's piece.

While Kilmer creates his image of trees by using personification with phrases including "A hungry mouth," "leafy arms," and "hair," the Division's piece factually states that "some trees like basswood will sprout regardless of age," "the way the seeds are produced is the basis for classifying plants," and "Jack pine is especially interesting because it protects its seeds from fire." Both authors divide their work into smaller sections. Nonetheless, Kilmer's couplets are small packages of delicate thought while the Division's heading represent different characteristics of forest trees. It may have been possible for Kilmer to categorize each of his couplets. However, that would have taken away the rhythm and the flow of his poem. The Division's categories allow the reader to divide the information into more manageable pieces. Kilmer's poem is meant to inspire while the Division's prose is meant to inform.

In this essay

- The author catches the reader's attention by directly addressing the prompt's statement that "Joyce Kilmer and the Wisconsin Division of Forestry had a different purpose in mind when writing about trees."

- The student contrasts Kilmer's "heartfelt picture" of the tree that "pales in comparison to a poem" with the Division's factual statements about the trees.

- Tone is contrasted with Kilmer's soft style running counter to the Division's unemotional prose.

- Citations are made directly from the text throughout both paragraphs: "A poem lovely as a tree" from Kilmer and "Trees...grow mature and die..." in the Division's work.

- There is good length to the essay. The paragraphs contain sufficient examples to support each point being raised.

- Academic vocabulary is evident throughout as the writer uses phrases including "heartfelt," "unemotional," "regardless," and "couplets."

- Transitions including "In contrast," "While," and "However" are used.

- There are no grammar or spelling mistakes.

Sample Response 2/Essay for Poetic Devices

Joyce Kilmer in *Trees* wrote a poem, but the guys in the Wisconsin Division didn't. Kilmer used poetry language like "hungry mouth" and "leafy arms." Nobody has leafy arms. Anyway, the Division uses phrases like "Cuttings from small branches" and "Seeds of pine, maple and basswood have wings." That last phrase actually sounds a little like poetry. Anyway, Kilmer gets all romantic while the Division is serious at all times.

Kilmer makes his tree sound like a human. That's personification. He says phrases like "A poem lovely as a tree." That's a simile! He also says "A tree that may in Summer wear / A nest of robins in her hair." That's personification. The Division doesn't do any of that. Besides, Kilmer's poem isn't a fable with a moral. It's a short statement with lots of description. But the Division writes stuff that might be in a textbook so they're not going to use poetry. That wouldn't make sense.

In this essay

- The prompt is weakly addressed.

- The contrast in the two styles of writing considers each style separately rather than in contrast.

- The language is much too casual, rather than academic: "Kilmer gets all romantic" rather than "Kilmer's images generate a sense of romanticism."

- The author makes some good points about the Division's unintended poetry: "Seeds of pine, maple and basswood have wings" and Kilmer's use of personification and simile.

- There are no spelling and grammar mistakes, but the use of phrases like "guys" and "stuff" are not appropriate in an academic piece.

- The essay writer actually uses text references, but these are not properly showcased in a mindful essay.

- There is an attempt to use transitional phrases ("Anyway" and "Besides," for example), but they need to be used in a stronger essay context.

Chapter 2: Reading: Informational (Everyday Text)

Things Had Really Changed (pages 85–86)

1. Part A: The correct answer is **D.** "All events are listed in sequence" since Answers A. "First, 'Jonathan had quickly written a note in his planner as he sat down at his desk,'" B. "Second, Jonathan 'was assigned to cover the school's wrestling matches,'" and C. "Third, Jonathan 'had received the highest grade in the class on the last test'" all follow the correct sequence.
    Part B: The correct answers are **B.** "logical order" and **D.** "particular arrangement." Answer A. "randomness" is an antonym (opposite), and C. "inductive reasoning" refers to reasoning from facts to get generalizations. Answer E. "cohesion" refers to the process of forming a unified object or idea.

2. Part A: The correct answer is **B.** "He thought his friends wouldn't think he was 'cool.'" Answer A. "His best friend had been thrown off the team" is not mentioned in the text. Answers C. "He thought Katie wouldn't think he was 'cool'" and D. "He thought his teachers wouldn't think he was 'cool'" are proven wrong by Answer A.
    Part B: The correct answer is **C.** "attempting not to lose his friends." This is supported in the text by the sentence, "Jonathan had never gone to a school event before because his friends would think he wasn't cool." Answer A. "implying" is incorrect, since it means "hinting." Answer B. "investigating" is incorrect since it means "looking into." Answer D. "showing Katie he was better than she" has no basis in the story and Answer E. "both B. and D." is incorrect since neither of the two answers is correct.

3. Part A: The correct answer is **D.** "the school newspaper." Answers A. "the principal's newsletter" and B. "the parent-teacher group's newsletter" are wrong because he writes for a newspaper, not a newsletter. Don't be fooled by Answer C. "the class newspaper." Even though Miss Rumson supported Jonathan, there is no mention of a class newspaper.
    Part B: The correct answer is **C.** "report on." Answers A. "disregard," B. "incorporate," and D. "instigate" do not mean the same as "report on."

Suggestions for Essay for Details and Sequence of Events (page 87)

You should mention that things in school "really began to change for Jonathan" after he had joined the school newspaper. Point out that when he began to study, "he received the second highest grade on Miss Rumson's test." Mention that the head cheerleader "Katie asked him if he would study with her for the next test." Explain that his friends didn't tease him for being on the school newspaper because the "older brother of one of his friends was on the team." Add that Miss Rumson had called Jonathan's mom to tell her "that he had received the highest grade in the class on the last test" and that she had recommended him to the editor of the local newspaper. Be sure to conclude by stating that through hard work, things in school indeed had "really began to change for Jonathan."

Vacation (pages 92–93)

1. Part A: The correct answer is **D.** "When you take a vacation, you should look to your own country first" since it is supported by the text. Answer A. "You should take a vacation" is too general and therefore incorrect. Answers B. "Vacations are overrated" and C. "When you take a vacation, you should look outside of your state" are not supported by the text.
    Part B: The correct answer is **D.** "mountains in the Delaware Water Gap can be fun for a vacation if they interest you" because it is supported in the text ("If the mountains interest you..."). All of the other answer choices are not supported in the text.

2. Part A: The correct answer is **B.** "The North Carolina seashore has swimming, shopping, food, and more." Answer A. "It's hot at the seashore" is incorrect because it's not the main point. Answer C. "All of the historic areas are located at the seashore" is not true. Answer D. "The seashore doesn't get many visitors in the winter" is not mentioned anywhere in the passage and is not a main point.
    Part B: The correct answers are **A.** "eclectic" and **B.** "diverse" since they reflect the variety mentioned in Part A. "The North Carolina seashore has swimming, shopping, food, and more." Answers C. "implausible" means "not convincing," D. "isolated" means "alone," E. "sweltering" means "excessively hot," and F. "uniform" means "the same." None of these answers reflect the variety, and each is therefore incorrect.

3. The correct answer is **C.** "There are swimming pools in many towns" because it is not included in the paragraph. Answers A. "Madison Square Garden is the home of various professional sports teams," B. "There are eight different professional league parks for baseball," and D. "There are auto racetracks that sponsor NASCAR and NHRA races" are mentioned in the paragraph.

4. The correct answer is **A.** "Your own state may be the best place to take a vacation." Answers B., C., and D. are all included as supporting details in the paragraph.

Essay for Main Idea or Theme (page 94)

You should write, "you could take a vacation without leaving your own state" as your main idea. Be sure that you include the mountains, the seashore, and the areas of sports and history" as vacation options and various states you may have visited. Also, mention some of your favorite activities and places of interest in these areas. Use resources you know of from different parts of the country.

The Parting of the Ways (pages 99-100)

1. Part A. The correct answer is **D.** "friend" since "chum" is slang for "friend." Answer A. "bait" is incorrect. Although "chum" is an expression used to describe a type of bait for fishermen, the context of the sentence indicates no connection with fishing. Answer B. "relative" is incorrect since a "relative" is not always a friend. Answer C. "frenemy" is a colloquial (modern) expression that is not only slang, but also contains the concept of "enemy."
   Part B: The correct answers are **D.** "pal" and **G.** "buddy." Answers A. "lure" and B. "hook" are correct only if the word "chum" was being used to indicate items used to catch fish. (*Be aware that test designers will sometimes put two synonyms together in an attempt to trick you into connecting the two words in your own mind.*) Answer C. "cousin" is incorrect since the term indicates a blood relative and not necessarily a "friend." Answer E. "graduate" is a person who has completed a course of study and who may or may not be a "friend." Answer F. "rival" is an antonym for "friend."
2. The correct answer is **B.** "Mary and Marjorie are beginning to realize that they will not be seeing each other regularly anymore." There is no evidence in the story to support Answers A. "Mary is suspicious of Marjorie," C. "Marjorie is jealous of Mary," and D. "Mary and Marjorie had grown tired of each other."
3. The correct answers are **B.** "Miss Fielding, a popular teacher, would be missed by Marjorie" (since the text refers to Miss Fielding as the "idol of the school") and **F.** "Marjorie was trying to avoid having to leave school and soon afterwards, Mary" (since Marjorie "had clung to Mary" and her friendship). There is nothing in the text to support all the other answers.
4. Part A: The correct answer is **C.** "submitted." Answer A. "triumphed" is incorrect because it means being victorious. Answer B. "overwhelmed" is incorrect because it means struggling to handle a situation. Conceding defeat is not implied, however. Answer D. "became inspired" would lead to action, not concession.

Part B: The correct answers are **B.** "conquer" and **D.** "defend." Answers A. "capitulate," C. "accede," and E. "demise" are synonyms for "succumb." Answer F. "extant" means still existing.

5. The correct answers are **A.** "A Painful Move" and **E.** "Friendship Can Sometimes Be Challenging." Answer B. "You're Finally Leaving" belies the friendship that Marjorie and Mary have. Answer C. "Even Best Friends Keep Secrets From Each Other" does not relate to an issue in the text. Answer D. "High School Adventures" is much too general for a passage dealing with two close friends who will be attending different schools. Answer F. "Deception" does not relate at all to the actions of Marjorie and Mary, who are both sad to be leaving each other.

Suggestions for Essay for Questioning, Clarifying, and Predicting (page 101)

You should mention the following:

- Marjorie and Mary's summer may be a sad one because the two girls are parting ways. Marjorie is moving away from her friend the summer before they go to high school.
- They have a few more weeks to spend together, so Marjorie and Mary will spend the little time they have left together, doing activities they like to do.
- The girls will write to each other after Marjorie moves and they will remain friends.
- From Mary's letters to Marjorie, she may send her encouraging words and about fun times they had in their old school to remind Marjorie that she will make new friends in her new one.
- Marjorie visits Mary or Mary comes back to visit Marjorie.

A Letter to the Mayor (pages 106–107)

1. Part A: The correct answer is **A.** "Victoria Martinez wrote the letter to Mayor Patel." Answer B. "Victoria Martinez wrote the letter to her friends" is incorrect because Victoria talked about her friends but she didn't write them a letter. Answers C. "Mayor Patel wrote the letter to Victoria Martinez and her friends" and D. "Mayor Patel wrote the letter to Victoria Martinez" are wrong because Victoria wrote the letter.
    Part B: The correct answers are **B.** "authenticity" meaning "being real" and **C.** "palpability" meaning "easily seen." Answers A. "versatility" meaning "having different skills or qualities," D. "precluding" meaning "making impossible," E. "presiding" meaning "occupying a place of authority or control," and F. "abject" meaning "wretched or miserable" are incorrect.

2. The correct answer is **A.** "I believe that we should have a place in town...." The word believe is an opinion word. Answers B. "...the building is closed," C. "Mr. Ross used to volunteer his time on the weekends," and D. "Mr. Ross 'retired and moved to Florida'" are all facts that can be proven.

3. The correct answer is **C.** "...we go to the movies." Answers A. "The security guards are 'always chasing us away'" and B. "...the security guards are mean to us" are Victoria's opinions. Answer D. "...large groups of teens cause trouble" is not always true and is therefore an opinion.

4. Part A: The correct answer is **B.** "...there were too many kids hanging out in the Maple Grove Shopping Center parking lot." Answers A. "'...we came to a town council meeting,'" C. "'We asked 'for a teen center,'" and D. "'...nine teenagers had been arrested for fighting during the last month'" are all facts that can be proven.

    Part B: The correct answers are **A.** "sentiment" which means "a feeling about something" and **F.** "conjecture" which means "a somewhat educated guess." Answers B. "certainty" meaning "being sure," C. "credibility" meaning "believability," D. "conscientious" meaning "thorough and vigilant," and E. "foreboding" meaning "impending" are incorrect.

Suggestions for Essay for Fact vs. Opinion (page 108)

You should mention the following:

*   Victoria is giving an opinion.
*   Her promise that "there wouldn't be any more trouble in town" can't be guaranteed because she doesn't control the behavior of all the teens in town.
*   Her statement that "we'd be off the streets" is an opinion for the same reason.
*   Victoria's statement that she and the teens in town would "all want to be with our friends" is her perception rather than fact.

Guided Reading Book Report, Choice Fiction (pages 113–114)

1. The correct answer is **B.** "free choice fiction." Answer A. "free choice" is incorrect because the word "fiction" is not included. Answers C. "free choice non-fiction" and D. "free choice biography" are wrong. Even though they contain the phrase "free choice," the genres (types) are wrong.

2. The correct answer is **D.** "Return your book permission slip to Mr. Rhoades by February 26." Answer A. "Find a friend who also wants to read the same book" is wrong because it is the step before, not after, the second one. Answers B. "Ask a parent/guardian to help you select a book" and C. "Have your partner sign your book permission slip" are not part of the list of steps.

3. Part A: The correct answer is **C.** "your parent/guardian's signature." Answers A. "your name," B. "your reading partner's name," and D. "the title and author of the book that you and your partner are reading" all need to be included in the reading log.
    Part B: The correct answers are **A.** "essential" meaning "absolutely necessary," **B.** "imperative" meaning "vital or crucial," and **C.** "requisite," meaning required. Answers D. "superfluous," E. "extraneous," and F. "fundamental" are antonyms (opposites) and are therefore incorrect.
4. The correct answer is **C.** "two 'C' grades." Answer A. "two 'A+' grades" is assigned for the completion of all three sections, not two. Answer B. "two 'C+' grades" is not a grade option. Answer D. "two 'D' grades" is assigned if only one section is completed.

Suggestions for Essay for Following Directions (page 115)

You should mention the following:

- The student and his/her partner meet "for no more than 20 minutes with another pair of students who are reading a different book."
- One student "will serve as a group facilitator who will keep the discussion 'on track.'"
- A recorder will also be chosen to "take notes that will be signed by all group members and submitted to Mr. Rhoades."

Professional Sports Broadcasting—My Dream Job (pages 120–121)

1. Part A: The correct answer is **C.** Answers A. "Phil's dream to go to college," B. "Phil's dream to be a professional sports manager," and D. "Phil's dream to be a hip hop artist" are incorrect because they contradict the opening sentence: "I've always wanted to become a professional sports broadcaster." Part B: The correct answers are **B.** "aspiration" meaning "hope" and **F.** "ambition" meaning "a strong desire to fulfill a dream." Answers A. "nightmare" is "a disturbing dream," C. "conscience" is "an inner voice of right and wrong," D. "reciprocity" is "exchanging for mutual benefit (quid pro quo)," and E. "inveigle" is "enticing through flattery." These four answers are all incorrect.
2. The correct answer is **A.** "autobiographical" because it is written by Philip about himself. Answer B. "biographical" is incorrect because nobody else wrote about Philip's life. Answer C. "fictional" is incorrect because the information is factual. Answer D. "poetic" is wrong because the structure does not follow poetic structure.

3. Part A: The correct answer is **D.** "The books feature sportscasters who never cared about playing the game." Answers A. "The books feature sportscasters who enjoy sports," B. "The sportscasters received training before they began to broadcast," and C. "The sportscasters enjoy working with people" are all traits of successful sportscasters.

    Part B: The correct answers are **B.** "counterfeit" meaning "illegally copied" and **E.** "fraudulent" meaning "misleading to appear real or accurate." Answers A. "bona fide" meaning "genuine" (from the Latin "in good faith"), C. "veracity" meaning "accuracy," D. "genuine" meaning "real or actual," and F. "authentic" meaning "not an imitation" are all synonyms of the word "true." Be sure that you read the question carefully and remember that antonym means *opposite* while synonym means *same.*

4. The correct answer is **B.** "a school literary magazine." Answer A. "a professional broadcasting magazine" is not possible since the piece would not have enough interest for a professional audience. Answer C. "a university literary magazine" is not the place a seventh-grade essay would be published. Answer D. "a national weekly sports magazine" is wrong for the same reason.

Suggestions for Essay for Recognizing Literary Forms and Information Sources (page 122)

You should mention the following:

- A short story could be fictional, but that is an option.
- There needs to be at least one main character who's facing a conflict.
- This conflict needs to be resolved.
- There will be a theme (main idea), which may actually teach a lesson.

Guidelines for Making a Class Presentation (pages 128-129)

1. Part A: The correct answer is **D.** "conjugating verbs" since it was not included in the list. Answers A. "transitive verbs," B. "intransitive and linking verbs," and C. "helping (auxiliary) verbs" are all part of the list.

    Part B: The correct answers are the synonyms **A.** "category" and **D.** "class." Answer B. "assignment" is incorrect since it refers either to classwork or homework in general. Answers C. "preposition" and F. "conjunction" are parts of speech, making the answer incorrect. Answer E. "diagram" is a technique used in the past to parse sentences and is not a "verb division."

2. The correct answer is **B.** "movie screen" because slides are shown on a screen. Answer A. "audio headset" is incorrect because it is not necessary. Answers C. "spiral notebook" and D. "chalk eraser" are wrong because they have no direct use for a computer slide show.

3. The correct answer is **C.** "The student will receive a lower grade." Answer A. "No one will notice because the information is the most important part of the presentation" is wrong since Miss Ostrovsky has said that "your information and the way you present it are both important." There is neither evidence nor prior knowledge to lead one to conclude that Answers B. "Miss Ostrovsky will give the student one more chance to do better" and D. "The student will receive a detention" are anything but incorrect.

4. Part A: The correct answer is **D.** "She understands that teaching with media helps to improve learning." Answer A. "She just bought a new computer" is wrong because the entire class could not complete their projects by using only Miss Ostrovsky's computer. Answer B. "She's punishing the students for misbehaving" is incorrect because this lesson is designed to help the students with their learning. Answer C. "She's going on maternity leave" is wrong because there is no connection between the assignment and a maternity leave. Part B: The correct answers are **A.** "probable" meaning "likely to occur" and **B.** "feasible" meaning "possible." Answer C. "incomprehensible" means "difficult to understand," D. "implausible" means "not reasonable or likely," E. "insincere" means "not showing genuine feelings," and F. "inconceivable" means "difficult if not impossible to understand." These four answers are therefore incorrect.

Suggestions for Essay on Finding Information and Answering with Prior Knowledge (page 130)

You should mention the following:

- The definitions of the verb concepts being covered will give the students the basic information they will need to understand the concepts.
- The rules will help the students to learn the right way to use the concepts.
- The use of examples will provide the students with the chance to practice the concepts.
- Looking at exceptions will help the students to avoid making mistakes in the future.

Chapter 3: The Research Simulation Task

Steps to Resolve Problems with Purchases (pages 143–144)

1. Part A. The correct answer is **D.** "problem and solution."
   Part B. The correct answers are **C.** "therefore" and **F.** "in conclusion." Answers A. "on the other hand" is common in a comparison and contrast piece, B. "consists of" is common in a description piece, D. "first of all" is common in a sequence piece, and E. "if…then" is common in a problem and solution piece.
2. Part A. The correct answer is **D.** "instructional" since the author is looking to explain a strategy.
   Part B. The correct answer is **D.** "advisory" since the author of the article seeks to give advice. Answer A. "mandatory" is incorrect because advice is not a requirement, as are Answers B. "misappropriated" (usually used with funds placed or used incorrectly), and C. "ad hoc" (usually used to describe a committee with a temporary life span).
3. The correct answer is **B.** "Follow This Plan When You Make a Customer Complaint to a Company." Answer A. "How Not to Get Scammed by Companies" is incorrect because there is no mention of "scamming." Answer C. "Getting Your Money Back from a Company" may be one step in getting customer satisfaction, but it is never mentioned in the article. Answer D. "An Insider's Look at Getting Satisfaction for a Faulty Product or Service" is wrong because the concept of being an "insider" is not mentioned.
4. The correct answers are **C.** "If you are experiencing shoulder pain while you wear your backpack that is filled with an amount of weight that does not exceed the suggested amount, then you are justified in making a complaint" and **F.** "This gesture emphasizes the point that you are a reasonable individual who wishes to resolve this problem in a reasonable manner." Answer A. "Imagine saving your money over a period of a few months because you are hoping to make a special purchase" is incorrect since it refers to the time before the purchase was made. Answer B. "Often, the product description includes terms such as 'durable' and 'convenient' to describe the product" is incorrect since it is referring to a claim for the product and not the product's performance. Answer D. "Rather, the cause of the problem is your fault for not following directions" would indicate that the customer is not justified in making a claim since (s)he is at fault. Answer E. "If there is any assembly or special procedure to follow concerning your product or service, then it may be wise to take the following steps" is incorrect since the advice refers to the product's "assembly or special procedure" to be followed rather than a cause for the customer to file a complaint.

5. The correct answer is **D.** "Customers should carefully examine a number of steps to resolve a problem with a company." This is the entire focus of the article. The points made in Answers A. "Companies are often taking advantage of their customers," B. Only aggressive customers get satisfaction when dealing with companies," and C. "Reasonable customers sometimes get help from companies, but not often" are details.

6. The correct answers are **B.** "a newspaper" (probably in the lifestyle section) and **E.** "a blog" (likely one dealing with consumer issues). Answer A. "a business journal" is incorrect since the target audience is the business community, not consumers. Answer C. "an almanac" is incorrect because this type of publication contains events pertaining to the weather and astronomy. Answer D. "a numismatist journal" is incorrect because this type of publication is written for collectors of objects including coins, paper money, and stock certificates. Answer F. "an instructional manual" is incorrect since the article is presenting a set of directions.

Steps to File a Complaint Against a Company (pages 147–148)

7. The correct answers are **D.** "When you have a complaint, you should contact the company" and **E.** "You should gather supporting documents before you contact a company." Answer A. "When you have a complaint, always go right to the top to get satisfaction" is incorrect since the passage advises the reader to "try going higher up to the national headquarters" only after contacting a "salesperson or customer service representative" and "a supervisor or manager" has failed. Answer B. "Don't complain unless you really have no other way to resolve your problem" is incorrect since it contradicts the title. Answer C. "It is your right and duty under the U.S. Constitution to complain" is incorrect since it is never mentioned in the article. Answer F. "You don't really need to gather supporting documents before you contact a company" contradicts the first step in the process: "Gather supporting documents."

8. The correct answers are **D.** "anecdotal notes of phone calls" and **E.** "previous correspondence" since these contain information from the customer's contact with company representatives. The information has been logged. Answer A. "business ledgers" is incorrect because these are financial records created by accountants. Answer B. "newspapers" is incorrect since these report news on a daily basis and have nothing to do with an individual's complaint. Answer C. "pieces of firewood" is an alternate meaning for the word when used to refer to fuel for the fireplace. Answer F. "product advertisements" is incorrect because they are not records of correspondence between the customer and the company.

Although they may be used to support or dispute a claim, they do not reflect the interaction between the customer and the company.

9. Part A: Answer **C.** "Tips about Getting Customer Satisfaction" is correct because the article deals with the steps you need to take to file a complaint in pursuit of getting customer satisfaction for the complaint. Answer A. "Get Your Money Back!" is incorrect because that advice is only one alternative to be sought. Answer B. "How to Get the Best Prices" is incorrect because the article deals with customer satisfaction after, not before a purchase. Answer D. "Making a Profit" is not mentioned.

Part B: The correct answers are **B.** "consumers, complaints, redress" (a remedy or compensation for a grievance) and **E.** "consumers, complaints, resolution." Answer A. "consumers, price wars, justice system" has nothing to do with price wars. Answer C. "consumers, the law, the courts" is incorrect because the law and the courts are never mentioned in the article. Answer D. "consumers, complaints, lawyers" is incorrect since lawyers are never mentioned. Answer F. "consumers, the law, the Supreme Court" is incorrect because neither the law nor the Supreme Court is mentioned.

10. Part A: The correct answer is **B.** "a sector." Answers A. "a math process," C. "a sports team," and D. "a treaty" are incorrect.

Part B: The correct answers are **E.** "branch" and **F.** "group." Answer A. "a math process" is incorrect since it refers to the entire company and not a division. Answers B. "the addition of integers and fractions" and C. "associative properties" are incorrect because they refer specifically to math.

Essay for The Research Simulation Task: Sample Response (page 149)

Here is an example of an essay using text evidence to show similarities and differences to help compare and contrast the two pieces.

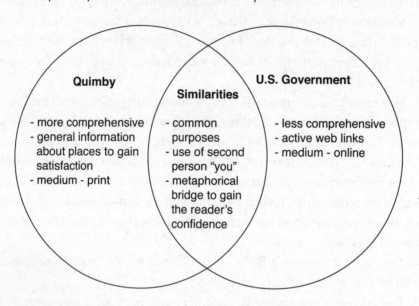

Two Approaches Leading to One Solution

In everyday life, situations are often faced in which there are similarities and differences between two attempts to give advice. When comparing "Steps to Resolve Problems with Purchases" by Fiona Quimby and "Steps to File a Complaint Against a Company" from the U.S. Government's Website, one must address the similarities and differences in their approach to giving advice. This essay will examine the manner in which these two pieces contain both common and opposite elements.

The most apparent similarity of the two pieces seems to be rooted in their common purpose: giving advice to the consumer who is dissatisfied with a product. Each piece uses the second person "you" when addressing the reader, thereby providing a more inviting and personalized tone. This style gives the impression that the author is speaking directly to the reader. Furthermore, the author of each piece attempts to gain the reader's confidence by creating a metaphorical bridge between the author/sponsor of the piece and the frustrated reader who is seeking advice. Both pieces, therefore, maintain their intended mission: they provide sound advice for customers who want satisfaction rather than frustration when dealing with a complaint concerning a product.

Not only do these two pieces have similarities, but they also contain significant differences. The piece by Ms. Quimby is more comprehensive than the one provided by the U.S. Government. It includes steps to follow before considering the filing of a complaint. In contrast, the U.S. Government's piece begins with the filing since it presumes that the consumer seeking this information wishes to begin the complaint process. Ms. Quimby's piece presents general information about ways to gain satisfaction. This advice includes contacting "the help line," writing "a letter to the customer service department," considering "filing a complaint with the Better Business Bureau," and finally hiring "a lawyer if you have not received satisfaction through other avenues." The U.S. Government's piece contains active Web links including those to access a "sample complaint letter," the "Better Business Bureau (BBB)," and a list of "appropriate federal agenc(ies)." The reason for this particular difference may be the medium through which each is presented. Ms. Quimby's piece may be more typical of the format found in a magazine. It contains multiple headings with a step-by-step approach that is supplemented with panel and box copy, or extra inserted material, accompanied by a chart. The government piece, on the other hand, uses bullet points to organize the steps for its advice.

As stated, the pieces created by Flona Quimby and the U.S. Government have a number of similarities and differences. Both pieces intend to provide a dissatisfied customer with the proper steps to resolve a problem with a product. Both pieces speak directly to the reader while they use the second person pronoun "you," and both attempt to provide alternatives for a customer to use when dissatisfied with a product. As for differences, the piece by Ms. Quimby is more comprehensive and print-oriented while the piece from the U.S. Government avoids addressing the steps prior to the decision to seek satisfaction, uses a number of online links to supplement the information presented, and is organized with bullet points rather than steps. The needs of the consumer are addressed in both pieces while each maintains its focus. The ultimate goal of each article is the same: customer satisfaction.

Explanation of Student Response

This essay is a very comprehensive comparison of two different pieces with similar intent but differing purposes and structures. The author establishes a direction for the essay with a title that captures the main idea: "Two Approaches Leading to One Solution." This title is also reinforced in the opening statement which also serves to gain the reader's attention: "In everyday life, situations are often faced in which there are similarities and differences between two attempts to give advice." The author mentions "both the similarities and differences in the approaches" of each work while presenting the intention to "examine the manner in which these two pieces contain both common and opposite elements." The second paragraph is dedicated to the development of the similarities while the third is dedicated to the development of the differences. The level of comparisons and contrasts shows academic vigor. This is especially evident when the author addresses voice with the statement "the second person "you," the "metaphorical bridge between the author/sponsor of the piece and the frustrated reader who is seeking advice," and the "comprehensive" aspect of Ms. Quimby's piece when compared to that of the U.S. Government. The generous use of "Web links" by the U.S. Government and "the medium on which each (of the pieces) may be presented" further supports the differences between the two pieces. The final paragraph summarizes some of the major similarities and differences while additionally providing a bit of insight with the statements: "The needs of the consumer are addressed in both these pieces. The ultimate goal of each article is the same: customer satisfaction."

There are additional areas to be commended. This essay uses well-constructed paragraphs that are appropriately indented. The logic of the explanation by the author follows the pattern of an opening paragraph that introduces the information, a second paragraph that examines the similarities of each piece, a third paragraph that examines the differences, and a fourth paragraph that includes a summary and the author's insight. There are numerous examples of transitions throughout the piece including "Furthermore," "Also," "not only ... but ... also," and "on the other hand." The citations from the text are not only appropriate and academically appropriate, but they are also direct quotes to ensure that the test examiner must notice them. A variety of sentence structure including simple ("It includes steps to follow before considering the filing of a complaint"), compound ("Not only do these two written pieces have similarities, but they also do contain significant differences"), and complex ("The needs of the consumer are addressed in both these pieces while each piece maintains its focus"). The vocabulary used by the writer is academically sophisticated. This is evidenced by the use of words and phrases including "supplemented," "dissatisfied," "ultimately," "common and opposite elements," and "intended mission." Finally, there are neither grammar nor spelling mistakes. Therefore, this essay would receive a score of **4**.

Chapter 4: The Narrative Writing Task

Narrative Writing Task Essay Sample Response (page 170)

Frisky Saves the Day

As the sun came up, JJ looked at the alarm clock as she lay in bed. She had been asleep when she was woken up by the music from her clock radio and some other noise. The noise was coming from downstairs, and it seemed to be loud. She figured her mom would take care of it, but the noise kept going. How would JJ be able to sleep with all that noise?

JJ was known as being trustworthy. She always helped out people who needed help. She had stopped some kids at school from bullying another kid one time. She had taken care of a neighbor's dog while the neighbor was away. "I probably should help out in my house, too," she thought.

As she walked out of her room, she was able to tell that the noise that she had been hearing was coming from Frisky, her puppy. Frisky sounded excited, but JJ figured that her puppy was acting the way it always did. This puppy would run around nonstop for almost ten minutes at a time. The barking was probably just Frisky's way of being excited.

When JJ got downstairs, however, she noticed that it smelled as if something was burning. JJ called to her mom to ask if anything was wrong, but her mom didn't answer since she had just stepped outside for a moment. JJ called again, but still didn't get an answer. "Maybe something really is wrong," she said.

As JJ opened the door to the kitchen, the sun that would usually be in JJ's eyes was blocked since her mom had pulled down the shade. At once, JJ noticed that Frisky was barking and running around in circles. Before she could try to calm down her puppy, JJ noticed that there was smoke coming from the oven. JJ had to act quickly.

She started to fill up a bucket with water, but then JJ remembered a conversation she had last week with her Uncle Ralph.

JJ asked him, ""Should you throw water on a fire?"

Her Uncle Ralph had replied, "Not if the fire is a grease fire—you know, like the ones in a kitchen. Then you should open a box of salt and throw the salt on the fire."

Luckily, the muffins hadn't caught fire yet. JJ was able to take a box of salt, look through the oven door to make sure the fire hadn't started yet, cautiously open the door, and remove the muffins before they caught fire. JJ turned off the oven as her mom raced into the kitchen.

"What happened, JJ?"

"Frisky's barking woke me up, and I came down just in time to turn off the oven and prevent a fire. Frisky's a hero, mom," JJ said with relief.

"You're a hero too, JJ. You may have saved our lives."

"Mom, please don't go outside again if the oven is on. It's dangerous."

"I promise," said JJ's mom.

Both JJ and her mom learned a valuable safety lesson that morning: never leave the stove or the oven unattended.

Notice that in this essay, the writer made the following improvements. The title relates directly to the main events in the story.

- There is more detailed description.

  – "As the sun came up, JJ looked at the alarm clock as she lay in bed."
  – "She had taken care of a neighbor's dog while the neighbor was away."

- The entire "scene" is painted completely.

  – "JJ was known as being trustworthy. She always helped out people who needed help. She had stopped some kids at school from bullying another kid one time. She had taken care of a neighbor's dog while the neighbor was away. "I probably should help out in my house, too," she thought."

- There is dialogue.

  – "What happened, JJ?"
    "Frisky's barking woke me up, and I came down just in time to turn off the oven and prevent a fire. Frisky's a hero, mom," JJ said with relief.

- There are specifics.

- The original sentence was "JJ was able to take as box of salt, make sure the fire hadn't started, open the door, and take out the muffins. JJ's mom raced into the kitchen."
- It has been replaced by "JJ was able to take a box of salt, look through the oven door to make sure the fire hadn't started yet, cautiously open the door, and remove the muffins before they caught fire."

- There is a lesson that JJ and her mom both learn: "never leave the stove or the oven unattended." **(Insight)**

Independent Writing Practice/Narrative Writing Task

Suggested Main Points

Possible information to include in your essay.

- The main conflict deals with the following problem: should the narrator Jean take the present and keep it, or should she try to find the person whose name is on the present?
- The plot (story line) deals with Jean walking down the street on the way to the store on Saturday morning around 10:00 A.M. Jean turns a corner and sees the wrapped birthday present. There is no one around on this clear summer morning.
- The setting is a small town in the summer. There is no one on the street where Jean finds the present. In the town, most people know each other. However, even this fact doesn't help Jean to know for whom the present is intended since the name on the tag has been smeared by the moisture from the morning dew.
- Jean is an honest seventh grader who always tries to do the right thing. She is a member of the student council at school, and she has been a girl scout since she was eight years old. She also won the award for most reliable student at school last year when she was in sixth grade.
- Jean tries to find someone to ask for advice about whether or not she should try to find the owner of the present. She first meets Harriet from school, who advises Jean to keep the present. Jean's too honest and doesn't think that Harriet's advice is good.
- Jean's best friend Miriam comes by and tells her that Jean should follow the advice she always gives to Miriam: "Honesty is the best policy." Jean agrees with Miriam, and the two girls walk one block to the police station to turn in the present they have found.
- The working title for the story is "Jean Finds a Present." The final title is "Jean Takes Her Own Advice."

Chapter 5: Grammar the Write Way

Number, Case, and Gender (page 179)

Number

1. *Are*
My Friend and I Is Going to the Video Game Store

After school today, my friend Sam and I don't plan to go straight home. Instead,

2. *plan*   3. *are*
we **plans** to go to the video game store. We **is** going to walk down Main Street and

then turn right on Maple Avenue. There are three new games being released today,

and we're going to be at the store to try them out with our friends.

Explanation
1. The subject "**My friend and I**" is plural so the verb must also be plural: "**Are.**"
2. The subject "**we**" is plural so the verb must also be plural: "**plan.**"
3. Again, the subject "**we**" is plural so the verb must also be plural: "**are.**"

Part A: Gender (page 182)
1. Mrs. Cairo asked Mary to pick up (**her**, its) books.
2. Jackson took (**his**, its) brother to the movies.
3. The table can hold (her, **its**) own weight.

Explanation
1. The correct answer is "**her**" since Mary is a girl.
2. The correct answer is "**his**" since Jackson is a boy.
3. The correct answer is "**its**" since the table is neuter: neither a girl nor a boy.

Misplaced Modifiers (page 188)
Part A
1. A suggested answer is "**In her desk, Savannah found a lady's blue bracelet.**" The bracelet is blue, not the lady.
2. A suggested answer is "**I once met a one-armed man named Rashawn.**" The man is named Rashawn, not his arm.
3. A suggested answer is "**I heard on the evening news that the burglar has been captured.**" The evening news is the place where the news was heard, not the location where the capture took place.

Voice (page 192)
Part B
1. A suggested answer is "**Students filled every desk in the library yesterday.**" The students do the action in an active voice sentence.
2. A suggested answer is "**At my favorite ice cream store, the new owner prepared my sundae.**" The new owner is doing the action.
3. A suggested answer is "**My parents scolded me when I didn't do all my chores yesterday.**" The parents are doing the scolding.

Sentence Variety (page 194)
The following is one sample of the way this paragraph could have used more sentence variety.

Getting in Trouble

1.   **2.**
Yesterday I unexpectedly got into some trouble. My friends and I forgot our

3.
manners, and we cut across our neighbor's lawn. He became very upset, and then

4.   **5.**
he started yelling at us. We tried to explain to him that we weren't hurting anything.

6.
He said that somebody stole his lawn chair as a prank. Now he's blaming us, even

7.
though we're innocent. I guess we shouldn't have walked on his lawn.

Explanation
1. Change the position of the adverb "Yesterday" and add the word "**unexpectedly.**"
2. Change the sentence to a compound sentence.
3. Combine the next two sentences into a compound sentence.
4. Change the simple sentence into a complex one ("…that we weren't hurting anything" can't stand alone as a sentence because of the word "that.")
5. No change was made.
6. Combine the next two sentences to make a complex sentence.
7. No change was made.

(Remember that these changes are suggestions. Your answers may be different.)

Fragments and Run-ons (pages 195–196)

Fragments

1. A suggested answer is "**My cousin and I walked through the park.**"
2. A suggested answer is "**My best friend from Vineland is visiting me today.**"
3. A suggested answer is "**Exercising every morning keeps me in shape.**"

Run-ons

1. A suggested answer is "**Come to my birthday party because it will be fun.**"
2. A suggested answer is "**Because I'm doing my homework now, I can't talk to you.**"
3. A suggested answer is "**I'll take out the trash, and then I'll walk the dog.**"

Punctuation with Commas and End Marks (pages 199–200)

Commas

1. I had a hamburger, and you had pizza.
2. My mom asked me to go to the store, mail a letter, and put my dirty clothes in the wash.
3. Because I earned all "A's" and "B's" on my report card, I'm getting a reward.
4. We moved to New Jersey from Springfield, Ohio.
5. "Sincerely yours, Allen" is the ending I used for my letter.
6. No, I won't make fun of the new student in our class.
7. The winner of the fund raising challenge was Nicole, a student from my class.

Punctuating Sentences

1. I just won a million dollars! (Exclamatory Sentence)
2. Please take care of yourself. (Imperative Sentence)
3. Did you eat the last piece of cake? (Interrogative Sentence)
4. The class project will be due on March 3. (Declarative Sentence)

Homophones and Homographs (pages 202–204)

Homophones

Part A

1. The correct answer is "**sew,**" which means to use "a needle and thread to join together cloth or other similar material. The homonym "so" means "thus" or "therefore."
2. The correct answer is "**They're,**" which is the contraction of "They are." "Their" is a pronoun showing ownership by more than one person, and "There" refers to a direction that is usually not close by.

3. The correct answer is "**to**," which is a preposition usually meaning a direction. "Too" means "also," and "Two" is the number following one.
4. The correct answer is "**hear**," which means receiving communication through the ear. "Here" means a nearby location.
5. The correct answer is "**flower**," which is the blossom of a plant. "Flour" is grain that is very finely milled (ground).

Homographs

Part A
1. The correct answer is **B.** "the covering of a tree"
2. The correct answer is **A.** "not heavy"
3. The correct answer is **A.** "admirer"
4. The correct answer is **B.** "skin cut"
5. The correct answer is **B.** "happening in the present time"

Grammar Demons

Unusual Order (page 205)

Part A
1. The correct answer is "**are**" since the subject is "tickets."
2. The correct answer is "**is**" since the subject is "outfit."
3. The correct answer is "**is**" since the subject is "rip."
4. The correct answer is "**are**" since the subject is "gloves."

Adjective or Adverb (page 207)

Part A
1. The correct answer is "**good**" since this adjective modifies the noun "meal."
2. The correct answer is "**well**" since we are referring to health.
3. The correct answer is "**bad**" since this adjective modifies the noun "test."
4. The correct answer is "**badly**" since this adverb modifies the verb "performed."
5. The correct answer is "**really**" since this adverb modifies the adjective "good."
6. The correct answer is "**real**" since this predicate adjective follows the linking verb "**is**" and modifies the subject "wish."

Quotations (page 209)
1. The correct answer is: **The principal said over the intercom, "Students, please report to the cafeteria at the end of second period today."**
2. The correct answer is: **"Write your homework assignment in your notebooks,"said Mrs. Hudson.**

3. The correct answer is: **"Are we there yet?" said my brother after every five minutes of our trip**.
4. The correct answer is: **"Should we go to the park?" said Carrie, "or should we go to the ball field?"**
5. The correct answer is: **I answered, "We should go to the park. They're having a special program there. Besides, all our friends will be there too."**
6. The correct answer is: **"That's sounds great!" said Carrie.**

Underlining or Quotation Marks (page 210)

Part A

1. The correct answer is: **My sister is reading <u>Great Expectations</u>, a novel by Charles Dickens.**
2. The correct answer is: **In class we read "Dream Deferred," a poem by Langston Hughes.**
3. The correct answer is: **Before the play-off game, we stood and took off our caps as the loudspeakers played "God Bless America."**
4. The correct answer is: **In class today, Mr. Porter read an article from <u>The New York Times</u>.**

Spelling Demons (pages 214–215)

Part A

1. The correct answer is **"If you don't bring a note to excuse your absence from school, you'll get a detention."**
2. The correct answer is **"Let's buy some balloons for our party."**
3. The correct answer is **"I am assigned the job of changing the date on the class calendar."**
4. The correct answer is **"The month after January is February."**
5. The correct answer is **"Do we have any grammar homework tonight?"**
6. The correct answer is **"Oops, my shoelaces are loose."**
7. The correct answer is **"Our town's parade occurred last weekend."**
8. The correct answer is **"Mom asked me to get the butter for the mashed potatoes."**
9. The correct answer is **"Our music class is studying rhythm and blues artists from the 1970s."**
10. The correct answer is **"I used the vacuum to pick up the dirt that spilled on the rug."**

PARCC ELA/Literacy Practice Test

Now you will take a PARCC Grade 7 ELA/Literacy practice test. Try your best and remember to time yourself to see how long it takes you to complete a unit.

Remember, there are three units: The Literary Analysis Task, The Research Simulation Task, and The Narrative Writing Task. You will most likely see all three types of questions (EBS, TECR, and PCR) that you previously read in the Introduction of this book. Some directions may include prompts for TECRs *and* paper test questions.

> **IMPORTANT NOTE:** Barron's has made every effort to create sample tests that accurately reflect the PARCC Assessment. However, the tests are constantly changing, but each sample test will still provide a strong framework for seventh-grade students preparing for the assessment. Be sure to consult *www.parcconline.org* for all the latest testing information.

Unit 1 (110 minutes)

Literary Analysis Task

Directions: You will be asked to read a literary passage and then answer questions.

"Mother to Son"

by Langston Hughes

Well, son, I'll tell you:
Life for me ain't been no crystal stair.
It's had tacks in it,
And splinters,
(5) And boards torn up,
And places with no carpet on the floor—Bare.
But all the time
I'se been a-climbin' on,
And reachin' landin's,
(10) And turnin' corners,
And sometimes goin' in the dark
Where there ain't been no light.
So boy, don't you turn back.
Don't you set down on the steps
(15) 'Cause you finds it's kinder hard.
Don't you fall now—
For I'se still goin', honey,
I'se still climbin',
And life for me ain't been no crystal stair.

1. When the son's mother tells him in line 2 that "life for me ain't been no crystal stair," she means that

   ○ A. she has lived her life on the ground floor of her house.
   ○ B. she is someone who has always desired stairs made from crystal.
   ○ C. she is poor and cannot afford an easy life of luxury.
   ○ D. she is a maid who is forced to clean up "tacks" and "splinters."

2. Select the words listed below that describe the actions of the mother when she says in lines 8–10 that she's, "a climbin' on,/ And reachin' landin's,/ And turnin' corners" and drag (write) them into the boxes.

A. persevering

B. resigned

C. incoherent

D. determined

E. agnostic

3. In lines 11–12 when the mother speaks of "sometimes goin' in the dark/Where there ain't been no light," she is speaking of

○ A. her home without electricity.
○ B. her job in the evening when it is dark.
○ C. her boredom with her life and desire for the excitement that the night life has.
○ D. her being forced to live a difficult life.

4. In lines 14–15 the mother tells her son, "Don't you set down on the steps / 'Cause you finds it's kinder hard." She means that since life is hard

○ A. the son should just give up now and avoid the inevitable disappointment.
○ B. the son should keep trying and not quit.
○ C. life is unpredictable, and there is no formula for success.
○ D. even though you may try your best, there is little hope for success in this cruel world.

5. In lines 16–19 the mother says, "Don't you fall now—/For I'se still goin', honey, / I'se still climbin', And life for me ain't been no crystal stair" because she is trying to _____ her point to her son.

☐ A. reinforce
☐ B. undermine
☐ C. underscore
☐ D. intimidate
☐ E. improvise

Directions: You will be reading a fable titled "The Ant and the Grasshopper" and an essay, "Getting Ready for Winter." You will then be asked questions based on both selections.

The Ant and the Grasshopper

by Aesop

1   In a field one summer's day a Grasshopper was hopping about, chirping and singing to its heart's content. An Ant passed by, bearing along with great toil an ear of corn he was taking to the nest.

2   "Why not come and chat with me," said the Grasshopper, "instead of toiling and moiling in that way?"

3   "I am helping to lay up food for the winter," said the Ant, "and recommend you to do the same."

4   "Why bother about winter?" said the Grasshopper; we have plenty of food at present." But the Ant went on its way and continued its toil. When the winter came the Grasshopper had no food and found itself dying of hunger, while it saw the ants distributing every day corn and grain from the stores they had collected in the summer. Then the Grasshopper knew:

5   **It is best to prepare for the days of necessity.**

Source: http://www.bartleby.com/17/1/36.html

6. Which of these statements is **not** part of the plot?

   O A.   The Grasshopper was hopping in a field.
   O B.   The Grasshopper met the Ant.
   O C.   The Grasshopper helped the Ant.
   O D.   The Ant stored food for the winter.

7. Who are the main characters in the fable?

   O A.   the Ant and the Grasshopper
   O B.   the Ant and the other ants
   O C.   the Grasshopper and the other ants
   O D.   the Grasshopper, the Ant, the other ants, and the ear of corn

8. Which of the following words **best** describes the traits of the Grasshopper? Select all the correct statements.

    ○ A. The Grasshopper has exactly the same traits as those of the Ant.

    ○ B. The Grasshopper is conscientious.

    ○ C. The Grasshopper is somber and disillusioned.

    ○ D. The Grasshopper believes throughout the fable that his idea of chirping and singing throughout the summer is a smart one.

9. Part A

Select from the following the settings in the fable, "The Ant and the Grasshopper."

    ☐ A. a field in the spring

    ☐ B. a barn in the spring

    ☐ C. a field in the summer

    ☐ D. a nest in the summer

    ☐ E. a barn in the summer

    ☐ F. a nest in the fall

    ☐ G. a barn in the fall

    ☐ H. a field in the winter

    ☐ J. a nest in the winter

Part B

Select the following statements that **best** describe the reason for Aesop's choice of settings in Part A.

    ☐ A. He wanted to add a lot of description, and using more than one setting gave him that opportunity.

    ☐ B. He wanted to develop his characters fully with extensive conflicts.

    ☐ C. He wanted to use humor to clarify his point.

    ☐ D. He wanted to extend the length of his fable.

    ☐ E. He wanted to connect the actions of the main characters to the differences of the seasons.

    ☐ F. He wanted to use the idea of careless behavior to make his point.

10. During the summer, what did the ants store?

- ○ A. bread
- ○ B. milk
- ○ C. corn
- ○ D. hay

11. Which of these would be the **best** theme for this fable?

- ○ A. Always plan ahead.
- ○ B. Cheaters never prosper.
- ○ C. Take life one day at a time.
- ○ D. Always tell the truth.

12. Which of the following were effects of the Grasshopper **not** listening to the Ant's advice?

- ☐ A. The Grasshopper and the Ant became bitter enemies.
- ☐ B. The Grasshopper lost its sight.
- ☐ C. The Grasshopper and the Ant became friends.
- ☐ D. The Grasshopper was dying of hunger.
- ☐ E. The Grasshopper declared war on the Ant.
- ☐ F. The Ant stored food for the winter.
- ☐ G. The Grasshopper realized that he was wrong not to store food in the summer.
- ☐ H. The Grasshopper was saved when the Ant invited the Grasshopper to spend the winter with the other ants.

13. Select the **two** statements that are true about the point of view in this fable.

- ☐ A. It is told in the first person.
- ☐ B. It is told in the second person.
- ☐ C. It is told in the third person.
- ☐ D. The narrator is the Ant.
- ☐ E. The narrator is the Grasshopper.
- ☐ F. The narrator is omniscient.
- ☐ G. The narrator is antagonistic.
- ☐ H. The narrator is neutral and does not take sides.

Getting Ready for Winter: My Three "Musts"

J. C. Mann

1 Summertime is a time when the cold temperatures of winter seem like distant memories. The gentle breezes, the warming sun rays, and the temperatures well above freezing serve to provide comfort and a welcomed escape from the harsh realities of winter.

2 Nonetheless, when the days of summer begin to become shorter and the temperatures begin to fall, the reality of the approach of winter becomes quite clear. At that point in time, it is wise to begin to prepare for the harshness of winter. Not to do so would be a grave mistake. I believe that as winter approaches, there are three "musts" for all my friends and me.

3 First of all, we must make sure that our winter clothing is prepared to be worn again. Some items like wool sweaters and corduroy jackets usually need to be taken to the cleaners to be refreshed. Other clothing may need to be washed and dried, according to the individual needs of the fabrics or materials. If we wash our clothing, fold it neatly, and put it away in a moth-proof container, then the amount of ironing and freshening needed before wearing our clothing next summer will be minimal.

4 Additionally, we must consider the family lawnmower. It is a good idea to drain out all the gasoline before moving the mower to a safe storage place like a shed or garage. The mower should also be run for a short time since this will ensure that the gasoline in the fuel lines is fully drained. Otherwise, condensation may occur when the gasoline is stored for a long time. The result is usually a gas line that has frozen ice crystals and possibly water in both the gas lines and tank. If the fuel is not going to be drained, then a fuel stabilizer should be added to prevent condensation.

5 Finally, we need to store all our summer sports equipment properly. Our roller blades need to have the leather cleaned and treated, the laces replaced, and the blades checked for excess wear and maybe repaired. Our baseball gloves need to be cleaned with a gentle leather cleaner and treated with a good preservative. Our basketball should be deflated, cleaned off, and put away for the following summer. If we plan on using the basketball on an indoor court during the winter, then we should clean it with an appropriate cleaning agent and check it for excess wear. Any other sports equipment, clothing, or footwear should be stored in appropriately as instructed by the manufacturers.

6 If we take the time to treat our clothing, our lawnmowers, and our summer sports equipment properly, then we shall get many years of enjoyment from them. Should we choose to take the easy way out and just toss everything into a pile and worry about the items the following summer, then we are designing a plan for disappointment. A little bit of effort can go a long way in helping us to keep our seasonal clothing and equipment in great shape.

14. What organizational pattern is used for Mann's essay?

- ○ A. chronological
- ○ B. problem and solution
- ○ C. cause and effect
- ○ D. compare and contrast

15. **Part A**

Select the **two** statements that are true about Mann's essay.

- ☐ A. Mann loathes winter.
- ☐ B. Mann prefers summer to any season.
- ☐ C. Mann is conscientious about his possessions.
- ☐ D. Mann takes a laissez-faire attitude toward his possessions.
- ☐ E. Mann believes that planning for the future is overrated.
- ☐ F. Mann believes that planning ahead is a smart thing to do.

Part B

Given your answers to Part A, which **two** statements below match with Aesop's fable?

- ☐ A. Kindness overcomes all obstacles.
- ☐ B. Good planning leads to good results.
- ☐ C. Don't wait until the last minute to take action.
- ☐ D. Always keep a calendar handy and follow it.
- ☐ E. No one should take advantage of another.
- ☐ F. If you see someone in need, then lend them a hand.
- ☐ G. Honesty is the best policy.

16. Which **two** statements are true of both J. C. Mann and Aesop's Ant?
Drag (write) the correct statements and drop them in the boxes below.

    A. They are both careful planners.
    B. They are both respected in their communities.
    C. They both belong to local civic organizations.
    D. They both begin their planning and preparation well in advance.
    E. They both gather a cadre of helpers to assist them with their plans.
    F. They both have doubts that their actions are appropriate, but they overcome these and are successful.

    ```

    ```

    ```

    ```

17. The term **condensation** in paragraph 4 refers to

    ○ A. animal infestation.
    ○ B. dry rotting.
    ○ C. fissures.
    ○ D. moisture build-up.

18. Which **two** statements apply to both passages?

    ☐ A. Aesop and Mann are contemporaries, and the experiences they have written about come from the same era.
    ☐ B. Both Aesop and Mann advocate the benefit of good planning.
    ☐ C. While Aesop's advice deals mainly with nutritional considerations, Mann's advice focuses on possessions.
    ☐ D. Mann has decided not to use a fable to make his point because he believes that writing a fable is equal to "designing a plan for disappointment." (paragraph 6)
    ☐ E. Mann has learned his lesson from his own frivolous behavior and has therefore decided to advise people about the best way to prepare for winter.

19. Select all of the statements that are accurate.

☐ A. Aesop and Mann are angry with those who do not take the time to plan.

☐ B. Aesop would have written a longer piece if he had known more about the behavior of grasshoppers.

☐ C. Mann wrote an informational piece because his audience would not understand fables.

☐ D. The advice each author gives is based on evidence from his writing.

☐ E. Both Aesop and Mann are advocates with a clearly stated position.

☐ F. Neither Aesop nor Mann has ever taken the advice being given in his passage.

Reading and Vocabulary

Directions: Read the following passage and answer the questions that follow.

1. *At the beginning of the school year, my teachers met* with all of us *students from the play we had staged during the previous* school year. 2. *I was hoping* to get a principal part in the cast this year, and I told my best friend Emma about my wish. 3. *Because she was not interested in the play, she shrugged her shoulders and she wished me luck.* 4. Undaunted, *I became more excited* as the time for rehearsals neared. 5. *Listening carefully, I knew that I was being challenged.* 6. I wanted to make sure that *I didn't miss one thing* that our director Miss Skyler said as she explained the parts. 7. If I tried my best during rehearsals, then I could possibly earn a principal part in the *play.* 8. *Wondering about my chances, I hoped for the best.* 9. When Miss Skyler mentioned that *the* lead role required good dancing skills, I became excited since I have been taking dance lessons for four years.

20. Select the phrases that are prepositional phrases.

- ☐ A. *At the beginning*
- ☐ B. *of the school year*
- ☐ C. *my teachers met*
- ☐ D. *students*
- ☐ E. *from the play*
- ☐ F. *we had staged*
- ☐ G. *during the previous*

21. Which of the following answers are contained in the phrase *"I was hoping"*?

- ☐ A. subject verb
- ☐ B. direct object
- ☐ C. helping verb
- ☐ D. indirect object
- ☐ E. conjunction
- ☐ F. main verb

22. Part A

What type of phrase is the word **play** in the passage a part of?

- ○ A. object of a preposition
- ○ B. direct object
- ○ C. indirect object
- ○ D. subject

Part B

Select the similar phrase(s) to the one in which **play** is contained to support the answer to Part A.

- ○ A. "If I tried"
- ○ B. "I tried my best"
- ○ C. "during rehearsals"
- ○ D. "a principal part"

23. Which of the following **two** words from sentence 9 are adjectives? Drag and drop them into the boxes.

- A. *"When"*
- B. *"Miss Skyler"*
- C. *"the"*
- D. *"good"*
- E. *"became"*
- F. *"dance"*

Unit 2 (110 minutes)

Research Simulation Task

Directions: Today you will read the following texts and view a video: *The Highwayman* by Alfred Noyes, *Highwaymen—Romantic Heroes or Common Criminals?* by Jeremiah Justice, Professional video recording called "The Highway Man." After you read the passages and answer the questions, you will write an essay that compares and contrasts each text.

The Highwayman

By Alfred Noyes

Part One

1   The wind was a torrent of darkness among the gusty trees.
The moon was a ghostly galleon tossed upon cloudy seas.
The road was a ribbon of moonlight over the purple moor,
And the highwayman came riding—
     Riding—riding—
The highwayman came riding, up to the old inn-door.

2   He'd a French cocked-hat on his forehead, a bunch of lace at his chin,
A coat of the claret velvet, and breeches of brown doe-skin.
They fitted with never a wrinkle. His boots were up to the thigh.
And he rode with a jewelled twinkle,
     His pistol butts a-twinkle,
His rapier hilt a-twinkle, under the jewelled sky.

3   Over the cobbles he clattered and clashed in the dark inn-yard.
He tapped with his whip on the shutters, but all was locked and barred.
He whistled a tune to the window, and who should be waiting there
But the landlord's black-eyed daughter,
     Bess, the landlord's daughter,
Plaiting a dark red love-knot into her long black hair.

4   And dark in the dark old inn-yard a stable-wicket creaked
Where Tim the ostler listened. His face was white and peaked.
His eyes were hollows of madness, his hair like mouldy hay,
But he loved the landlord's daughter,
     The landlord's red-lipped daughter.
Dumb as a dog he listened, and he heard the robber say—

5 "One kiss, my bonny sweetheart, I'm after a prize to-night,
   But I shall be back with the yellow gold before the morning light;
   Yet, if they press me sharply, and harry me through the day,
   Then look for me by moonlight,
        Watch for me by moonlight,
   I'll come to thee by moonlight, though hell should bar the way."

6 He rose upright in the stirrups. He scarce could reach her hand,
   But she loosened her hair in the casement. His face burnt like a brand
   As the black cascade of perfume came tumbling over his breast;
   And he kissed its waves in the moonlight,
        (O, sweet black waves in the moonlight!)
   Then he tugged at his rein in the moonlight, and galloped away to the west.

Part Two

7 He did not come in the dawning. He did not come at noon;
   And out of the tawny sunset, before the rise of the moon,
   When the road was a gypsy's ribbon, looping the purple moor,
   A red-coat troop came marching—
        Marching—marching—
   King George's men came marching, up to the old inn-door.

8 They said no word to the landlord. They drank his ale instead.
   But they gagged his daughter, and bound her, to the foot of her
        narrow bed.
   Two of them knelt at her casement, with muskets at their side!
   There was death at every window;
        And hell at one dark window;
   For Bess could see, through her casement, the road that *he* would ride.

9 They had tied her up to attention, with many a sniggering jest.
   They had bound a musket beside her, with the muzzle beneath her
        breast!
   "Now, keep good watch!" and they kissed her. She heard the doomed
        man say—
   Look for me by moonlight;
        Watch for me by moonlight;
   I'll come to thee by moonlight, though hell should bar the way!

10   She twisted her hands behind her; but all the knots held good!
     She writhed her hands till her fingers were wet with sweat or blood!
     They stretched and strained in the darkness, and the hours crawled by
       like years
     Till, now, on the stroke of midnight,
           Cold, on the stroke of midnight,
     The tip of one finger touched it! The trigger at least was hers!

11   The tip of one finger touched it. She strove no more for the rest.
     Up, she stood up to attention, with the muzzle beneath her breast.
     She would not risk their hearing; she would not strive again;
     For the road lay bare in the moonlight;
           Blank and bare in the moonlight;
     And the blood of her veins, in the moonlight, throbbed to her love's
       refrain.

12   *Tlot-tlot; tlot-tlot!* Had they heard it? The horsehoofs ringing clear;
     Tlot-tlot; tlot-tlot, in the distance? Were they deaf that they did not hear?
     Down the ribbon of moonlight, over the brow of the hill,
     The highwayman came riding—
           Riding—riding—
     The red coats looked to their priming! She stood up, straight and still.

13   *Tlot-tlot*, in the frosty silence! *Tlot-tlot*, in the echoing night!
     Nearer he came and nearer. Her face was like a light.
     Her eyes grew wide for a moment; she drew one last deep breath,
     Then her finger moved in the moonlight,
           Her musket shattered the moonlight,
     Shattered her breast in the moonlight and warned him—with her death.

14   He turned. He spurred to the west; he did not know who stood
     Bowed, with her head o'er the musket, drenched with her own blood!
     Not till the dawn he heard it, and his face grew grey to hear
     How Bess, the landlord's daughter,
           The landlord's black-eyed daughter,
     Had watched for her love in the moonlight, and died in the darkness
       there.

15 Back, he spurred like a madman, shouting a curse to the sky,
With the white road smoking behind him and his rapier brandished
   high.
Blood red were his spurs in the golden noon; wine-red was his velvet
   coat;
When they shot him down on the highway,
     Down like a dog on the highway,
And he lay in his blood on the highway, with a bunch of lace at his
   throat.

16 *And still of a winter's night, they say, when the wind is in the trees,*
When the moon is a ghostly galleon tossed upon cloudy seas,
When the road is a ribbon of moonlight over the purple moor,
A highwayman comes riding—
     Riding—riding—
A highwayman comes riding, up to the old inn-door.

17 *Over the cobbles he clatters and clangs in the dark inn-yard.*
He taps with his whip on the shutters, but all is locked and barred.
He whistles a tune to the window, and who should be waiting there
But the landlord's black-eyed daughter,
     Bess, the landlord's daughter,
Plaiting a dark red love-knot into her long black hair.

1. **Part A**

   In paragraph 1, Alfred Noyes mentions a "ghostly galleon." The use of this phrase indicates which of the literary devices listed below?

   ○ A. onomatopoeia
   ○ B. alliteration
   ○ C. hyperbole
   ○ D. compositional Risk

   Part B

   Which of the following choices is also an example of the literary device correctly mentioned in Part A?

   ○ A. "His rapier hilt a-twinkle" (paragraph 2)
   ○ B. "Plaiting a dark red love-knot" (paragraph 3)
   ○ C. "His eyes were hollows of madness" (paragraph 4)
   ○ D. "his hair like mouldy hay" (paragraph 4)

2. **Part A**

   In paragraph 4, "Tim the ostler listened" to the conversation between the highwayman and Bess, the landlord's daughter. Why did Tim's face become "white and peaked"?

   ○ A. Tim always wanted to be a highwayman, and this was his chance to make his dream come true.
   ○ B. Tim was Bess's cousin, and he had promised his aunt to keep her out of danger.
   ○ C. Tim was also in love with Bess, but he didn't have the flair that the highwayman had.
   ○ D. Tim was a member of the king's army, and he was preparing to arrest the highwayman.

   Part B

   Select the phrase from paragraph 4 that supports Part A.

   ☐ A. "Tim the ostler listened."
   ☐ B. "His eyes were hollows of madness"
   ☐ C. "his hair like mouldy hay"
   ☐ D. "he heard the robber say"
   ☐ E. "dumb as a dog he listened"

3. **Part A**

Which one of the following could serve as an alternate title to
"The Highwayman"?

- ○ A. "True Love Never Ends Well"
- ○ B. "Never Be Kind to Strangers"
- ○ C. "True Love Knows No Boundaries"
- ○ D. "Every Man for Himself

Part B

Which of the following can support the alternative title?

- ○ A. "Over the cobbles he clattered and clashed in the dark inn-yard."
  (paragraph 3)
- ○ B. "Then he tugged at his rein in the moonlight, and galloped away to
  the west. (paragraph 6)
- ○ C. "The tip of one finger touched it! The trigger at least was hers!"
  (paragraph 10)
- ○ D. "Back, he spurred like a madman, shouting a curse to the sky."
  (paragraph 15)

Highwaymen—Romantic Heroes or Common Criminals?

Jeremiah Justice

Overview

1   Much has been written over the years about the highwaymen of the past.
Some were portrayed as free-spirited rogues who were the anti-heroes of
their times. They rode on horses and robbed from travelers, who were mostly
on foot. These disadvantaged travelers had no choice but to succumb to the
will of the swift and unprovoked attacks of these scoundrels on horseback.

Historical Eras

2   When did these highwaymen parlay their "talents" into unearned
riches? Highwaymen were said to be roaming the countryside and wreaking
their havoc on unsuspecting travelers from Elizabethan times until the
beginning of the 1800s. Sometimes known as common thieves and brigands,
these scoundrels were also known by more euphemistic names including
"knights of the road" and "gentlemen of the road." Phrases used by these
highwaymen included "Stand and deliver" and "Your money or your life."
Although some worked alone, many highwaymen worked in gangs so it was

easier to intimidate their victims. The highwaymen would prowl the less-travelled areas of roads leading from London since those negotiating these roads were often men of means. Most importantly, the king's soldiers, who served the same role as today's police forces, did not patrol these roads often since they themselves would be in danger of an attack.

Du Vall—A Gentleman or a Thief?

3 Not all highwaymen approached their position in the same manner. A highwayman who was truly a gentleman as well as a thief was Claude Du Vall. The son of a miller who worked as a stable boy and a footman, he learned his manners by being around nobility. Du Vall was famous not only for his skill as a highwayman, but also for his gentlemanly manners. He was such a charmer that when he was captured and sent to trial, the ladies of the Court pleaded for his release. When Judge Sir William Morton found Du Vall to be guilty of his crimes, even Charles II attempted to have Du Vall pardoned. Only Morton's threat to resign made Charles II rescind his request for clemency.

Highwaymen—Common Criminals?

4 Many of these highwaymen were gentlemen themselves. Often, wealthy gentlemen would surround themselves with a group of thieves and criminals who would rob from the general public and then share the wealth with the particular gentleman who "commanded" them. Should these criminals run afoul of the law, the gentleman for whom they worked would "influence" the local law enforcers through bribery and other unseemly means. The lure of the criminal life seemed to be far too enticing for both the gentlemen and the highwaymen.

A Place for a Woman?

5 It is interesting to note that women also masqueraded as highwaymen. It was not considered to be ladylike for a woman to be a criminal of any sort. However, the women could hide their identities under their clothing, their hats, and their masks. These women had to be sure that the fashionably long hair that helped to define their beauty in polite society was hidden artfully under their hats. Moreover, they knew that they could not speak much since the lightness of their voices would indicate their femininity.

4. **Part A**

When Justice in paragraph 1 speaks of the travelers having *"no choice but to succumb to the will"* of the highwaymen, he uses the word **succumb** to mean

- ○ A. defy.
- ○ B. define.
- ○ C. surrender.
- ○ D. challenge.

Part B

The word in the first paragraph that supports the correct answer to Part A is

- ○ A. disadvantaged.
- ○ B. choice.
- ○ C. will.
- ○ D. swift.

5. **Part A**

Claude Du Vall was unique as a highwayman because

- ○ A. he was a foreigner living in England.
- ○ B. he gave back the money he had stolen.
- ○ C. he never robbed from poor people but only from the rich.
- ○ D. he was considered to be a true gentleman who was well liked by different classes.

Part B

Select the lines from the text that support the correct answer to Part A.

- ☐ A. "...many highwaymen worked in gangs so it was easier to intimidate their victims." (paragraph 2)
- ☐ B. "...he learned his manners by being around nobility." (paragraph 3)
- ☐ C. "...he was captured and sent to trial." (paragraph 3)
- ☐ D. "...the ladies of the Court pleaded for his release." (paragraph 3)

6. Which of the following statements is accurate?

   ○ A. Many women wanted to be highwaymen, but they just weren't strong enough.
   ○ B. Women were better highwaymen than the men themselves and admired for it.
   ○ C. A woman who was a highwayman was praised by society.
   ○ D. Women who were highwaymen had to hide their femininity.

7. Choose the statement that supports the reason why women highwaymen had to hide their femininity.

   ○ A. Women who were highwaymen actually outnumbered the men.
   ○ B. Women never disguised themselves when they became highwaymen because they were admired as heroes.
   ○ C. Women were forced to disguise themselves as men if they wanted to be highwaymen.
   ○ D. Women weren't interested in being highwaymen so the question is irrelevant.

Please note: A video based on a similar topic or theme is often added to the paired passages on the PARCC. You may wish to view a video of one of the professional singers who recorded "The Highwayman" and use that in your response.

8. **Essay**

Directions: Highwaymen can be viewed in different ways. Compare and contrast the point of view of the two authors, Alfred Noyes and Jeremiah Justice and how they write about highwaymen. Moreover, consider the structure of each text and the manner in which it affects the way the highwaymen are portrayed.

Write your essay here.

Unit 3 (90 minutes)

Narrative Writing Task

Directions: Today, you will read a short story by O. Henry. As you read, pay attention to the main character, his traits, and a transformation that occurs.

"A Retrieved Reformation"

by O. Henry

1   In the prison shoe-shop, Jimmy Valentine was busily at work making shoes. A prison officer came into the shop and led Jimmy to the prison office. There Jimmy was given an important paper. It said that he was free.

2   Jimmy took the paper without showing much pleasure or interest. He had been sent to prison to stay for four years. He had been there for ten months. But he had expected to stay only three months. Jimmy Valentine had many friends outside the prison. A man with so many friends does not expect to stay in prison long.

3   "Valentine," said the chief prison officer, "you'll go out tomorrow morning. This is your chance. Make a man of yourself. You're not a bad fellow at heart. Stop breaking safes open, and live a better life."

4   "Me?" said Jimmy in surprise. "I never broke open a safe in my life."

5   "Oh, no," the chief prison officer laughed. "Never. Let's see. How did you happen to get sent to prison for opening that safe in Springfield? Was it because you didn't want to tell where you really were? Perhaps because you were with some lady, and you didn't want to tell her name? Or was it because the judge didn't like you? You men always have a reason like that. You never go to prison because you broke open a safe."

6   "Me?" Jimmy said. His face still showed surprise. "I was never in Springfield in my life."

7   "Take him away," said the chief prison officer. "Get him the clothes he needs for going outside. Bring him here again at seven in the morning. And think about what I said, Valentine."

8   At a quarter past seven the next morning, Jimmy stood again in the office. He had on some new clothes that did not fit him, and a pair of new shoes that hurt his feet. These are the usual clothes given to a prisoner when he leaves the prison.

9   Next they gave him money to pay for his trip on a train to the city near the prison. They gave him five dollars more. The five dollars were supposed to help him become a better man.

10   Then the chief prison officer put out his hand for a handshake. That was the end of Valentine, Prisoner 9762. Mr. James Valentine walked out into the sunshine. He did not listen to the song of the birds or look at the green trees or smell the flowers. He went straight to a restaurant. There he tasted the first sweet joys of being free.

11   He had a good dinner. After that he went to the train station. He gave some money to a blind man who sat there, asking for money, and then he got on the train.

12   Three hours later he got off the train in a small town. Here he went to the restaurant of Mike Dolan.

13   Mike Dolan was alone there. After shaking hands he said, "I'm sorry we couldn't do it sooner, Jimmy my boy. But there was that safe in Springfield, too. It wasn't easy. Feeling all right?"

14   "Fine," said Jimmy. "Is my room waiting for me?"

15   He went up and opened the door of a room at the back of the house. Everything was as he had left it. It was here they had found Jimmy, when they took him to prison. There on the floor was a small piece of cloth. It had been torn from the coat of the cop, as Jimmy was fighting to escape.

16   There was a bed against the wall. Jimmy pulled the bed toward the middle of the room. The wall behind it looked like any wall, but now Jimmy found and opened a small door in it. From this opening he pulled out a dust-covered bag.

17   He opened this and looked lovingly at the tools for breaking open a safe. No finer tools could be found any place. They were complete; everything needed was here. They had been made of a special material, in the necessary sizes and shapes. Jimmy had planned them himself, and he was very proud of them.

18   It had cost him over nine hundred dollars to have these tools made at a place where they make such things for men who work at the job of safe-breaking.

19 In half an hour Jimmy went downstairs and through the restaurant. He was now dressed in good clothes that fitted him well. He carried his dusted and cleaned bag.

20 "Do you have anything planned?" asked Mike Dolan.

21 "Me?" asked Jimmy as if surprised. "I don't understand. I work for the New York Famous Bread and Cake Makers Company. And I sell the best bread and cake in the country."

22 Mike enjoyed these words so much that Jimmy had to take a drink with him. Jimmy had some milk. He never drank anything stronger.

23 A week after Valentine, 9762, left the prison, a safe was broken open in Richmond, Indiana. No one knew who did it. Eight hundred dollars were taken.

24 Two weeks after that, a safe in Logansport was opened. It was a new kind of safe; it had been made, they said, so strong that no one could break it open. But someone did, and took fifteen hundred dollars.

25 Then a safe in Jefferson City was opened. Five thousand dollars were taken. This loss was a big one. Ben Price was a cop who worked on such important matters, and now he began to work on this.

26 He went to Richmond, Indiana, and to Logansport, to see how the safe-breaking had been done in those places. He was heard to say: "I can see that Jim Valentine has been here. He is in business again. Look at the way he opened this one. Everything easy, everything clean. He is the only man who has the tools to do it. And he is the only man who knows how to use tools like this. Yes, I want Mr. Valentine. Next time he goes to prison, he's going to stay there until his time is finished."

27 Ben Price knew how Jimmy worked. Jimmy would go from one city to another far away. He always worked alone. He always left quickly when he was finished. He enjoyed being with nice people. For all these reasons, it was not easy to catch Mr. Valentine.

28 People with safes full of money were glad to hear that Ben Price was at work trying to catch Mr. Valentine.

29 One afternoon Jimmy Valentine and his bag arrived in a small town named Elmore. Jimmy, looking as young as a college boy, walked down the street toward the hotel.

30   A young lady walked across the street, passed him at the corner, and entered a door. Over the door was the sign, "The Elmore Bank." Jimmy Valentine looked into her eyes, forgetting at once what he was. He became another man. She looked away, and brighter color came into her face. Young men like Jimmy did not appear often in Elmore.

31   Jimmy saw a boy near the bank door, and began to ask questions about the town. After a time the young lady came out and went on her way. She seemed not to see Jimmy as she passed him.

32   "Isn't that young lady Polly Simpson?" asked Jimmy.

33   "No," said the boy. "She's Annabel Adams. Her father owns this bank."

34   Jimmy went to the hotel, where he said his name was Ralph D. Spencer. He got a room there. He told the hotel man he had come to Elmore to go into business. How was the shoe business? Was there already a good shoe-shop?

35   The man thought that Jimmy's clothes and manners were fine. He was happy to talk to him.

36   Yes, Elmore needed a good shoe-shop. There was no shop that sold just shoes. Shoes were sold in the big shops that sold everything. All business in Elmore was good. He hoped Mr. Spencer would decide to stay in Elmore. It was a pleasant town to live in and the people were friendly.

37   Mr. Spencer said he would stay in the town a few days and learn something about it. No, he said, he himself would carry his bag up to his room. He didn't want a boy to take it. It was very heavy.

38   Mr. Ralph Spencer remained in Elmore. He started a shoe-shop. Business was good.

39   Also he made many friends. And he was successful with the wish of his heart. He met Annabel Adams. He liked her better every day.

40   At the end of a year everyone in Elmore liked Mr. Ralph Spencer. His shoe-shop was doing very good business. And he and Annabel were going to be married in two weeks. Mr. Adams, the small-town banker, liked Spencer. Annabel was very proud of him. He seemed already to belong to the Adams family.

41 One day Jimmy sat down in his room to write this letter, which he sent to one of his old friends:

42 Dear Old Friend: I want you to meet me at Sullivan's place next week, on the evening of the 10th. I want to give you my tools. I know you'll be glad to have them. You couldn't buy them for a thousand dollars. I finished with the old business—a year ago. I have a nice shop. I'm living a better life, and I'm going to marry the best girl on earth two weeks from now. It's the only life—I wouldn't ever again touch another man's money. After I marry, I'm going to go further west, where I'll never see anyone who knew me in my old life. I tell you, she's a wonderful girl. She trusts me.

Your old friend, Jimmy.

43 On the Monday night after Jimmy sent this letter, Ben Price arrived quietly in Elmore. He moved slowly about the town in his quiet way, and he learned all that he wanted to know. Standing inside a shop, he watched Ralph D. Spencer walk by.

44 "You're going to marry the banker's daughter, are you, Jimmy?" said Ben to himself. "I don't feel sure about that!"

45 The next morning Jimmy was at the Adams home. He was going to a nearby city that day to buy new clothes for the wedding. He was also going to buy a gift for Annabel. It would be his first trip out of Elmore. It was more than a year now since he had done any safe-breaking.

46 Most of the Adams family went to the bank together that morning. There were Mr. Adams, Annabel, Jimmy, and Annabel's married sister with her two little girls, aged five and nine. They passed Jimmy's hotel, and Jimmy ran up to his room and brought along his bag. Then they went to the bank.

47 All went inside—Jimmy, too, for he was one of the family. Everyone in the bank was glad to see the good-looking, nice young man who was going to marry Annabel. Jimmy put down his bag.

48 Annabel, laughing, put Jimmy's hat on her head and picked up the bag. "How do I look?" she asked. "Ralph, how heavy this bag is! It feels full of gold."

49 "It's full of some things I don't need in my shop," Jimmy said. "I'm taking them to the city, to the place where they came from. That saves me the cost of sending them. I'm going to be a married man. I must learn to save money."

50   The Elmore bank had a new safe. Mr. Adams was very proud of it, and he wanted everyone to see it. It was as large as a small room, and it had a very special door. The door was controlled by a clock. Using the clock, the banker planned the time when the door should open. At other times no one, not even the banker himself, could open it. He explained about it to Mr. Spencer. Mr. Spencer seemed interested but he did not seem to understand very easily. The two children, May and Agatha, enjoyed seeing the shining heavy door, with all its special parts.

51   While they were busy like this, Ben Price entered the bank and looked around. He told a young man who worked there that he had not come on business; he was waiting for a man.

52   Suddenly there was a cry from the women. They had not been watching the children. May, the nine-year-old girl, had playfully but firmly closed the door of the safe. And Agatha was inside.

53   The old banker tried to open the door. He pulled at it for a moment. "The door can't be opened," he cried. "And the clock—I hadn't started it yet."

54   Agatha's mother cried out again.

55   "Quiet!" said Mr. Adams, raising a shaking hand. "All be quiet for a moment. Agatha!" he called as loudly as he could. "Listen to me." They could hear, but not clearly, the sound of the child's voice. In the darkness inside the safe, she was wild with fear.

56   "My baby!" her mother cried. "She will die of fear! Open the door! Break it open! Can't you men do something?"

57   "There isn't a man nearer than the city who can open that door," said Mr. Adams, in a shaking voice. "My God! Spencer, what shall we do? That child—she can't live long in there. There isn't enough air. And the fear will kill her."

58   Agatha's mother, wild too now, beat on the door with her hands. Annabel turned to Jimmy, her large eyes full of pain, but with some hope, too. A woman thinks that the man she loves can somehow do anything.

59   "Can't you do something, Ralph? Try, won't you?"

60 He looked at her with a strange soft smile on his lips and in his eyes.

61 "Annabel," he said, "give me that flower you are wearing, will you?"

62 She could not believe that she had really heard him. But she put the flower in his hand. Jimmy took it and put it where he could not lose it. Then he pulled off his coat. With that act, Ralph D. Spencer passed away and Jimmy Valentine took his place.

63 "Stand away from the door, all of you," he commanded.

64 He put his bag on the table, and opened it flat. From that time on, he seemed not to know that anyone else was near. Quickly he laid the shining strange tools on the table. The others watched as if they had lost the power to move.

65 In a minute Jimmy was at work on the door. In ten minutes— faster than he had ever done it before—he had the door open.

66 Agatha was taken into her mother's arms.

67 Jimmy Valentine put on his coat, picked up the flower and walked toward the front door. As he went he thought he heard a voice call, "Ralph!" He did not stop.

68 At the door a big man stood in his way.

69 "Hello, Ben!" said Jimmy, still with his strange smile. "You're here at last, are you? Let's go. I don't care, now."

70 And then Ben Price acted rather strangely.

71 "I guess you're wrong about this, Mr. Spencer," he said. "I don't believe I know you, do I?"

72 And Ben Price turned and walked slowly down the street.

Source: http://americanenglish.state.gov/files/ae/resource_files/a-retrieved-reformation.pdf (free domain)

1. **Part A**

   Read the following from the second paragraph of the story. "He had been sent to prison to stay for four years. He had been there for ten months. But he had expected to stay only three months." The literary device being used in this sentence is

   ○ A. personification.
   ○ B. irony.
   ○ C. alliteration.
   ○ D. metaphor.

   Part B

   Which of the **three** following lines also contain the same technique used in the line cited in Part A?

   ☐ A. "The five dollars were supposed to help him become a better man." (paragraph 9)
   ☐ B. "It was here they had found Jimmy, when they took him to prison." (paragraph 15)
   ☐ C. "Everything easy, everything clean." (paragraph 26)
   ☐ D. "'You're going to marry the banker's daughter, are you, Jimmy?'" said Ben to himself." (paragraph 44)
   ☐ E. "'There isn't a man nearer than the city who can open that door,'" said Mr. Adams, in a shaking voice." (paragraph 57)
   ☐ F. "A woman thinks that the man she loves can somehow do anything." (paragraph 58)

2. **Part A**

What literary device is being featured in "Fine," said Jimmy. "Is my room waiting for me"? (paragraph 14)

- ○ A. consonance
- ○ B. simile
- ○ C. repetition for effect
- ○ D. personification

Part B

Which of the following contains an example of this literary device mentioned in Part A?

- ○ A. "There he tasted the first sweet joys of being free." (paragraph 10)
- ○ B. I don't understand. I work for the New York Famous Bread and Cake Makers Company. And I sell the best bread and cake in the country." (paragraph 21)
- ○ C. "...he himself would carry his bag up to his room. He didn't want a boy to take it. It was very heavy." (paragraph 37)
- ○ D. "And the fear will kill her." (paragraph 57)

3. Which **two** sentences from the passage are compound sentences?

- ☐ A. "You never go to prison because you broke open a safe." (paragraph 5)
- ☐ B. "At a quarter past seven on the next morning, Jimmy stood again in the office." (paragraph 8)
- ☐ C. "They were complete; everything needed was here." (paragraph 17)
- ☐ D. "She looked away, and brighter color came into her face." (paragraph 30)
- ☐ E. "I'm living a better life, and I'm going to marry the best girl on earth two weeks from now." (paragraph 42)
- ☐ F. "Jimmy took it and put it where he could not lose it." (paragraph 62)

4. **Part A**

Which word is the correct definition for **retrieved**?

- ○ A. lost
- ○ B. abandoned
- ○ C. regained
- ○ D. renovated

Part B

Which **two** words are synonyms for **retrieved**?

- ☐ A. rescued
- ☐ B. designated
- ☐ C. incorporated
- ☐ D. salvaged
- ☐ E. endangered
- ☐ F. forfeited

5. Which **two** answers **best** reflect the theme of this story?

- ☐ A. If you are clever enough, then you can get away with all crimes.
- ☐ B. It's never too late to change.
- ☐ C. Slow and steady wins the race.
- ☐ D. The grass is always greener on the other side of the fence.
- ☐ E. Love is a powerful force that can alter one's outlook on life.
- ☐ F. You plan to fail when you fail to plan.

6. **Essay**

Imagine that O. Henry doesn't end his story with the last line. Consider how this story would continue after Jimmy Valentine had been allowed to go free by the detective Ben Price. Be sure to consider all the prior events in the story, as well as the characters' personalities.

Write your essay here.

PRACTICE TEST ANSWERS

Unit 1

Literary Task Analysis

"Mother to Son"

1. The correct answer is **C.** "she is poor and cannot afford an easy life of luxury." The "crystal stair" represents wealth, which the mother does not have. Answers A. "she has lived her life on the ground floor of her house," B. "she is someone who has always desired stairs made from crystal," and D. "she is a maid who is forced to clean up 'tacks' and 'splinters'" are incorrect.

2. The correct answers are **A.** "persevering" and **D.** "determined" since they represent the mother's strong desire to succeed in her quest for a better life. Answer B. "resigned" means that the mother has given up, which is incorrect. Answer C. "incoherent" would mean that the mother is not making any sense at all. Answer E. "agnostic" is wrong because an agnostic is one who is unsure about an established position.

3. The correct answer is **D.** "her being forced to live a difficult life." Answers A. "her home without electricity," B. "her job in the evening when it is dark," and C. "her boredom with her life and desire for the excitement that the night life has" have no basis in the text.

4. The correct answer is **B.** "the son should keep trying and not quit." Answer A. "the son should just give up now and avoid the inevitable disappointment" is the opposite of the correct answer and is therefore wrong. Answers C. "life is unpredictable, and there is not a formula for success" and D. "even though you may try your best, there is little hope for success in this cruel world" have no basis in the text.

5. The correct answers are **A.** "reinforce" and **C.** "underscore" because they both demonstrate the mother's desire to emphasize her point strongly to her son. Answer B. "undermine" means the opposite of the mother's intention. Answer D. "intimidate" represents a much more aggressive action while Answer E. "improvise" indicates an action that is unplanned.

"The Ant and the Grasshopper"

6. **C.** "The Grasshopper helped the Ant." The grasshopper wanted the Ant to stop and chat with him instead of finding food for the winter.

7. **A.** "the Ant and the Grasshopper"

8. **D.** "The Grasshopper believes throughout the fable that his idea of chirping and singing throughout the summer is a smart one." He asks the Ant why be bothered with toiling and moiling away with an ear of corn.

9. Part A: The correct answers are **D.** and **J.** When we meet the Grasshopper and the Ant they are in a field during the summer time. When we catch up with the characters at the end of the fable, it is winter and the Ant is passing food out from the nest.

   Part B: Answers **E.** and **F.** are correct. The author wanted to connect the actions of the main characters with the seasons to show the idea of what careless behavior does over time and to make his point.

10. **C.** "Corn." The Ant was toiling and moiling with an ear of corn.

11. **A.** "Always plan ahead." The Grasshopper ended up starving during the winter.

12. **D.** and **G.** The Grasshopper was dying of hunger during the winter realizing that he was wrong to not store food during the summer months for the winter.

13. **C.** and **H.** It is told in the third person by a narrator who is neutral and does not take sides.

Getting Ready for Winter: My Three "Musts"

14. **A.** The organizational pattern of this essay is chronological. The author uses language, such as, first of all, additionally, and finally.

15. Part A: **B.** and **F.** Mann prefers the summer months and believes that planning ahead is a smart thing to do. Then Mann proceeds to explain how best to prepare from the summer months for the winter months ahead.

    Part B: **B.** and **C.** Good planning leads to good results and not waiting until the last minute to take an action is best. The Ant did not wait for the cold weather to start preparing for the winter. When winter came, he had enough food and was not starving like the Grasshopper. Mann states that "it is wise to begin to prepare for the harshness of winter."

16. **A.** and **E.** They are both careful planners and believe in preparing and planning for events in advance. The Ant prepared to have food before the winter and Mann describes a plan on how to prepare yourself and your belongings for the harsh winter months.

17. **D.** Condensation is a "moisture build-up."

18. The correct answers are **B.** and **C.** Both Aesop and Mann advocate the benefit of good planning. While Aesop's advice deals mainly with nutritional considerations, Mann's advice focuses on possessions. Aesop has The Ant advise The Grasshopper "to lay up food for the winter." Mann advises his reader that "it is wise to begin to prepare for the harshness of winter."

19. The correct answers are **D.** and **E.** The advice each author gives is based on evidence from his writing. Both Aesop and Mann are advocates with a clearly-stated position. Aesop supports his position with The Grasshopper's frivolousness and the change of the seasons while Mann speaks of the "three musts."

Vocabulary

20. **A.** and **G.** are prepositional phrases.
21. The correct answers are **A.**, **C.**, and **F.**
22. Part A: The correct answer is **A.** "object of a preposition."
    Part B: The correct answer is **D.** "a principal part."
23. The correct answers are **D.** "good" and **F.** "dance."

Unit 2

Research Simulation Task

"The Highwayman"

1. Part A: The correct answer is **B.** "alliteration" since the initial "g" sound in "ghostly galleon" is repeated.
   Part B: The correct answer is **D.** "his hair like mouldy hay" since the initial "h" sound in "hair" and "hay" is repeated.

2. Part A: The correct answer is **C.** "Tim was also in love with Bess, but he didn't have the flair that the highwayman had." Tim was jealous of the highwayman, who was more handsome, dynamic, and daring. Being an ostler was an honest profession for Tim, but his mundane job of stableman paled in comparison to the highwayman, whose success was shown by his "French cocked-hat on his forehead, a bunch of lace at his chin, / A coat of the claret velvet, and breeches of brown doe-skin. / They fitted with never a wrinkle." Answer A. "Tim always wanted to be a highwayman, and this was his chance to make his dream come true" is incorrect since Tim's actions mainly demonstrated jealousy. Answers B. "Tim was Bess's cousin, and he had promised his aunt to keep her out of danger" and D. "Tim was a member of the king's army, and he was preparing to arrest the highwayman" are incorrect.
   Part B: The correct answers are **B.** "His eyes were hollows of madness" (paragraph 4) and **C.** "his hair like mouldy hay," since these traits are not attractive like the highwayman. Answers A. "Tim the ostler listened" and D. "he heard the robber say" are events in the story, not traits.

3. Part A: The correct answer is **C.** "True Love Knows No Boundaries" because Bess gave up her own life to save the highwayman. Answer A. "True Love Never Ends Well" is not correct because the word never is an "absolute." The statement can be true in many instances. Answer B. "Never Be Kind to Strangers" has no basis in the text. Answer D. "Every Man for Himself" is the opposite of the correct answer since Bess dies to save the highwayman, who dies to avenge her death.

Part B: The correct answer is **C.** "The tip of one finger touched it! The trigger at least was hers." This answer tells of Bess's preparation to warn the highwayman by killing herself and the highwayman's blind rage when he learns of Bess's death. Answer A. "Over the cobbles he clattered and clashed in the dark inn-yard" simply refers to an earlier visit by the highwayman while Answer B. "Then he tugged at his rein in the moonlight, and galloped away to the west" refers to the highwayman galloping away after visiting Bess.

"Highwaymen—Romantic Heroes or Common Criminals?"

4. Part A: The correct answer is **C.** "surrender" since it is a synonym for "succumb." Answer A. "defy" is an antonym, B. "define" refers to clarifying, and D. "challenge" is an antonym.

   Part B: The correct answer is **A.** "disadvantaged" since one who succumbs is indeed at a disadvantage. Answer B. "choice" is more general than "disadvantaged" and therefore not as good a word to use. Answer C. "will" indicated the opposite of being willing to "succumb." Answer D. "swift" deals with speed.

5. Part A: The correct answer is **D.** "he was considered to be a true gentleman who was well liked by different classes." This is proven by the fact that "the ladies of the Court pleaded for his release," as did Charles II. Answer A. "he was a foreigner living in England" is inaccurate. Answer B. "he gave back the money he had stolen" refers to Robin Hood, not Claude Du Vall. Answer C. "he never robbed from poor people but only from the rich" has no basis in the text.

   Part B: The correct answers are **B.** "...he learned his manners by being around nobility" and **D.** "...the ladies of the Court pleaded for his release." Neither Answer A. "...many highwaymen worked in gangs so it was easier to intimidate their victims" nor Answer C. "...he was captured and sent to trial" support the statement. In fact, Answer A. is from the paragraph prior to the one about Du Vall.

6. The correct answer is **D.** "Women who were highwaymen had to hide their femininity." This is supported in paragraph 5: "However, the women could hide their identities under their clothing, their hats, and their masks." Answers A. "Many women wanted to be highwaymen, but they just weren't strong enough" and B. "Women were better highwaymen than the men themselves and admired for it" have no support in the text. Answer C. "A woman who was a highwayman was praised by society" is a completely false statement.

7. Answer **C.** "Women were forced to disguise themselves as men if they wanted to be highwaymen" is correct. Answer A. "Women who were highwaymen actually outnumbered the men" has no basis in the text. Answer B. "Women never disguised themselves when they became highwaymen because they were

admired as heroes" is the opposite of the correct answer. Answer D. "Women weren't interested in being highwaymen so the question is irrelevant," has no basis in the text.

8. Research Simulation Task Sample Response

Noyes vs. Justice   Differing Opinions

Two different people with two different purposes may be likely to view either something or someone in two different ways. These two authors do indeed see criminals through completely different lenses.

In "The Highwayman," Alfred Noyes portrays the character in a romantic fashion. Even before he appears to Bess, the landlord's daughter, the setting is described romantically. In the opening of the poem, Noyes uses the setting to entice the reader with details including "The wind was a torrent of darkness among the gusty trees. / The moon was a ghostly galleon tossed upon cloudy seas. / The road was a ribbon of moonlight over the purple moor." (paragraph 1) Before the highwayman even appears, the setting creates a mood of intrigue, darkness, and suspense—all traits of the highwayman who wreaks havoc across the countryside while maintaining an air of elegance and mystery. This masked "intruder" who wishes to "steal" the heart of the smitten Bess approaches her while wearing "a French cocked-hat on his forehead, a bunch of lace at his chin, / A coat of the claret velvet, and breeches of brown doe-skin. / They fitted with never a wrinkle." (paragraph 2) Moreover, he wore "boots (that) were up to the thigh. / And he rode with a jewelled twinkle, / His pistol butts a-twinkle, / His rapier hilt a-twinkle, under the jewelled sky." (paragraph 2)

Jeremiah Justice does not condone this romance of thieves, however. Rather than praise the highwaymen for their daring feats and dashing personalities, Justice notes the highwaymen's reputations "as free-spirited rogues who were the anti-heroes of their times." (paragraph 2) Unlike Noyes, Justice spends little time with elevating the highwaymen to a praiseworthy status. Instead, he immediately refers to the fact that "They rode on horses and robbed from travelers, who were mostly on foot." (paragraph 1) He reinforces this point by stating in simple, non-romantic terms that "These disadvantaged travelers had no choice but to succumb to the will of the swift and unprovoked attacks of these scoundrels on horseback." (paragraph 1)

Noyes focuses on the romance of Bess and the highwayman while Justice exhibits disdain for those who "were said to be roaming the countryside and wreaking their havoc on unsuspecting travelers." (paragraph 2) Noyes portrays the highwayman in most admirable terms as he describes the playful scoundrel who "clattered and clashed in the dark inn-yard," and who "whistled a tune" to call to Bess, who was waiting for his arrival while "Plaiting a dark red love-knot into her long black hair." (paragraph 3) Tim the Ostler, whose "hair like mouldy hay" and eyes that "were hollows of madness" is forced to watch the highwayman kiss Bess and listen to the highwayman's plans to avoid any pursuers and return "by moonlight, though hell should bar the way." (paragraphs 4 and 5)

Justice takes a different approach, describing highwaymen as "common thieves and brigands," as well as "scoundrels." (paragraph 2) Furthermore, he speaks unflatteringly of these criminals who used phrases such as "Stand and deliver (your possessions)" and "Your money or your life." In addition, Justice illustrates his point further by explaining that "many highwaymen worked in gangs so it was easier to intimidate their victims" and "The highwaymen would prowl the less-travelled areas of roads leading from London since those negotiating these roads were often men of means." (paragraph 2)

Noyes describes Bess's "noble" act when "Her musket shattered the moonlight, / Shattered her breast in the moonlight and warned him—with her death." He further makes the highwayman a sympathetic character by having him killed in an attempt to avenge Bess's death "With the white road smoking behind him and his rapier brandished high." (paragraph 17) Justice, on the other hand, portrays the "gentlemanly" Claude Du Vall as "such a charmer that when he was captured and sent to trial, the ladies of the Court pleaded for his release." (paragraph 3) Even Charles II pleaded for his release.

Finally, using a poem to tell the tall of the highwayman gives his story a sense of romance and a musical tone. In fact, the poem ends with the image of Bess "Plaiting a dark red love-knot into her long black hair.

(paragraph 19) Justice, on the other hand, uses paragraphs, headings, and phrases including "thieves," "brigands," and "criminals" to demonstrate his disdain. One can easily infer that Justice believes there is no romance for those who are the victims of these criminal charmers.

Noyes romanticizes the highwayman while Justice feels disdain for all highwaymen, even the charming Claude Du Vall. Need more proof? Just look at the two titles. Noyes' work is entitled "The Highwayman" while Justice's is entitled "Highwaymen—Romantic Heroes or Common Criminals?"

Explanation of Student Response

This begins with a compositional risk to engage the interest of the reader by making a statement that relates directly to the "Differing Opinions" stated in the title. The author then proceeds to methodically diagnose the differences in the two authors' philosophies by first demonstrating Noyes' romanticizing of the highwayman by using a mood of "intrigue, darkness, and suspense." He furthers the point by citing provocative details of the highwayman including descriptions of his clothing and the "twinkle" reflecting off his pistol and rapier. Justice's opposing point of view in introduced in the next paragraph to contrast Noyes' romanticizing. Justice uses terms including "free-spirited rogues" and "anti-heroes (who) rode on horses and robbed from travelers, who were mostly on foot." The third and fourth paragraphs continue this diametrical opposition as "Noyes focuses on the romance of Bess and the highwayman while Justice exhibits disdain for those who 'were said to be roaming the countryside and wreaking their havoc on unsuspecting travelers.'" Furthermore, the "music" of Noyes' poetry of praise is contrasted directly with the matter-of-fact approach of Justice's unemotional textbook style. The author adds insight at the end by contrasting the titles that each author uses. There is thorough development of the topic, and academic vocabulary is evident with words including "elegance," "praiseworthy," and "sympathetic."

Unit 3

Narrative Writing Task

"A Retrieved Reformation"

1. Part A: The correct answer is **B.** "irony" since Jimmy Valentine stayed longer in prison than he had "expected." Remember, irony is the difference between what is expected and what actually occurs. Answer A. "personification" is incorrect because there are no life-like qualities being bestowed through personification. Answer C. "alliteration" is incorrect because there is no repetition of initial sound required with alliteration. Answer D. "metaphor" is incorrect. Although there is a comparison being made concerning time, the lengths of time are not unrelated and therefore do not serve as metaphors.

   Part B: The correct examples of irony are **A.** "The five dollars were supposed to help him become a better man" (his act of saving the young girl trapped in the safe made him a better man), **D.** "'You're going to marry the banker's daughter, are you, Jimmy'?" said Ben to himself" (safecrackers don't usually marry bankers' daughters), and **E.** "'There isn't a man nearer than the city who can open that door,'" said Mr. Adams, in a shaking voice." (Jimmy is standing right there in the bank.) Answer B. "It was here they had found Jimmy, when they took him to prison" is incorrect since it is simply a statement of fact. Answer C. "Everything easy, everything clean" is incorrect since it is an example of alliteration. Answer F. "A woman thinks that the man she loves can somehow do anything" is incorrect since it is more an example of hyperbole (exaggeration).

2. Part A: The correct answer is **D.** "personification" since Jimmy's room could not be waiting for him. Answers A. "consonance" (repetition of consonant sounds), B. "simile" (comparison using "like" or "as"), C. "repetition for effect" (repeating something one or more times purposefully) are incorrect.

   Part B: The correct answer is **D.** "And the fear will kill her" since fear is being given a lifelike quality. Answers A. "There he tasted the first sweet joys of being free" (metaphor), B. "I don't understand. I work for the New York Famous Bread and Cake Makers Company. And I sell the best bread and cake in the country" (irony), C. "…he himself would carry his bag up to his room. He didn't want a boy to take it. It was very heavy" (description).

3. Answers **C.** "They were complete; everything needed was here" (two sentences joined by a semicolon and no coordinating conjunction), **D.** "She looked away, and brighter color came into her face," and **E.** "I'm living a better life, and I'm going to marry the best girl on earth two weeks from now" (two sentences joined by a comma and the coordinating conjunction "and") are correct. Answers A. "You never go to prison because you broke open a safe" (two

sentences joined by "because" = complex sentence), B. "At a quarter past seven on the next morning, Jimmy stood again in the office." (simple sentence), and F. "Jimmy took it and put it where he could not lose it" (simple sentence with a compound predicate) are incorrect.

4. Part A: The correct answer is **C.** "regained." Answers A. "lost" (unfound), B. "abandoned" (cast off or left behind), and D. "renovated" (repaired) are incorrect.
   Part B: The correct answers are **A.** "rescued" and **D.** "salvaged." B. "designated" (named or assigned), C. "incorporated" (mixed in), E. "endangered" (put at risk), and F. "forfeited" (given up) are incorrect.

5. The correct answers are **B.** "It's never too late to change" and **E.** "Love is a powerful force that can alter one's outlook on life." Answers A. "If you are clever enough, then you can get away with all crimes" (Jimmy has already been in prison many times), C. "Slow and steady wins the race" (not an issue), D. "The grass is always greener on the other side of the fence" (not an issue), and F. "You plan to fail when you fail to plan" (Jimmy never failed to plan) are incorrect.

6. Narrative Writing Task

"And Ben Price turned and walked slowly down the street."

Jimmy couldn't believe his eyes. He thought he was mistaken. He and Ben Price had a long history. Jimmy would constantly avoid Ben's pursuit while cracking open safes. Ben, however, had been determined to catch up with Jimmy one more time. And now he was letting him go free. Why? Why was Ben letting Jimmy go free?

While Jimmy pondered this unlikely turn of events, things suddenly became more clear in his mind as he listened to the muffled sounds behind him. Annabel Adams, the woman who had changed his entire life. She was the woman whom he was going to marry. Annabel Adams was heard sobbing uncontrollably while she hugged little Agatha, who had moments before been trapped in a safe that was thought to be burglar proof. Losing her dear Agatha would have been devastating to Annabel. She would never have been able to go on. Agatha was so much like Annabel when she herself was young.

Jimmy could hear Annabel comforting Agatha while both sobbed.

"Agatha, you'll be fine. Don't be afraid, my little one. You'll be fine."

"I'm afraid, Auntie. It was so cold and dark in there. I just wanted to get out."

"There, there. You're safe now."

Agatha innocently asked, "Where's Uncle Jimmy?"

While courageously battling a pending cascade of tears, Annabel somehow managed to say, "He had to leave to go somewhere important. He'll be back someday."

Agatha looked a bit puzzled, but she was too afraid to ask any more questions. She just wanted to be held closely in her auntie's arms.

Nonetheless, what could Jimmy do now to console himself? He knew that he could never return to Annabel. He had completely violated the trust that she and her entire family had placed in him. Why, her father had even showed Jimmy the new features on the safe because he trusted Jimmy. And he did so with pride for a future son-in-law who was making his daughter the happiest girl on earth.

Now that Jimmy has shattered the heart of Annabel, Mr. Adams would never be able to forgive him. Oh, he was surely grateful that young Agatha was saved by Jimmy, but how would Mr. Adams ever be able to forgive Jimmy for the deceit he had perpetrated on both Mr. Adams' beloved Annabel and the entire Adams family? Why, the entire town of Elmore had viewed Jimmy as a hero, a role model. Jimmy had shattered the hearts of an entire town.

Knowing that he could never return to Elmore, Jimmy climbed aboard a stagecoach that was preparing to leave and left the fond memories of Elmore behind. Never again would he be able to find another young woman with Annabel's purity of heart and deep love for him. Yes, Jimmy was sadly now a broken man. He reflected on his life and wondered whether things could have been different had he decided not to save young Agatha. That would not have been a choice, however, because Jimmy was always a man who strived to be the best. He dressed in the best clothes, ate the best food, and lived in a manner that he determined.

Jimmy had always determined the direction of his life. He was not an easy criminal to catch. He usually had his sentences shortened because he had the right "connections." One might venture to say that he pursued an "I'll-live-my-life-the-way-I-choose" type of lifestyle. This always seemed to make him happy. However, he would now be faced with living a life without his most treasured gift: Annabel Adams.

When Jimmy would be caught and forced to serve time in prison, he always knew that this discomfort would be temporary and often, short-lived. Now that he had lost his beloved Annabel, the one person who in his own words was "a wonderful girl" who trusted him, he would no longer be able to steal his way to happiness. Jimmy had to reveal himself as a thief so he could save young Agatha. In the process, however, he lost the love of his life: Annabel.

By taking the proper action and saving Agatha, Jimmy saved himself from a life of guilt. Had he remained silent and decided not to rescue Agatha, Jimmy would have been able to live the rest of his life in wedded bliss. However, he somehow knew that lying to his beloved would continue to haunt him. Thus, he had no other choice. He decided to take the right action   even though it would cost him a penalty worse than any prison sentence he might ever have to serve.

Explanation of Student Response

This essay follows directly from the short story. The author wisely quotes the final line of the story before beginning the continuation. This directly established a clearly-defined connection between O. Henry's efforts and those of the author. This tactic also underscores for a reviewer the commitment to continue the story from its stated ending.

The reflection that Jimmy has as he wonders about Ben Price's decision not to arrest him is a logical one. These two individuals were adversaries. Ben was in pursuit of Jimmy—"he was waiting for a man" whom he hoped to capture (Jimmy) and take to prison. For a lawman to step aside and allow the criminal he was pursuing to go free, the criminal had to have committed an extraordinary act of valor.

The author of the essay continues the piece from the perspective of Jimmy's reflections. With phrases including "Why was Ben letting Jimmy go free?" and "…what could Jimmy do now to console himself?" the author of the essay reflects

Jimmy's angst (deep anxiety) as he deals with this life-altering situation. Had the essayist brought Jimmy and Annabel back together again, then the depth of O. Henry's characters would be compromised by a mundane, simple ending.

The structure of the sentences is varied both in length and type (simple, compound, and complex). Transitions are used throughout the piece to build "bridges" between thoughts and paragraphs. Some of the transitions include "Nonetheless," "However," and "In the process." Neither grammar nor spelling mistakes are found throughout the piece. Furthermore, the dialogue is punctuated properly, and paragraphs are used during the exchange between Annabel and Agatha.

For the reason noted, this piece is an outstanding one. Thus, the grade it deserves is a **"4"**.

Narrative Writing

Topic:		Audience:

Sights:
Sounds:
Smells:
Textures:
Tastes:

What happened?
(In order)

1.

2.

3.

4.

5.

The characters learned:

Compare and Contrast

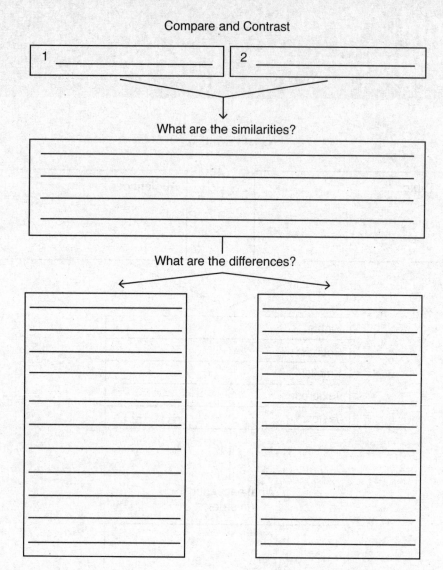

Reading Literature

Key Ideas and Details:

CCSS.ELA-LITERACY.RL.7.1
Cite several pieces of textual evidence to support analysis of what the text says explicitly as well as inferences drawn from the text.

CCSS.ELA-LITERACY.RL.7.2
Determine a theme or central idea of a text and analyze its development over the course of the text; provide an objective summary of the text.

CCSS.ELA-LITERACY.RL.7.3
Analyze how particular elements of a story or drama interact (e.g., how setting shapes the characters or plot).

Craft and Structure:

CCSS.ELA-LITERACY.RL.7.4
Determine the meaning of words and phrases as they are used in a text, including figurative and connotative meanings; analyze the impact of rhymes and other repetitions of sounds (e.g., alliteration) on a specific verse or stanza of a poem or section of a story or drama.

CCSS.ELA-LITERACY.RL.7.5
Analyze how a drama's or poem's form or structure (e.g., soliloquy, sonnet) contributes to its meaning.

CCSS.ELA-LITERACY.RL.7.6
Analyze how an author develops and contrasts the points of view of different characters or narrators in a text.

Integration of Knowledge and Ideas:

CCSS.ELA-LITERACY.RL.7.7
Compare and contrast a written story, drama, or poem to its audio, filmed, staged, or multimedia version, analyzing the effects of techniques unique to each medium (e.g., lighting, sound, color, or camera focus and angles in a film).

313

CCSS.ELA-LITERACY.RL.7.8
(RL.7.8 not applicable to literature)

CCSS.ELA-LITERACY.RL.7.9
Compare and contrast a fictional portrayal of a time, place, or character and a historical account of the same period as a means of understanding how authors of fiction use or alter history.

Range of Reading and Level of Text Complexity:

CCSS.ELA-LITERACY.RL.7.10
By the end of the year, read and comprehend literature, including stories, dramas, and poems, in the grades 6–8 text complexity band proficiently, with scaffolding as needed at the high end of the range.

Reading Informational Text

Key Ideas and Details:

CCSS.ELA-LITERACY.RI.7.1
Cite several pieces of textual evidence to support analysis of what the text says explicitly as well as inferences drawn from the text.

CCSS.ELA-LITERACY.RI.7.2
Determine two or more central ideas in a text and analyze their development over the course of the text; provide an objective summary of the text.

CCSS.ELA-LITERACY.RI.7.3
Analyze the interactions between individuals, events, and ideas in a text (e.g., how ideas influence individuals or events, or how individuals influence ideas or events).

Craft and Structure:

CCSS.ELA-LITERACY.RI.7.4
Determine the meaning of words and phrases as they are used in a text, including figurative, connotative, and technical meanings; analyze the impact of a specific word choice on meaning and tone.

CCSS.ELA-LITERACY.RI.7.5
Analyze the structure an author uses to organize a text, including how the major sections contribute to the whole and to the development of the ideas.

CCSS.ELA-LITERACY.RI.7.6
Determine an author's point of view or purpose in a text and analyze how the author distinguishes his or her position from that of others.

Integration of Knowledge and Ideas:

CCSS.ELA-LITERACY.RI.7.7

Compare and contrast a text to an audio, video, or multimedia version of the text, analyzing each medium's portrayal of the subject (e.g., how the delivery of a speech affects the impact of the words).

CCSS.ELA-LITERACY.RI.7.8

Trace and evaluate the argument and specific claims in a text, assessing whether the reasoning is sound and the evidence is relevant and sufficient to support the claims.

CCSS.ELA-LITERACY.RI.7.9

Analyze how two or more authors writing about the same topic shape their presentations of key information by emphasizing different evidence or advancing different interpretations of facts.

Range of Reading and Level of Text Complexity:

CCSS.ELA-LITERACY.RI.7.10

By the end of the year, read and comprehend literary nonfiction in the grades 6–8 text complexity band proficiently, with scaffolding as needed at the high end of the range.

Writing

Text Types and Purposes:

CCSS.ELA-LITERACY.W.7.1

Write arguments to support claims with clear reasons and relevant evidence.

CCSS.ELA-LITERACY.W.7.1.A

Introduce claim(s), acknowledge alternate or opposing claims, and organize the reasons and evidence logically.

CCSS.ELA-LITERACY.W.7.1.B

Support claim(s) with logical reasoning and relevant evidence, using accurate, credible sources and demonstrating an understanding of the topic or text.

CCSS.ELA-LITERACY.W.7.1.C

Use words, phrases, and clauses to create cohesion and clarify the relationships among claim(s), reasons, and evidence.

CCSS.ELA-LITERACY.W.7.1.D

Establish and maintain a formal style.

CCSS.ELA-LITERACY.W.7.1.E

Provide a concluding statement or section that follows from and supports the argument presented.

CCSS.ELA-LITERACY.W.7.2

Write informative/explanatory texts to examine a topic and convey ideas, concepts, and information through the selection, organization, and analysis of relevant content.

CCSS.ELA-LITERACY.W.7.2.A

Introduce a topic clearly, previewing what is to follow; organize ideas, concepts, and information, using strategies such as definition, classification, comparison/contrast, and cause/effect; include formatting (e.g., headings), graphics (e.g., charts, tables), and multimedia when useful to aiding comprehension.

CCSS.ELA-LITERACY.W.7.2.B

Develop the topic with relevant facts, definitions, concrete details, quotations, or other information and examples.

CCSS.ELA-LITERACY.W.7.2.C

Use appropriate transitions to create cohesion and clarify the relationships among ideas and concepts.

CCSS.ELA-LITERACY.W.7.2.D

Use precise language and domain-specific vocabulary to inform about or explain the topic.

CCSS.ELA-LITERACY.W.7.2.E

Establish and maintain a formal style.

CCSS.ELA-LITERACY.W.7.2.F

Provide a concluding statement or section that follows from and supports the information or explanation presented.

CCSS.ELA-LITERACY.W.7.3

Write narratives to develop real or imagined experiences or events using effective technique, relevant descriptive details, and well-structured event sequences.

CCSS.ELA-LITERACY.W.7.3.A

Engage and orient the reader by establishing a context and point of view and introducing a narrator and/or characters; organize an event sequence that unfolds naturally and logically.

CCSS.ELA-LITERACY.W.7.3.B

Use narrative techniques, such as dialogue, pacing, and description, to develop experiences, events, and/or characters.

CCSS.ELA-LITERACY.W.7.3.C

Use a variety of transition words, phrases, and clauses to convey sequence and signal shifts from one time frame or setting to another.

CCSS.ELA-LITERACY.W.7.3.D

Use precise words and phrases, relevant descriptive details, and sensory language to capture the action and convey experiences and events.

CCSS.ELA-LITERACY.W.7.3.E

Provide a conclusion that follows from and reflects on the narrated experiences or events.

Production and Distribution of Writing:

CCSS.ELA-LITERACY.W.7.4

Produce clear and coherent writing in which the development, organization, and style are appropriate to task, purpose, and audience. (Grade-specific expectations for writing types are defined in standards 1–3 above.)

CCSS.ELA-LITERACY.W.7.5

With some guidance and support from peers and adults, develop and strengthen writing as needed by planning, revising, editing, rewriting, or trying a new approach, focusing on how well purpose and audience have been addressed. (Editing for conventions should demonstrate command of language standards 1–3 up to and including grade 7 here.)

CCSS.ELA-LITERACY.W.7.6

Use technology, including the Internet, to produce and publish writing and link to and cite sources as well as to interact and collaborate with others, including linking to and citing sources.

Research to Build and Present Knowledge:

CCSS.ELA-LITERACY.W.7.7

Conduct short research projects to answer a question, drawing on several sources and generating additional related, focused questions for further research and investigation.

CCSS.ELA-LITERACY.W.7.8

Gather relevant information from multiple print and digital sources, using search terms effectively; assess the credibility and accuracy of each source; and quote or paraphrase the data and conclusions of others while avoiding plagiarism and following a standard format for citation.

CCSS.ELA-LITERACY.W.7.9

Draw evidence from literary or informational texts to support analysis, reflection, and research.

CCSS.ELA-LITERACY.W.7.9.A

Apply *grade 7 Reading standards* to literature (e.g., "Compare and contrast a fictional portrayal of a time, place, or character and a historical account of the same period as a means of understanding how authors of fiction use or alter history").

CCSS.ELA-LITERACY.W.7.9.B

Apply *grade 7 Reading standards* to literary nonfiction (e.g., "Trace and evaluate the argument and specific claims in a text, assessing whether the reasoning is sound and the evidence is relevant and sufficient to support the claims").

Range of Writing:

CCSS.ELA-LITERACY.W.7.10

Write routinely over extended time frames (time for research, reflection, and revision) and shorter time frames (a single sitting or a day or two) for a range of discipline-specific tasks, purposes, and audiences.

Speaking and Listening

Comprehension and Collaboration:

CCSS.ELA-Literacy.SL.7.1

Engage effectively in a range of collaborative discussions (one-on-one, in groups, and teacher-led) with diverse partners on grade 7 topics, texts, and issues, building on others' ideas and expressing their own clearly.

CCSS.ELA-Literacy.SL.7.1.A

Come to discussions prepared, having read or researched material under study; explicitly draw on that preparation by referring to evidence on the topic, text, or issue to probe and reflect on ideas under discussion.

CCSS.ELA-Literacy.SL.7.1.B

Follow rules for collegial discussions, track progress toward specific goals and deadlines, and define individual roles as needed.

CCSS.ELA-Literacy.SL.7.1.C

Pose questions that elicit elaboration and respond to others' questions and comments with relevant observations and ideas that bring the discussion back on topic as needed.

CCSS.ELA-Literacy.SL.7.1.D

Acknowledge new information expressed by others and, when warranted, modify their own views.

CCSS.ELA-Literacy.SL.7.2

Analyze the main ideas and supporting details presented in diverse media and formats (e.g., visually, quantitatively, orally) and explain how the ideas clarify a topic, text, or issue under study.

CCSS.ELA-Literacy.SL.7.3

Delineate a speaker's argument and specific claims, evaluating the soundness of the reasoning and the relevance and sufficiency of the evidence.

Presentation of Knowledge and Ideas:

CCSS.ELA-Literacy.SL.7.4

Present claims and findings, emphasizing salient points in a focused, coherent manner with pertinent descriptions, facts, details, and examples; use appropriate eye contact, adequate volume, and clear pronunciation.

CCSS.ELA-Literacy.SL.7.5

Include multimedia components and visual displays in presentations to clarify claims and findings and emphasize salient points.

CCSS.ELA-Literacy.SL.7.6

Adapt speech to a variety of contexts and tasks, demonstrating command of formal English when indicated or appropriate.

Language

Conventions of Standard English:

CCSS.ELA-Literacy.L.7.1

Demonstrate command of the conventions of standard English grammar and usage when writing or speaking.

CCSS.ELA-Literacy.L.7.1.A

Explain the function of phrases and clauses in general and their function in specific sentences.

CCSS.ELA-Literacy.L.7.1.B

Choose among simple, compound, complex, and compound-complex sentences to signal differing relationships among ideas.

CCSS.ELA-Literacy.L.7.1.C

Place phrases and clauses within a sentence, recognizing and correcting misplaced and dangling modifiers.

CCSS.ELA-Literacy.L.7.2

Demonstrate command of the conventions of standard English capitalization, punctuation, and spelling when writing.

CCSS.ELA-Literacy.L.7.2.A

Use a comma to separate coordinate adjectives (e.g., *It was a fascinating, enjoyable movie* but not *He wore an old[,] green shirt*).

CCSS.ELA-Literacy.L.7.2.B

Spell correctly.

Knowledge of Language:

CCSS.ELA-Literacy.L.7.3

Use knowledge of language and its conventions when writing, speaking, reading, or listening.

CCSS.ELA-Literacy.L.7.3.A

Choose language that expresses ideas precisely and concisely, recognizing and eliminating wordiness and redundancy.*

Vocabulary Acquisition and Use:

CCSS.ELA-Literacy.L.7.4

Determine or clarify the meaning of unknown and multiple-meaning words and phrases based on *grade 7 reading and content*, choosing flexibly from a range of strategies.

CCSS.ELA-Literacy.L.7.4.A

Use context (e.g., the overall meaning of a sentence or paragraph; a word's position or function in a sentence) as a clue to the meaning of a word or phrase.

CCSS.ELA-Literacy.L.7.4.B

Use common, grade-appropriate Greek or Latin affixes and roots as clues to the meaning of a word (e.g., *belligerent, bellicose, rebel*).

CCSS.ELA-Literacy.L.7.4.C

Consult general and specialized reference materials (e.g., dictionaries, glossaries, thesauruses), both print and digital, to find the pronunciation of a word or determine or clarify its precise meaning or its part of speech.

CCSS.ELA-Literacy.L.7.4.D

Verify the preliminary determination of the meaning of a word or phrase (e.g., by checking the inferred meaning in context or in a dictionary).

CCSS.ELA-Literacy.L.7.5

Demonstrate understanding of figurative language, word relationships, and nuances in word meanings.

CCSS.ELA-Literacy.L.7.5.A

Interpret figures of speech (e.g., literary, biblical, and mythological allusions) in context.

CCSS.ELA-Literacy.L.7.5.B

Use the relationship between particular words (e.g., synonym/antonym, analogy) to better understand each of the words.

CCSS.ELA-Literacy.L.7.5.C

Distinguish among the connotations (associations) of words with similar denotations (definitions) (e.g., *refined, respectful, polite, diplomatic, condescending*).

CCSS.ELA-Literacy.L.7.6

Acquire and use accurately grade-appropriate general academic and domain-specific words and phrases; gather vocabulary knowledge when considering a word or phrase important to comprehension or expression.

Scoring Rubrics

Narrative Task

	Construct Measured
	Writing and Expression
Score Point 4	The student response **is effectively** developed with narrative elements and is **consistently appropriate** to the task; is **effectively organized** with clear and coherent writing; establishes and maintains an **effective** style.
Score Point 3	The student response is **mostly effectively** developed with narrative elements and is **mostly appropriate** to the task; is **organized** with mostly clear and coherent writing; establishes and maintains a **mostly effective** style.
Score Point 2	The student response is developed with **some** narrative elements and is **generally appropriate** to the task; demonstrates **some organization** with somewhat coherent writing; has a style that is **somewhat effective**.
Score Point 1	The student response is **minimally developed** with few narrative elements and is **limited** in its **appropriateness** to the task; demonstrates **limited organization** and coherence; has a style that has **limited effectiveness**.
Score Point 0	The student response is **undeveloped** and/or **inappropriate** to the task; **lacks** organization and coherence; has an **inappropriate** style.

Construct Measured	
Writing Knowledge of Language and Conventions	
Score Point 3	The student response to the prompt demonstrates **full command** of the conventions of standard English at an appropriate level of complexity. There may be **few minor errors** in mechanics, grammar, and usage, but **meaning is clear**.
Score Point 2	The student response to the prompt demonstrates **some command** of the conventions of standard English at an appropriate level of complexity. There **may** be errors in mechanics, grammar, and usage that **occasionally impede understanding**, but the **meaning is generally clear**.
Score Point 1	The student response to the prompt demonstrates **limited command** of the conventions of standard English at an appropriate level of complexity. There **may** be errors in mechanics, grammar, and usage that **often impede understanding**.
Score Point 0	The student response to the prompt **does not demonstrate command** of the conventions of standard English at the appropriate level of complexity. **Frequent and varied errors** in mechanics, grammar, and usage **impede understanding**.

Research Simulation Task and Literary Analysis Task

Construct Measured	
Reading Comprehension and Written Expression	
Score Point 4	The student response demonstrates **full comprehension** of ideas stated explicitly and inferentially by providing **accurate** analysis; addresses the prompt and **provides effective** and comprehensive development of the claim or topic that is **consistently appropriate** to task, purpose, and audience; uses **clear reasoning** supported by relevant text-based evidence in the development of the claim or topic; is **effectively organized** with clear, coherent writing; establishes and maintains an effective style.
Score Point 3	The student response demonstrates **comprehension of ideas** stated explicitly and/or inferentially by providing a **mostly accurate** analysis; addresses the prompt and provides mostly **effective** development of claim or topic that is mostly appropriate to task, purpose, and audience; uses **mostly clear** reasoning supported by relevant text-based evidence in the development of the claim or topic; **is organized** with **mostly clear** and coherent writing; establishes and maintains a **mostly effective** style.
Score Point 2	The student response demonstrates **basic comprehension** of ideas stated explicitly and/or inferentially by providing a generally **accurate** analysis; addresses the prompt and provides some development of claim or topic that is **somewhat appropriate** to task, purpose, and audience; uses **some** reasoning and text-based evidence in the development of claim or topic; demonstrates **some organization** with **somewhat** coherent writing; has a style that is **somewhat effective**.
Score Point 1	The student response demonstrates **limited comprehension** of ideas stated explicitly and/or inferentially by providing **minimally accurate** analysis; addresses the prompt and provides minimal development of claim or topic that is **limited** in its **appropriateness** to task, purpose, and audience; uses **limited reasoning** and text-based evidence; demonstrates **limited organization** and coherence; has a style that is **minimally effective**.
Score Point 0	The student response demonstrates **no comprehension** of ideas by providing an **inaccurate** or no analysis; is **undeveloped** and/or **inappropriate** to task, purpose, and audience; includes little to no text-based evidence, **lacks** organization and coherence; has **inappropriate** style.

Construct Measured	
Knowledge of Language and Conventions	
Score Point 3	The student response to the prompt **demonstrates full command** of the conventions of standard English at an appropriate level of complexity. There may be **few minor errors** in mechanics, grammar, and usage, but **meaning is clear**.
Score Point 2	The student response to the prompt demonstrates **some command** of the conventions of standard English at an appropriate level of complexity. There **may** be errors in mechanics, grammar, and usage that **occasionally impede understanding**, but the **meaning is generally clear**.
Score Point 1	The student response to the prompt demonstrates **limited command** of the conventions of standard English at an appropriate level of complexity. There **may** be errors in mechanics, grammar, and usage that **often impede understanding**.
Score Point 0	The student response to the prompt **does not** demonstrate command of the conventions of standard English at the appropriate level of complexity. **Frequent and varied errors** in mechanics, grammar, and usage **impede understanding**.

Index